The Invention of Europe in French Literature and Film

The Invention of Europe in French Literature and Film

Edward Ousselin

THE INVENTION OF EUROPE IN FRENCH LITERATURE AND FILM
Copyright © Edward Ousselin, 2009.

All rights reserved.

First published in 2009 by PALGRAVE MACMILLAN® in the United States—a division of St. Martin's Press LLC, 175 Fifth Avenue, New York, NY 10010.

Where this book is distributed in the UK, Europe and the rest of the world, this is by Palgrave Macmillan, a division of Macmillan Publishers Limited, registered in England, company number 785998, of Houndmills, Basingstoke, Hampshire RG21 6XS.

Palgrave Macmillan is the global academic imprint of the above companies and has companies and representatives throughout the world.

Palgrave® and Macmillan® are registered trademarks in the United States, the United Kingdom, Europe and other countries.

ISBN-13: 978-0-230-60553-4
ISBN-10: 0-230-60553-2

Library of Congress Cataloging-in-Publication Data

Ousselin, Edward.
The invention of Europe in French literature and film / Edward Ousselin.
    p. cm.
  Includes bibliographical references.
  ISBN 0-230-60553-2 (alk. paper)
  1. French literature—History and criticism. 2. Motion pictures—France. 3. Europe—In literature. 4. Europe—In motion pictures. I. Title.

PQ145.7.E87O97 2008
840.9—dc22

A catalogue record of the book is available from the British Library.

Design by Scribe Inc.

First edition: March 2009

10 9 8 7 6 5 4 3 2 1

Printed in the United States of America.

For Catherine

Contents

Acknowledgments		ix
Introduction		1
1	Voltaire's Europe	7
2	The European Spirit of Germaine de Staël	33
3	Victor Hugo's European Utopia	57
4	The Shrunken Europe of Maurice Barrès	81
5	Europe Onscreen: Jean Renoir	109
6	Institutionalizing the Dream: Denis de Rougemont	137
Afterword		151
Notes		159
Works Cited		175
Index		187

Acknowledgments

At a personal level, this book is a distant echo of my dissertation. It would not have been possible without the guidance and encouragement of my advisor, Jean-François Fourny, to whom I would like to express my gratitude.

I am grateful to Judith Mayne and Karlis Racevskis for their advice and suggestions concerning this study and for their assistance in my work on previous articles.

I thank Shubho Bhattacharya and Keith Wright for their stimulating discussions. Also, many thanks to Petra Fiero for her suggestions and careful proofreading.

Three chapters of this book include sections that were previously published in earlier versions. I am grateful to the editors of the following publications for their permission to include portions of these articles:

"Victor Hugo's European Utopia." *Nineteenth-Century French Studies* 34.1–2 (Fall–Winter 2005–6): 32–43.
"Latin Connections and Ordinary Immigrants: Jean Renoir's *Toni*." *French Review* 75.4 (March 2002): 688–96.
"Denis de Rougemont and the Literary Construction of Europe." *Dalhousie French Studies* 76 (Fall 2006): 73–84.

All translations from French to English are mine. Most of the book titles are left in the original form, as are some quotes that mainly contain easily identifiable cognates.

Introduction

Europe has never existed. It does not constitute an easily definable entity in geographic, historical, political, social, cultural, ethnic, or religious terms. The word "Europe," whose origin remains unclear, has been used to cover multiple and competing meanings over time, varying from merely a neutral appellation for a loose geographical concept, to an identification with Christendom and civilization, and to its current usage in a developing historical and cultural sense, as a designation and implicit rationale for a transnational political organization. To this day, few of the continent's inhabitants—if it is a continent—would identify themselves primarily as "Europeans."[1] Despite its long interrelated history and literary traditions, what Paul Valéry, after the trauma of the First World War, called "a sort of promontory of the old continent, a western appendage of Asia" (1004), remains a largely unknown quantity, an amorphous multinational entity that seems to be engaged in a continuous but inconsistent quest for some form of common identity. Valéry's question, "So who is European?" (1007), has yet to find an answer that is commonly agreed upon.

And yet, there is today such a thing as the European Union, with its established institutions and its recognized symbols.[2] The concept or issue of Europe, meanwhile, and the evolving notion of a "European identity" have for centuries constituted important themes for a wide-ranging series of writers and, more recently, film directors. Indeed, to a great extent, the textual production on and about Europe has announced and accompanied—that is, helped to bring about—the current process of European integration.[3] While Europe remains difficult to define, and therefore study, as a historical reality, its diverse representations can be analyzed as literary and filmic topoi. As Edgar Morin noted (196–97), citizens of established nation-states generally base their sense of collective identity, their personal and societal links, on a common *past*, whether real or partly imagined. The currently evolving experiment, which finds its institutional expression in the European Union, instead posits an emerging multinational/multicultural identity based on its *future* prospects—and on the explicit renunciation of much of its past. These prospects or expectations did not recently arise ex nihilo, but were developed over time by artists and philosophers, who articulated a wide variety of conceptions of Europe, some of which will be discussed in the following chapters.

Textual Europes

This study explores the conceptions of Europe found in the works of six authors: Voltaire, Germaine de Staël, Victor Hugo, Maurice Barrès, Jean Renoir, and Denis de Rougemont.[4] These authors were all well known during their lifetimes and influential in the cultural life of their day. Each of them experienced some form of internal or external exile. They also played political roles, most of them throughout their careers, and thus exerted a perceptible degree of direct or indirect influence on the development of Europe as a concept and as a practical project. Taken together, the literary and filmic production of these authors provides a historically continuous sampling of the principal representations of Europe, within France, since the eighteenth century. It is also indicative of the wide range of viewpoints expressed in the public discourse on the topic of European integration.

The following chapters are by no means intended as comprehensive studies of the works and lives of each author, nor do they constitute an attempt at a complete history of the idea of Europe from the eighteenth to the twentieth century in France. While highly influential, each of the authors I have chosen hardly constitutes the only relevant example within his or her lifetime. This study is thus limited in terms of its chronology, of its focus on France, and of the number of authors it covers. To be complete, a study of the literary traces of Europe should be a collective effort in comparative literature, encompassing a broad spectrum of European cultures. Obviously, authors as diverse as Dante, Erasmus, Hegel, Machiavelli, Leibniz, Nietzsche, and Ortega y Gasset have been influential in shaping the ancient and ongoing debate over the concept of European identity. It should be noted that several broader studies of the idea of Europe—by Jean-Baptiste Duroselle, Denys Hay, Bronislaw Geremek, Carl Pegg, Denis de Rougemont, and Bernard Voyenne, to cite only a few—provide useful and often insightful overviews over a much longer historical span.

In this study, the various representations of France's European neighbors will be one of the principal considerations. Some countries will receive more attention than others due to their importance in the authors' texts and in the relevant historical contexts. In particular, after the chapter on Voltaire, these French (or Francophone, in the case of Rougemont) authors' representations of Germany will be a central concern. While Europe is not reducible to the French-German relationship, it has been central to most of the historical period considered here. The antagonism between them contributed to the worst wars on the continent; and their reconciliation has been both the principal means and goal of the current process of European unification. Aside from European states and their inhabitants, an issue addressed in each chapter is the representation of transnational or trans-European minorities: groups whose collective identities are not immediately associated with individual nations, such as Jews or Gypsies. Another topic will be the ways in which groups perceived as non-European, such as Turks or Africans, are represented.

The chronological succession found in the following chapters is not designed to retrospectively designate the authors I have chosen as precursors or prophets of Europe. Of the six, only Hugo and Rougemont can be classified as having provided a "défense et illustration" of a united Europe. I have therefore not tried to superimpose a progressive or teleological pattern of evolution toward a united Europe onto the works of these authors. My approach has instead been archeological, a sustained attempt at extracting the changing and sometimes contradictory conceptions of Europe, through an examination of the texts. In this perspective, the idea of Europe is less a unitary historical fact to be retrospectively explored and more of a multifold corpus of literary and filmic constructs to be analyzed and contextualized.

Culture versus Civilization

Since the eighteenth century is the historical starting point for this study, and since the representations of Germany will be among the main topics discussed, it is useful at this stage to outline the controversy between two eighteenth-century German philosophers over what is still a contentious issue in our own day, an issue directly linked to that of European unification: the opposition between Immanuel Kant's defense of the notion of cosmopolitan or universal civilization, as expressed in his 1784 "Idea for a Universal History from a Cosmopolitan Perspective" (3–16), and Johann Herder's affirmation of differentiated individual cultures, in his 1774 "Yet Another Philosophy of History" (38–48).

Kant's keywords "universal" and "cosmopolitan" (which are of course associated with important literary and philosophical themes of the Enlightenment period) point toward a transcultural commonality to human historical development, inscribing all human societies within a generalized pattern of progress and unification: "The greatest problem for the human species to which nature compels it to seek a solution is the achievement of a civil society which administers right universally" (Fifth Proposition, 8). Unlike this future universal "civil society," individual societies that remain isolated and backward are inherently doomed to eventual failure. As rational individuals, all human beings, regardless of their social and cultural specificities, are thus impelled by nature along an inevitable progression, leading from primitive human folly to an advanced universal civilization. According to the Seventh Proposition, "Through wars, through the excessive and ceaseless preparation for war, through the resulting distress that every state, even in times of peace, must ultimately feel internally, nature drives humankind to make initially imperfect attempts, but finally, after the ravages of war, after the downfalls, and after even the complete internal exhaustion of its powers, [nature] impels humankind to take the step that reason could have told it to take without all these lamentable experiences: to abandon the lawless state of savagery and enter into a federation of peoples" (10).

While it is necessarily universal, Kant's pattern of progress does not evolve simultaneously and uniformly throughout the world. Unavoidably, some societies attain a quicker pace of historical advancement than others. Conveniently, Kant discerned a higher level of societal progress within the Europe of his day, and consequently posited its extension to the rest of the world, without specifying the means by which this civilizational extension would be accomplished: "one will discover a regular course of improvement in the constitution of the state in our part of the world (which is likely to provide all others with laws at some future point)" (Ninth Proposition, 15).

A former student of Kant and a major figure in the Sturm und Drang movement that prefigured French Romanticism, Herder produced a comprehensive critique of Kantian universalism and continuous progress. He proclaimed the radical, unbridgeable dissimilarities of individual cultures, each one progressing or declining according to its own internal logic, instead of following some universalistic pattern of generalized progress toward a common, unitary ideal or standard. Herder's exaltation of societal particularism discounts Kant's premise of rational individuals as a misleading abstraction. Human behavior remains in the Herderian schema largely irrational, determined by the historical contingencies of their specific culture: "Whenever the dispositions and spheres of happiness of two nations collide, there arises what we call prejudice, mob judgment, and narrow nationalism! But in its proper time and place prejudice is good, for happiness can spring from it. It thrusts people together toward their center, attaches them more firmly to their roots, causes them to flourish more fully in their own way, and makes them more ardent and therefore happier with their own tendencies and purposes" (43–44).

Any attempt at establishing a classification or hierarchy across cultures, which are by their nature radically distinct, is for Herder illusory and self-defeating: "Basically, then, all comparison is disastrous" (43). The figurative fixity of his metaphors—"roots" and "center"—connotes an inherent deterministic drive, verging on cultural autarchy, that is specific to each societal entity and that conditions the thoughts and behavior of individuals. Herder's skepticism and relativism directly countered Kant's notion of continuous progress spreading outward from a Europe construed as the civilizational standard, leading the rest of the world toward a state of generalized ideality: "The universal, philosophical, philanthropic tone of our century readily applies 'our own ideal' of virtue and happiness to each distant nation, to each remote period in history. But can one such single ideal be the sole standard for judging, condemning, or praising the customs of other nations or periods?" (44).

Both of these competing philosophic theses have become associated with repressive historical legacies: Herderian particularism with aggressive nationalism within Europe and Kantian universalism with colonial conquest and subjugation outside of the continent. Herder's revalorization of prejudice and irrationalism, his degree of tolerance for cultural isolationism, and his endorsement of ethnic or religious determinism as the main constituent element of national identity were later appropriated by Nazi propaganda, alongside some of Nietzsche's more bizarre pronouncements. In the eighteenth-century context of French cultural supremacy and German political division, Herder assailed the Kantian pattern of universal progress, arguing that it tended to establish an implicit hierarchy of nations and cultures while designating the more "advanced" as models to be emulated and relegating the more "primitive" to the correspondingly negative status of quaintly outdated stages that must be outgrown. As is indicated by the early example of Herder's denunciation of universalism as merely a disguised form of parochialism, the critique of Eurocentrism—more recently illustrated in various forms by the works of Samir Amin, Martin Bernal, Aimé Césaire, Frantz Fanon, or Edward Said—began within Europe, during the Enlightenment.

The opposition between the Herderian defense of differentiated cultures and Kantian enlightened cosmopolitanism, structured around a metaphor of deeply embedded roots and another of radiating light (or of solidity versus mobility), will reappear in some of the following chapters. Victor Hugo's reiterated appeals in favor of European unification provide the best illustration of Kantian universalism, with a clear Francocentric orientation. Meanwhile, Maurice Barrès's nationalistic ethos of "la terre et les morts," in the context of German political supremacy after the Franco-Prussian War, offers up an extreme form of Herderian particularism.[5]

How Is It Possible to Be European?

Valéry's question about who is European, which was quoted at the beginning of this introduction, recalls the famous exclamation of surprise at the encounter with incomprehensible foreignness or alterity, in the form of a question, from letter thirty of Montesquieu's 1721 epistolary novel, *Lettres persanes*: "How is it possible to be Persian?"[6] Through the device of the candid outsider's gaze, Montesquieu was able to satirize French institutions and, more widely, the "European manners and customs" that seemed so curious to his foreign visitors. The fictional clash of cultures that he orchestrated between Persia and France, or between Asia and Europe, produced much mutual puzzlement among his characters. For some of the French interlocutors of the Persian visitors, Rica and Usbek, the notion of an existing, unfamiliar culture in a foreign nation remained difficult to understand or even conceptualize. Visitors from such a nation could only be perceived as fantastical creatures. This type of lack of comprehension across cultures is of course hardly limited to the realm of fiction. Not surprisingly, the concept of intercultural commonality between adjoining nations, or the simultaneous acceptance of other cultures as at once neighboring and different, analogous and distinct, can produce a similar level of incomprehension. The conceptions of Europe presented in the following chapters constitute limited but influential examples of literary and cinematic encounters—producing reactions ranging from the enthusiastic to the xenophobic—with those other fantastical creatures, Europeans. It is through such encounters that Europe was invented, or that its conceptions evolved from the domain of myth, in the form of some long-lost common origin, to that of history, in terms of cultural links forged over time.[7]

CHAPTER 1

Voltaire's Europe

> The Enlightenment is Europe's most prestigious achievement, and it could not have come about without the presence of a European domain, at once unified and diverse.
>
> Tzvetan Todorov, *L'Esprit des Lumières*

Few writers have so dominated their period as Voltaire (1694–1778); even fewer have accomplished this beyond the borders of their country. While he was often skeptical about the possibility of sustained, peaceful cooperation among European states, Voltaire, the multilingual philosophe who corresponded with widespread segments of the European elites, occupied a central position in the literary and political crosscurrents of his day. Much of his work thus reflects or participates in the already active debates on the issues of European identity and integration. Perhaps the most famous (or infamous) man in Europe during his life, Voltaire announces, in positive or negative terms, the variations the European topos will undergo: a utopian community of nations that would establish perpetual peace; an imperialist continent colonizing the rest of the world; a racist Europe periodically ridding itself of undesirable minorities; a rough balance of power among a group of interconnected nation-states; and an expanding union based on social and cultural commonalities.

A prolific writer in almost all genres, Voltaire was originally a playwright, poet, and historian before becoming, during and after his lifetime, the embodiment of the Enlightenment. What Daniel Brewer referred to as the "Voltaire effect" (chapter 8) still reverberates to this day. Although his historical standing as the best-known and most influential eighteenth-century philosophe remains unchanged, most of Voltaire's texts are largely forgotten. While he wrote more plays than Shakespeare, for instance, they are today almost never performed. Considering the encyclopedic scope of Voltaire's written work—memorably described by Theodore Besterman as "enough to make twenty Bibles" (533)— any attempt at exhaustiveness within this study would be futile. This chapter will center on historical and polemical texts that are most relevant to the theme of Europe, a theme easily visible within the critical literature, which includes such titles as "England and Voltaire," "Voltaire's Russia," or "Voltaire and Holland."

Delineating "Voltaire's Europe" entails an examination of the ways in which he represented different European countries, how he situated Europe in relation to the rest of the world, and to what extent he assigned the status of alterity to individual human groups and geographical areas.

Such an examination does not constitute a simple or straightforward task. Due to the ever-present threat of censorship (along with imprisonment or worse), Voltaire often resorted to obfuscatory stratagems, such as using fictional masks to express different sides of an issue or disclaiming the authorship of dangerous texts. In addition, due to the sheer size of the Voltairean corpus, the extraordinary length of his literary career, and the often petty and vindictive attitudes he displayed when engaging in personal polemics, it is not unusual to find contradictory statements within his written work. The complex issue of European identity is no exception, especially in the eighteenth-century context of nearly continuous continental and colonial warfare.[1] At one level, Voltaire sought to puncture European self-satisfaction by stressing that Asian civilizations (especially China and India) had been more advanced than their European counterparts. However, Voltaire also unmistakably posited Europe as the dominant world power, not only in terms of military force, but also in the arts and sciences.

Voltaire was proud of his capacity to adapt to, and learn from, other cultures. In a letter written after his departure from the court of Frederick II (April 23, 1754), he touts his "chameleon's skin": "I had become an Englishman in London, I am a German in Germany" (D5786).[2] This was the cosmopolitan Frenchman who valued Newton and Locke above Descartes and Pascal, who perceived philosophical model societies in distant China and India, and who cast a Russian absolute monarch as the standard-bearer of the Enlightenment. Most durably, Voltaire championed an England where he saw the triumph of bourgeois values (religious toleration, free trade, meritocracy), against an archaically semifeudal France. In a letter written in English from London (April 11, 1728), he praises his place of refuge as a free country ruled by law, where he finds himself at home: "I think, I write like a free Englishman" (D330). Voltaire was a member of what Thomas Schlereth called the "international intellectual class" of the Enlightenment, a class notable for its rejection of narrow provincialism.[3] However, Voltaire also exhibited signs of patriotism, as when he produced a poem (8: 371–95) praising the French victory over British and Dutch troops at the 1745 Battle of Fontenoy, thus fulfilling his short-lived propagandistic role as royal historiographer.[4] Although his attempts at involving himself in court politics were generally unsuccessful, Voltaire played a political role outside the governmental processes of his day. During most of his career, he was engaged in campaigns, large or small, which he always conducted vigorously, whether it was against *l'Infâme* or in favor of smallpox inoculation. He described his writing as the means to a political end, while belittling Rousseau's literary output: "Jean-Jacques writes only for the sake of writing, whereas I write for a purpose" (D14117). The first writer to regularly appeal to public opinion, Voltaire invented a role for himself as the civic conscience of a nation and a continent that frequently reverted to barbarity and fanaticism.[5]

Voltaire's advocacy of judicial reform, religious toleration, and liberal constitutional principles stands in sharp contrast with his acceptance of absolutist monarchical institutions. He exhibited an unfortunate weakness for monarchs he imagined to be enlightened or at least progressively intentioned, especially Prussian king Frederick II and Russian empress Catherine II. However, Peter Gay (166–71) argued that Voltaire did not simply endorse "enlightened despotism." Like other philosophes, Voltaire attempted to influence European regimes from which he sought support for his campaigns (particularly anticlericalism). Never a democrat in the modern sense of the word, Voltaire felt he rightly belonged, by virtue of his wealth, education, and achievements, within the elite of his society. He had no trouble conceiving that since the largest part of the French population lacked the time and the means for learning, it was necessarily excluded from participating in public affairs: "Reasoning and manual labor do not mix" (*Essai sur les mœurs*, 12: 322). A similar expression of class-based *hauteur* is found in a letter explaining that the campaign against *l'Infâme* would only need to reach "forty thousand" enlightened readers (D13212).

Associating Europeans

Although Voltaire sought to undermine what would today be called a Eurocentric view of history, this did not prevent him from presenting most of the European continent as a discernible political entity in the form of an interrelated, if diverse, system of national and religious groups. The second chapter of the *Siècle de Louis XIV* provides an examination of the different countries of Europe before the Sun King's long reign. Voltaire begins by stressing their common characteristics: "Christian Europe (with the exception of Russia) could long since have been considered a sort of large republic divided into several states . . . all sharing a similar religious background, although divided into several denominations; all sharing the same principles of civil law and politics" (14: 159). While divergent in terms of constitutional organization, the "grande république partagée en plusieurs états" suggests a mosaic of contentious but interdependent nations. The associated notions of trans-European commonality and internecine conflict are found in several Voltairean texts. In *Essai sur les mœurs*, he draws a parallel between Europe in the fifteenth century and the Hellenistic period of interconnected city-states that alternated between cooperation and conflict: "l'Europe était en grand ce qu'avait été la Grèce" (12: 7). In *Précis du Siècle de Louis XV*, a temporarily peaceful Europe, in Voltaire's simile, is likened to a reconciled family after a series of feuds: "l'Europe ressemblait à une grande famille réunie après ses différends" (15: 335). One of the recurring topics in Voltaire's historical works is that a fragile but lasting balance of power had been established among the principal European states. While this uneasy equilibrium did not prevent rivalries or outbreaks of warfare, it protected Europe from total domination by one country. By positing both national independence and increasing European interdependence, Voltaire was not far from what would later become the Gaullist concept of "l'Europe des Etats."[6] In *Essai sur les mœurs*, the sixteenth-century antagonism between French king François I and Charles V of Spain is presented as the prefiguration of a multipolar balance of power: "Le système de l'équilibre était dès lors établi en Europe" (12: 262).

Voltaire was writing during a period of European economic integration, even though its effects—increased mobility, imported products, and cultural exchanges—were limited to a privileged segment of the population. The system of equilibrium and interdependency that he discerned within Europe remained visible only at the level of either governments or cultural elites. During the eighteenth century, there was no notion of "l'Europe des peuples"—nor would Voltaire have been inclined to envision it. What he perceived was an expansion of the links between scholars that had been established during the humanistic period of the sixteenth century. In his historical texts, Voltaire emphasized the effects of these exchanges across boundaries between artists and scientists, which strengthened the ties among European nations: "A literary republic was gradually established in Europe, in spite of wars and diverging religions. All sciences and arts thus received mutual support" (*Siècle de Louis XIV*, 14: 564). Literary and scientific exchanges were facilitated throughout the eighteenth century by the growing number of academies, several of which elected Voltaire as a member and which gradually formed a trans-European network of scholars and scientists. Among other social institutions or meeting places that facilitated contacts among the cosmopolitan elites were the freemasons and the literary salons.[7] European integration was thus primarily visible at the level of social interaction. During the age of cosmopolitanism, travel was relatively unhampered by border controls or regulations regarding citizenship. For those who had the means, it was possible to live and even obtain governmental positions in a foreign country. While travel was slow, uncomfortable, and often dangerous, there were fewer customs barriers.[8]

Like all French philosophes, Voltaire had the advantage of belonging to a wider European elite within which, as Marc Fumaroli has detailed, French language and culture were predominant. For Voltaire, this privileged cultural status was the lasting legacy of the reign of Louis XIV. Published in 1752, the *Siècle de Louis XIV* provides a panorama of European politics and wars. The central focus, however, is what Voltaire sees as the exceptional cultural flowering within France during the seventeenth century. Although he was not ordinarily inclined to panegyrize French accomplishments, Voltaire considered that during the Sun King's reign (1643–1715), the French were in literary and cultural terms "les législateurs de l'Europe" (14: 539). Along with the Greece of Pericles, Rome under Augustus, and the Italian Renaissance, the "century of Louis XIV" was for Voltaire one of the four historical moments of exceptional achievements within Europe—the one during which the influence of the French language and culture reached its peak. The idea of French as the appropriate language for European elites is a familiar one in the eighteenth century, one which Voltaire helped to disseminate: due to "les grands auteurs du siècle de Louis XIV," French had become "la langue de l'Europe" (14: 554).

This sort of retroactive logic, which finds inherent qualities within the French language in order to explain its dominance after the fact, was common among writers who were proud of its privileged status. An extreme case is found in Antoine de Rivarol's *L'Universalité de la langue française* (1783): "French is the language of humankind" (80). In a foolhardy prediction, Rivarol pronounced English, the only rival of French, as unlikely to ever supplant it as a universal language and vector of culture. Writing at a time when French cultural influence had already peaked, Rivarol provides an illustration of the conceptual risk inherent to any systematically universalizing postulate, which tends to proceed from de facto commonality to enforced uniformity: "The time seems to have come to speak of the French world, as in times past of the Roman world," henceforth united "under the domination of a common language" (27). During the Revolutionary and, especially, the Napoleonic regimes, French armies would serve as the instrument of overt political and cultural "domination." For his part, Voltaire was, with some notable exceptions, far from blindly systematic. The 1764 *Discours aux Welches* (25: 229–47), for instance, constitutes a wide-ranging assault on Francocentrism. France is compared, almost always unfavorably, to other European countries. The only exception—the continuing influence of French language and literature—was also formulated as a reproach, since it resulted mainly (along with the literary legacy of the "siècle de Louis XIV") from the expulsion of French Protestants in 1685. While Voltaire's violent tone derives in part from his battles against an oppressive legal system, what this text indicates is the permanence of his comparative European outlook. Even when conceding a preeminent role to French language and culture within the European "system," he seldom showed signs of outright nationalistic chauvinism, and he was consistent in his evaluation of other European countries, such as Holland and Great Britain, as more advanced and enlightened.

A Decentered History?

Published in 1756, the *Essai sur les Mœurs* constituted an attempt at providing a universal history, one not merely centered on the Bible and on Europe—as had been the work Voltaire derided, Jacques-Bénigne Bossuet's *Discours sur l'histoire universelle* (1681).[9] In terms of methodology, Voltaire outlined his refusal of traditional, event-based history, which was often reduced to a series of battles or a succession of monarchs. By foregrounding artistic, scientific, and economic achievements, by considering how most people lived out their lives in any given historical period, Voltaire became an innovator in the field of historiography: "I seek to examine how previous societies functioned, the ways in which their families lived, which arts were developed, rather than simply recount the innumerable disasters and battles" (*Essai sur les mœurs*, 12: 53). With such notable exceptions as France's Henri IV or Russia's Peter the Great, "les grands hommes" were therefore not the determining historical agents.[10] Along with his rejection of a purely event-based conception of historical study, Voltaire exhibited uncompromising skepticism when he encountered unproven accounts of the past that tended to reinforce local prejudices: "Among all nations, history is disfigured by fables" (13: 174). Scientific standards were therefore necessary: "Let us in physics consider only that which is proven, and in history only that which is of the highest recognized level of probability" (11: 164). This historical skepticism was also visible in his refusal to accept "our almost irresistible predisposition to glorify the past at the expense of the present" (12: 66). In Voltaire's version of historiography, the past generally provides a cautionary tale rather than a model. By distancing his historical work from the established model of Christian Europe and by partly shifting his discursive focus toward Asian nations, Voltaire tended to delegitimize the religious, if not the "scientific," basis for Eurocentrism.

When considering the best means by which to study world history "en philosophe," Voltaire begins by reversing Bossuet's focus on the development of Judaism and Christianity: "first consider the East, cradle of all arts, and which gave all to the West" (11: 158). From this Voltairean premise of *translatio studii* follows the organizational principle of his book: in order to grasp the historical development of the entire world, one must look beyond Europe, to the artistic and scientific achievements of older civilizations, particularly the Chinese and the Indians. By contrast, Voltaire highlights the backwardness of Europe during much of its recorded history, thereby undermining any notion of continuity or linear progress throughout European history. In his stark vision, the Middle Ages appear as a prolonged, benighted period of abject squalor situated between the glory of the Roman Empire and the sudden flowering of the Renaissance: "Europe was a chaos in which the strongest built over the ruins of the weakest, only to be later toppled by others. Throughout this period, we see only barbaric warlords struggling against bishops for mastery over backward serfs" (11: 304). Voltaire also finds no correlation between the fall of the decadent Byzantine Empire (1453) and the Renaissance: "It is not to those who fled Constantinople that we owe the Renaissance of the arts . . . What little physics and mathematics was known came from the Arabs" (12: 61).[11] In Voltaire's depiction, scientific progress within Europe was seldom self-sustaining, and often depended on outside contributions.

Another technique of Voltaire's campaign to reduce European arrogance was to attack the presupposition that non-Christian countries would necessarily practice a form of paganism or atheism: "the false idea that all those living beyond our tiny Europe, and our former Roman masters and lawgivers, and the Greeks who taught the Romans, and the ancient Egyptians who taught the Greeks, in sum all those who differ from us, have always been contemptible, ridiculous pagans" (12: 373). In his 1765 *Philosophie de l'histoire*, Voltaire praises the Persian book of Zend, which he describes as having predated the emergence of monotheism among the Hebrews: "Here is a useful religion, based on a belief in the immortal soul and on knowledge about the Creator" (11: 34). Indeed, not only do all Asian countries practice some form of religion, but many seem to Voltaire to be superior, in terms of their civilizing effects, to the European versions: "It is only in the religions of ancient India and of the Chinese sages that men were not barbarians" (11: 51). Along with history, the discipline of geography was one of Voltaire's tools for ridiculing French and European self-centeredness. In the article "Géographie" of the *Dictionnaire philosophique*, he opposed the provincialism of the inhabitants of a Parisian street to the vastness and diversity of the world: "Use a map to show them the vastness of Africa, the empires of Japan, China, India, Turkey, Persia, the Russian empire, larger than was its Roman counterpart . . . you will thus contrast the world with Saint-Jacques Street" (19: 256).

The Cosmopolitan Uses of Exoticism

Voltaire's foregrounding of the earlier achievements of Asian civilizations, as opposed to the comparatively recent emergence of European dominance, allowed him to surreptitiously subvert religious and historical rationalizations of European arrogance. China, with its lengthy recorded history, provided the philosophe with an opportunity to indirectly undermine the Biblical account of the creation of the world: "China certainly has the oldest historical records" (11: 151).[12] The first two chapters of the *Essai sur les mœurs* posit this vast country as the opposite of Europe: philosophical, tolerant, and deistic. The manners and religion of the ancient Chinese civilization—"the wisest empire in the world" (11: 180)—can be contrasted with those of "superstitious" Hebrews and (by implication) Christians. Voltaire eventually came to equate the teachings of Confucius with the deistic form of philosophy he espoused. In the Voltairean narrative, Chinese sages, with their non-Christian system of ethics founded on reason, thus embodied human wisdom, which was easily contrasted with European received dogma and obscure metaphysics. Continuing his examination of Asia, Voltaire devotes the next six chapters to India, Persia, and Arabia.[13] Countries that he had never visited and whose languages he did not speak thus became all the more useful as rhetorical foils against seemingly self-evident European practices and institutions.

As Basil Guy noted (232), there is a parallel between Voltaire's use of a philosophical China as a contrapuntal counterpart to Europe and the construction of a similarly tolerant Great Britain (versus France) in his *Lettres philosophiques*.

A similar parallel could be established in the case of Russia under Catherine the Great, to whom Voltaire dedicated the *Philosophie de l'histoire* and whom he persistently lauded as an enlightened monarch. Voltaire's comparative method allowed him to disguise attacks on French religious and secular institutions as mere exercises in dispassionate analysis, using instances of more humane cultural practices within non-European cultures as a means of deflating European pretensions of superiority. While he regularly employed exotic foreigners in order to satirize the absurdities of European societies—for instance, in the 1767 *L'Ingénu* (21: 247–304)—Voltaire made special rhetorical use of China, systematically presenting it as an exemplar of tolerance and rational organization.[14] The opposition between what Voltaire saw as the Chinese philosophical religion and European superstitions is highlighted in *Galimatias dramatique* (24: 75–77). In this short, ironic series of exchanges, the Chinese characters, who embody reason and common sense, are subjected to the self-righteous and contradictory preachings of a Jesuit, a Jansenist, a Quaker, an Anglican, a Lutheran, a Puritan, a Moslem, and a Jew. Predictably, the Chinese end up dismissing these absurd religious proselytizers as madmen.

Daniel Hawley paints a similar picture concerning the prevailing image of India within Voltaire's work. After reading the *Ezour-Védam* (which was only revealed to be a fake in the following century), Voltaire constructed an approbatory representation of Indian Brahmins, which he put to polemical uses resembling those he had already elaborated for Chinese Mandarins. A far older, non-European civilization, India became for Voltaire the authentic source of Jewish and Christian metaphysical principles, thereby reducing their spurious historical status to one of mere imitation of the established Indian philosophical model. In *Essai sur les mœurs*, Voltaire extends Indian scholarly influence to ancient Greece, characterizing the Greeks as a fairly recent civilization, who, like the Jews, copied more than they invented. Since the religion and cosmogony of the Brahmins predated Greek mythology, Voltaire felt the latter logically derived from the former: "The Greeks, in terms of their mythology, were only the disciples of India and Egypt" (11: 183). In *Précis du Siècle de Louis XV* (15: 325), Voltaire criticizes greedy Europeans who sent military expeditions abroad, seeking to conquer and plunder India instead of trying to learn from it. Voltaire's complementary themes of Indian historical precedence and European cupidity are found in more comic form in *Les Lettres d'Amabed*. In this epistolary *conte philosophique*, Shastasid, the Indian sage, delivers a biting satire of the "European barbarians" whose "true deity is gold" (21: 437). Overall, as discursive constructs, the Indians, the Chinese, and, to a lesser extent, the Japanese, Persians, and Arabs collectively participated in Voltaire's texts, extending his cosmopolitanism beyond the limits of Europe and helping to fashion a more rational, enlightened Other for Europeans to consider and perhaps emulate.

However, Voltaire unambiguously positioned Europe as the most advanced, and therefore "civilized," continent of the modern world, a view that was quite consistent with the European colonialism he sometimes decried. While Asian civilizations were more ancient, Voltaire made it clear they had been surpassed by European scientific accomplishments: "Of any civilized people of Asia, we can say: they preceded us, and we have surpassed them" (*Essai sur les mœurs*, 12: 444). Although he began by looking beyond Europe in order to forge a more balanced view of historical development, Voltaire in fact reestablished Europe as the central and dominant locus, not only of world power, but of most areas of human activity: "All these countries were formerly far superior to our Western countries in terms of arts and sciences, but we have clearly made up for lost time" (12: 366). Concerning China, Shun-Ching Song (213–26) detailed the Voltairean representation of a backward-looking society, as compared to rapid European progress in the arts and sciences since the Renaissance. Voltaire's unequivocal affirmation of eighteenth-century European superiority tends to attenuate Besterman's evaluation of his decentering intent: "Voltaire put Western man in his place by reminding him that there exist other parts of the world, occupied by pagans and savages whose behavior oddly resembled that of civilized Christians" (419). Overall, while Voltaire's pride in European technological achievements did not blind him to its destructive consequences, he retained Europe as the civilizational norm against which he judged others.

A Euroskeptic

If ever there was an illustrative instance of the opposition between Voltaire's ironic skepticism and Jean-Jacques Rousseau's instinctive enthusiasm, it is on the issue of peace and unity within Europe—as a practical possibility, not a mere dream. In 1761, Rousseau published his *Extrait du Projet de Paix perpétuelle de Monsieur l'Abbé de Saint-Pierre*, a text that updated, in glowing terms, one of the most comprehensive proposals for European unification: "No human mind ever conceived a greater, nobler, or worthier project than that of universal and perpetual peace among all the nations of Europe" (3: 563). The Abbé de Saint-Pierre's voluminous *Projet* (1713) was neither the first nor the last such proposal designed to promote peace and unity in Europe, but it became the best known, until Immanuel Kant's 1795 *Toward Perpetual Peace*, and therefore the object of much debate among the philosophes.[15] Saint-Pierre's detailed scheme combined utopianism with hard-headed politics, calling not just for lasting peace, but also for its enforcement by a supranational organization. In a bid to make his project more palatable to the French monarchy, Saint-Pierre described it as the mere development of the erstwhile "grand dessein" of King Henri IV (1589–1610) and Sully, his minister: "it was first conceived by Henri the Great" (165). Interestingly, Saint-Pierre's text repeatedly uses terms that are not far removed from those of Voltaire: "société européenne" and "système de l'union européenne."[16] Another similarity is that both designate the Ottoman Empire as the enemy of Europe. For Saint-Pierre, peace within Europe is not simply an end in itself: thanks to

European unity, "it will be profitable, simple, and glorious for the Christian monarchs to expel the Turks from Europe" (465).

Voltaire wrote about Saint-Pierre in *Siècle de Louis XIV*, ridiculing the Abbé as an idle dreamer: "He almost always presented the impossible as achievable" (14: 128). Not surprisingly, in a letter to Voltaire, Frederick II similarly dismissed Saint-Pierre's project as utopian: "It merely requires, among other trifles, that all of Europe concur" (D2602). Voltaire referred to Saint-Pierre's work throughout his career, most often disparagingly: "The only perpetual peace which could be instituted among humans is toleration: the peace dreamt of by the Abbé de Saint-Pierre is a pipedream" (*De la paix perpétuelle*, 28: 103). In his 1761 *Rescrit de l'Empereur de la Chine à l'occasion du projet de paix perpétuelle*, a satirical response to Rousseau's *Extrait*, Voltaire used a familiar rhetorical device in order to deflate European pretensions: the apparently puzzled musings of a foreign narrator encountering the narrow, self-serving European view of the rest of the world. This short text ridicules Rousseau's reformulation of the project put forward by Saint-Pierre, pointing out both its practical futility and its Eurocentrism: "The rest of the world had been forgotten" (24: 231).

For Voltaire, no supranational organization could prevent aggression initiated by states seeking territorial or other spoils, nor could it eliminate deep-seated divisions over competing religious dogmas, which lead to horrific civil wars. Europe was already ravaged by recurring conflicts when it was still largely dominated by Catholicism. During the Reformation, the level of mutual intolerance only increased with the emergence of Protestant denominations. In his epic poem *La Henriade* (1728), Voltaire depicted Henri IV, whom he admired for ending the sixteenth-century wars of religion in France, as refusing to choose between the twin dogmatic evils embodied by Geneva and Rome (8: 66). Through his evaluation of Saint-Pierre's project, Voltaire once again denounced the ingrained intolerance and fanaticism that gave rise to divisiveness, hatred, and wars (a campaign of course linked to his call to "Ecraser l'Infâme"): "The only way to bring about peace is to destroy the superstitions that divide people, and to restore the truth that unites them" (*De la paix perpétuelle*, 28: 128). While he ridiculed Saint-Pierre's utopianism, Voltaire obviously reflected on the preconditions for the eventual establishment of peace in Europe—and thereby commented upon Saint-Pierre's work at length. It is interesting that Voltaire wrote so often about a man he tended to dismiss as an ineffectual dreamer. A parallel could be made in the case of the Jews, whose historical status Voltaire strove to diminish, but about whom he produced so many texts.

Although he remained convinced that no supranational organization would be capable of preventing internecine wars, Voltaire's sarcastic criticism of Saint-Pierre's proposals did have a positive corollary, one that is linked to his view of the role of economic self-interest. For Voltaire, it is through the cultivation of trade and commerce, or the search for profits, that nations become politically strong. Continuous trade requires peace and the rule of law, not prolonged wars. Once enlightened people realize the advantages of peaceful development and the absurdity of religious divisions, they will tend to achieve an international balance of power, based on economically beneficial interdependence, that will curtail, if not eliminate, the use of warfare as a means of achieving political gains. In his commendatory characterization of international commerce as a contributing factor for mutual comprehension and cooperation, Voltaire was diametrically opposed to Rousseau, but quite close to Montesquieu.[17] As Merle Perkins argued (33), Voltaire's cautiously melioristic approach, which presumed the gradual diffusion of philosophic ideas, represented another form of idealism. As previously mentioned, the Voltairean vision of enlightened nations devoting their energies to economic development and maintaining a rough balance of power through a system of alliances was not inconsistent with the more recent Gaullist concept of "l'Europe des Etats." But neither was it incompatible with the continuation of European imperialism and colonialism throughout the world.

Holland and Freedom

In Voltaire's 1768 *La Princesse de Babylone* (21: 369–433), the star-crossed lovers Formosante and Amazan provide a review of the progress, or stagnation, of philosophical ideals as they chase each other over most of Europe.[18] Holland is one of the countries, along with England and Russia, that receives effusive praise in this *conte philosophique*. Voltaire visited Holland several times during a span of thirty years.[19] Although he never learned the language or came to know the country as well as England, he was obviously impressed with what he saw of Dutch religious, economic, and political life. In this bourgeois, Protestant republic, he found prosperity, relative freedom of expression, and peaceful coexistence among the believers of diverse religions. While Voltaire did not devote a separate historical text to "les Provinces-Unies," his observations are found throughout his works. A letter written during his second trip to Holland (October 7, 1722) provides a preview of the praise for British tolerance and industry—and the concomitant implied criticism of France—that Voltaire would develop in *Lettres philosophiques*: "They do not spend their time trying to curry favor at court, or lining up to watch a prince go by; they remain unpretentious and industrious" (D128). Praise for Holland is also found in *Essai sur les mœurs* (13: 116), where Voltaire contrasts the country's limited dimensions and lack of natural resources with its astounding achievements as a commercial and maritime power. As Jeroom Vercruysse points out (75–76), Voltaire could also be condescending or sarcastic in his descriptions of Dutch culture and manners. On the whole, however, Holland was for Voltaire a small-scale rhetorical societal model, in many ways a prototype for the more extensive model he would construct after his stay in England.[20]

For a French writer who often had to contend with the threat of censorship or worse, there were famous literary precedents to ponder when traveling to the Dutch republic. Holland had been home for René Descartes (from 1628 to 1649) and Pierre Bayle (from 1681 until his death in 1706). The *Discours de la méthode* (1637) and the *Dictionnaire historique et critique* (1697), two texts that, in different ways, profoundly influenced Voltaire, had both been published in that country. Voltaire was mindful of the comparative degree of literary and political freedom these exiled writers had found in Holland. In a letter (December 8, 1736), he complained of "persecutions" after his publication of *Le Mondain* and mused about seeking shelter abroad, "à l'exemple de Descartes et de Bayle" (D1220). Holland's principal attraction for Voltaire was as a place of refuge. Due to the relative lack of censorship, it was easier for him to have some of his works published there rather than in France.[21] While Voltaire was somewhat of a trailblazer as an eighteenth-century French writer traveling to England, this was not the case for Holland, which already constituted a privileged destination for travelers who were looking for a different religious and political model.[22] As a prosperous republic that was geographically close to France, but divergent in its religious and social structures, Holland offered an accessible case study for the philosophes.

An English Model

After the infamous *bastonnade* he suffered at the hands of the Chevalier de Rohan's lackeys, and after spending time in the Bastille because he vowed to avenge himself,[23] Voltaire lived in England from May 1726 to November 1728. His enthusiastic appreciation of its society and culture, his complex relationship with English thought and literature, and the role he played in shaping the image of that country in France have generated one of the largest sections of the critical literature devoted to his work. There is no doubt that, during his stay, Voltaire became deeply immersed in English literature and culture in general. He learned the language well enough to write two texts (*Essay on Epick Poetry* and *Essay on the Civil Wars in France*) as well as numerous letters in English. Having already met Bolingbroke in France, he would become acquainted with such authors as Alexander Pope, John Gay, and Jonathan Swift. He was received at court by both George I and George II. He frequently attended plays, including several by Shakespeare. He also attended the impressive funeral at Westminster Abbey of Isaac Newton, whose work Voltaire and Emilie du Châtelet would popularize in France.[24]

From the first, Voltaire's impressions of Great Britain were highly positive. In a letter written in English (October 26, 1726), he described its inhabitants as "fond of their liberty, learned, witty, despising life and death, a nation of philosophers" (D303). In *Lettres philosophiques* (1734), Voltaire reserved particular appreciation for the accomplishments—and the highly regarded societal status—of British scientists and philosophers Bacon, Newton, and Locke.[25] Gustave Lanson famously described this book as "the first bomb thrown against *l'ancien régime*" (52) because it indirectly attacked French social and political institutions by pointing out the comparative advantages of the more enlightened British model. Voltaire was severely punished for throwing his bomb: his book was condemned and burned shortly after its publication, and he had to flee to Emilie du Châtelet's residence at Cirey to avoid imprisonment by *lettre de cachet*. To no avail, Voltaire had adapted the relatively innocuous genre of the travel account to suit his polemical needs. The vignettes he drew of British religious, cultural, economic, and political life implied unfavorable comparisons with their French counterparts. For the philosophe, the superiority of British empiricism over French reverence for established tradition was readily visible: smallpox vaccination, religious tolerance, trade and industry, and science and rationalism. As Christiane Mervaud noted ("Des relations de voyage au mythe anglais des Lettres philosophiques," 15), Voltaire's image of the country as a whole, while based on observed facts, reaches the dimensions of a literary myth.

Voltaire's depictions of British particularisms were not always exempt from a tone of amused condescension, as in the case of the Quakers (the first four letters). Nor were his accounts of British institutions and political practices always accurate. As Gay pointed out, Voltaire's description of the country's constitutional system in particular "omitted some inconvenient facts" (59). The same could be said of his sanguine evaluation of British society in general. This selective form of description was, however, in keeping with Voltaire's polemical intent. By exaggerating the advantages of the British social order—religious tolerance, commercial prosperity, and rule of law—he could more effectively criticize the corresponding failings of the French system. Through the implicit contrast he established between progressive Great Britain and retrograde France, praise for one country could be clearly understood as criticism for the other, a technique he extended throughout his writings, across very diverse genres. In *L'Ingénu*, the opacity and arbitrariness of French justice is emphasized by a contrasting reference to the rule of law on the other side of the English Channel: "Are there no laws in this country? Men are condemned without a hearing! Such is not the case in England" (21: 285). In *Dictionnaire philosophique*, Voltaire compares a bourgeois, commercial, tolerant, forward-looking Great Britain with a static, dogmatic, aristocratic France: "Liberty and property: the English ralling-cry" ("Propriété," 20: 291). Chapter 83 of the *Essai sur les mœurs* provides a critique of the French system of three social orders, targeting the privileges of the nobility and particularly the power of the clergy: "France is the only country where the clergy constitutes a separate social order" (12: 70). The same chapter compares the rarely convened *Etats Généraux* to the more advanced British Parliament. As René Pomeau recounts (1: 262–64), the brutal contrast between the respective funeral rites accorded to two actresses—one French, one

English—was particularly distressing given Voltaire's reverence for the theater. In his poem *La Mort de Mlle Lecouvreur* (1730), Voltaire had another opportunity to rail against French "superstition" and the repressive power of the clergy, which had denied a decent burial to a distinguished French actress: "Is it only in England that one dare think?" (9: 370).

An especially important area of comparison was in the economic field, as well as in the conceptual interconnections Voltaire perceived between free trade, individual freedom, and national power and stability. During what was still largely a protectionist, mercantilist age, he praised liberal capitalism as a contributing factor in the development of toleration and freedom, as well as international integration. Overall, for Voltaire, the uninhibited development of free trade and enterprise generated beneficial social consequences. His positive view of economic activity generally did not take into account such real-world aspects of eighteenth-century European expansionism as colonialism and the slave trade, which he alternately condemned or countenanced. In the tenth letter, "Sur le commerce," Voltaire compares the energetically entrepreneurial spirit of the British elites, and its resulting social effects, to the obsession with aristocratic titles in Germany and France: "Trade, which made the citizens of England wealthy, also helped to make them free, and this freedom has in turn extended trade; thus was built a great nation" (*Lettres philosophiques*, 22: 109–10). By linking the ascendancy of Britain as a world power to its encouragement of trade and commerce, Voltaire articulated the connection, which has become axiomatic, between a nation's economic strength and its geopolitical power.

In economic matters, Voltaire—an astute businessman who became "one of the wealthiest private commoners in Europe" (Besterman 162)—did not exhibit the sort of amateurism that characterized his attempts to serve as a freelance diplomat for Louis XV. He wrote often on economics and on its links with the backward social and political situation in France. During the eighteenth century, in a situation that bears some resemblance to the late twentieth century, the level of international commerce was evolving at a quicker pace than the differing political and financial institutions of the countries it increasingly interconnected. In France, as recounted by Voltaire in his 1769 *Histoire du Parlement de Paris* (16: 58–67), the resounding failure of John Law's economic reforms during the Regency had slowed the much-needed modernization of the country's monetary system. Voltaire felt that, unlike France, Great Britain had successfully adapted its legal and constitutional framework in order to accommodate the economic changes resulting from the development of trade. These changes had in turn beneficially impacted the social and religious fabric of a potentially divided country. In a passage of the *Lettres philosophiques* that deserves close scrutiny, this impact was particularly visible at the London Stock Exchange: "Step into the London Stock Exchange, a more respectable place than many courts: you will there find assembled for useful purposes the representatives of all nations. There, Jews, Muslims, and Christians treat each other as if they were of the same religion, and only call infidels those who go bankrupt; there, Presbyterians trust Anabaptists, and Anglicans accept the word of Quakers" ("Sur les presbytériens," 22: 99).

By directly addressing his readers and figuratively asking them to step into the financial center of London, Voltaire progresses semantically from the stock exchange to the exchange of values, praising the symbol of British capitalism while disparaging the intolerance and corruption found in the churches and royal palaces of Europe. This passage is inserted within the first seven letters, which cover the different religious denominations Voltaire encountered during his stay in Britain. It implicitly establishes a contrast between that country's religious plurality and relative tolerance, and the religious and political hegemony of the Catholic Church in France. Voltaire thus elevates the stock exchange to the status of a benign social institution that encourages peaceful coexistence among diverse religious groups. The economic domain, as embodied by the temple of commerce, symbolically exerts a calming influence on the passions and the conflicts of the political and religious domains by providing a neutral, peaceful area for human activity, diminishing extraneous differences among religious groups and channeling collective energies toward productive ends. The stock exchange in effect becomes a relatively open and accessible locus of power, counterbalancing the arbitrary power of the courts and the churches. By associating London's financial market with the values he saw lacking in France—tolerance and reason—Voltaire metonymically established it as the unprejudiced arbitrator of feuding religious and political factions. In Holland, and especially in Great Britain, Voltaire found examples of unfettered, beneficial economic development that he could offer up as models for the eventual establishment of religious toleration and a rational political order within France.

Against Anglomania

Voltaire's admiration for the science, philosophy, and social system he discovered in Great Britain stands in stark contrast with his negative appraisal of the esthetic standards of its theatrical literature. Although he remained proud of having popularized British scientists and writers, Voltaire came to regret the cultural *anglomanie* he had helped to create. In particular, he sought to counter what he saw as the ill-deserved fame of British playwrights. Voltaire's choice of the theater as his polemical focus is not surprising, coming from a playwright whose work—which upheld the elaborate stylistic rules of seventeenth-century classicism—dominated French stages during the eighteenth century. His personal stake in artistic tastes partly accounts for the glaring discrepancy between his cross-cultural outlook in the political domain and the patriotism that undergirded his literary conservatism. As early as the *Lettres philosophiques*, he detected a striking disparity between the enlightened societal institutions of the British and their "barbaric" tastes. In his eighteenth letter, "Sur la tragédie," Voltaire attempts to translate excerpts from Shakespeare's work and declares British playwrights constitutionally incapable of producing tragedies that approach the established French standards of regularity and decorum: "Their plays, generally barbaric, devoid of propriety, show surprising flahes of light in the midst of their darkness" (22: 152). The same letter faintly praises Shakespeare while strongly denouncing his lack of taste and his ignorance of the accepted—that is, seventeenth-century French—rules of the theater: "His genius was strong and prolific, natural and sublime, without the slightest trace of good taste or knowledge of the rules" (22: 148).

Voltaire's mixed feelings led him to try to "improve" upon Shakespeare, producing one of his few dull texts, especially when compared to the original. *La Mort de César* (3: 297–366), his 1733 rewriting of *Julius Caesar*, eliminated Shakespeare's "barbarisms" and followed the rules of French tragic theater, thereby restricting the expansive scope of the original play and producing the sort of dry, passionless work the Romantics would later rail against. In 1761, Voltaire's *Appel à toutes les nations d'Europe* (24: 192–221) once again characterized Shakespeare's tragedies, particularly *Hamlet* and *Othello*, as barbaric in form and content, regardless of the English playwright's natural genius.[26] However, this traditional Voltairean lament was now part of a wider campaign against *l'anglomanie* and its corrosive effects on French tastes. For the greater part of his career, Voltaire was an influential cultural intermediary between Great Britain and France. With such texts as the *Appel*, he cast himself as the defender of French classical culture against the crudities of the stages of London, the imitation of which could only accelerate the decline of prevailing artistic standards. French literary classicism, with its elaborate stylistic rules, especially in the theatrical realm for which Voltaire felt a special affinity, reflected the rigid political order of the seventeenth century. Many of its esthetic codes would persist into the eighteenth century, including of course in Voltaire's own plays, even as the dominant focus of French letters shifted from the psychological to the political domain. The cosmopolitan Voltaire, who had been an innovator in other domains, staunchly remained the conservative voice of the French theatrical tradition, continuing to interpret English theater according to the constraining rules that governed what he considered to be the crowning glory of French—indeed world—literature.

Frederick the Great

It is clear that Voltaire was far less interested in German culture than he had been in the case of Great Britain. He did not seek contact with the intellectual life found outside Frederick's court, nor did he attempt to visit most of the kingdom. Germany as a cultural and (potentially) national entity, since it was divided into a series of mini-states, and the object of power struggles between Prussia, Austria, England, and France, seems to have attracted comparatively little attention on Voltaire's part. His best-known image of German principalities is the *Thunder-ten-tronckh* castle of *Candide*. The idle aristocracy of this *conte philosophique*, with its obsession on the required "quartiers de noblesse," is closer to a miniature version of the French monarchy than to the enlightened models Voltaire perceived in Holland and Great Britain. In his writings, no German state, aside from Prussia, seemed to hold any influence or promise. Chapter 178 of the *Essai sur les mœurs* characterizes Germany at the beginning of the seventeenth century as a politically inconsequential area: "It was impossible for this vast country, divided among so many principalities, with no trade or wealth, to have much influence over the European system" (13: 40). Voltaire's lengthy stay in Prussia (1750–53) followed the untimely death of Emilie du Châtelet. It also resulted from his sagging fortunes at the French court. However, it was mainly the myth of Frederick the Great, an enlightened monarch— "un roi philosophe"—and not the reality of Prussian political and intellectual life, that spurred Voltaire's desire to reside in Potsdam.[27] Perhaps because of his personal relationship with Frederick, Voltaire never constructed a Prussian or German model to use as a critical yardstick against France. He may also have sought out similarities instead of differences. Prussia, with its Francophone king and its Academy that deliberated in French, required less adjustment on the part of Voltaire: "This feels like France. Only our language is spoken. German is for soldiers and horses; it is useful only when traveling" (D4248).[28]

Before moving to Potsdam, Voltaire had tried to use his meetings and his epistolary ties with Frederick as a means of advancing French interests in the context of the power struggle between Prussia and Austria.[29] He had closely followed Frederick's military exploits, attempting to influence a king who had presented himself as a peace-minded philosophe during the early phase of their correspondence but who proved to be all too willing to use force in order to further his ambitions. Writing after one of Frederick's bloody victories, Voltaire showed concern but not condemnation (May 26, 1742): "Has the Solomon of the North become its Alexander?" (D2611). A few weeks later (June 30, 1742), Voltaire apparently wanted to believe that Frederick's genuine intent was one of lasting peace: "I believe that you will force all the warring powers to make peace, and that the hero of the century will be the pacifier of Germany and Europe" (D2623). Voltaire would of course be continually disappointed by the disparity between the Prussian king's philosophical pretensions and his cynical use of military power.[30] For his part, Frederick sought to make use of their friendship to further his aims of representing himself as the philosopher-prince who was transforming Berlin into "l'Athènes du nord." As the reigning prince of letters, Voltaire constituted the crowning glory of Frederick's efforts to enhance the cultural status of his court. As it turned out, Voltaire was not always the reliable panegyrist for Frederick that he would later become for Catherine II of Russia. Partly due to the lack of direct contact with Catherine and with the reality of her rule, Voltaire's fantasy of Frederick as a *roi philosophe*, working to bring enlightenment where there had only been barbarity, would later be transferred to the Russian empress. After leaving Frederick's court, Voltaire eventually settled near Geneva, effectively creating his own little principality at Ferney.

A Russian Fantasy

For Voltaire, Russia, since the reign of Peter the Great, had definitely become a part of Europe. Indeed, he saw Russia as having made such rapid progress that it had effectively overtaken some of its Western European societal models. Because the Russian empire had only recently emerged from barbarity, Voltaire was all the more enthusiastic about what appeared to be an immense laboratory for the application of philosophic principles. Long before French communists would find that "light comes from the East," Voltaire heralded a new dawn at the extremity of Europe based on the absolute power of monarchs determined to bring progress to their long-benighted country. The phrase used by Voltaire relied on the same metaphor, if not the same geographic direction: "It is from the North that light comes to us today" (*Epître à l'Impératrice de Russie, Catherine II*, 10: 435–38). Ironically for Voltaire, the historian of Russia, this vast country was in many ways terra incognita; he never traveled there and had no knowledge of the language. Since there was little or no French scholarship available, he relied on fragmentary information supplied by biased Russian officials.[31] The distant Russian empire was thus for Voltaire a European version of China and India onto which he could project the favorable image he needed, no matter how unrealistic it might be, in order to crititically reflect it back toward France and the rest of Europe. In Voltaire's literary landscape, Russia loomed as an awakening giant, energetically putting into practice the ideals of the Enlightenment, which many countries of Western Europe still stubbornly resisted. His enthusiastic endorsement of Russia's program of modernization constituted another instance of his well-honed rhetorical strategy of praising foreign cultures as a means of indirectly criticizing France and Europe: "Within half a century, the court of [Russia] became more enlightened than Greece or Rome had ever been" (*Philosophie de l'histoire*, 11: 43).

In *Voltaire's Russia* (chapter 2), Carolyn Wilberger recounted the circumstances under which Voltaire wrote his *Histoire de l'empire de Russie sous Pierre le Grand* (16: 377–639). Peter the Great had already been portrayed by Voltaire as the adversary of Charles XII, during the Great Northern War of 1700–21, in his 1731 *Histoire de Charles XII roi de Suède* (16: 123–354). Voltaire's interest in the Russian monarch is also visible in his 1748 *Anecdotes sur le czar Pierre le Grand* (23: 281–94). In his history of Russia, Voltaire painted a picture of a ruthless but well-intentioned czar single-handedly transforming the isolated, backward country he had inherited. Thanks to the work begun by Peter and continued by his successors, Russia had been rapidly modernized, growing in population and wealth. This Voltairean image of Peter's quasi-Promethean role as a visionary ruler dragging an entire country from the depths of barbarity is also found in *Essai sur les mœurs*: "Until Czar Peter, Russia, buried under despotism, remained almost unknown to the peoples of southern Europe" (13: 135). Along with technical modernization came social and cultural Europeanization, as Peter forced Russians to adapt to "the manners and customs of the countries he visited" (*Histoire de Russie*, 16: 468).

The issue of Russian efforts, ruthlessly initiated by Peter, to resemble the more advanced nations of Western Europe became the focus of one of the debates that pitted Voltaire against Rousseau.[32] In the article "Pierre le Grand et J.-J. Rousseau" of his *Dictionnaire philosophique* (20: 218–22), Voltaire ridiculed Rousseau's negative judgment on the forced modernization of Russian society. The eighteenth-century debate over Russia's transformation is eerily similar to current controversies concerning the presumed "threat" posed by European integration (or, for that matter, American pop culture) to the preservation of individual national identities. As Wilberger put it, "While Rousseau wanted to create 'Russians,' Voltaire wished to make 'Europeans'" (*Voltaire's Russia*, 233). Voltaire's position on Peter's efforts to Europeanize Russia provides the clearest instance of his universalizing tendency. Voltaire refuted Rousseau's insistence on the value of a distinct national character, arguing that excessive particularism would lead to xenophobia, intolerance, and war. Although he did not condone Peter's brutal methods, Voltaire found lasting intrinsic value in Russia's adoption of Western European cultural norms. By creating a civilized/savage dichotomy, he asserted the superiority of what he saw as universally valid European societal standards over primitive Russian practices.

Voltaire would find a worthy successor to Peter in Catherine the Great, with whom he of course corresponded and who would also supplant Frederick as his favorite enlightened monarch. The philosophe's praise for Catherine was even more lavish than that which he had bestowed on Peter: "She has deserved the title of mother of her country, and she will have that of benefactor of the human race, if she perseveres" (*La Princesse de Babylone*, 21: 404). Throughout the latter part of his career, he became Catherine's most fervent literary sycophant, as is visible, for example, in his *Lettres sur les panégyriques* (26: 307–14). Voltaire enthusiastically supported Catherine during the war she waged against the Ottoman Empire (1768–74). He wanted to see the Turks, oppressors of the Greeks, expelled from Europe. Voltaire's call for Greek independence prefigured the wider philhellenic movement within Western Europe. After having so vividly depicted the horror and absurdity of war in *Candide*, Voltaire did not hesitate to praise Catherine's Russia as a liberator throughout its war effort.[33]

Voltaire posited the Russian empire not only as a part of Europe but also as the instrument of the continent against the Turkish outsiders. Voltaire, who had long sought to revalorize Asian cultures and to deflate European arrogance, thus resorted to traditional prejudices against Moslems and Asians.[34] In several texts, he provided propaganda for the wars of "la Minerve du nord." In *Le Tocsin des rois* (1771), a tract for which he was paid by Catherine, Voltaire labels the Ottoman Empire "l'implacable ennemi de toute l'Europe" (28: 468). The same jingoistic image is found in *Traduction du poème de Jean Plokof* (1770): "Aux armes contre les ennemis de l'Europe!" (28: 365). In *Ode Pindarique* (8: 491–93), he issues a call to liberate Greece from the Ottoman Empire—as well as a call for a new crusade. While Voltaire resorted to outright warmongering in the case of Turkey, he limited himself to rationalizing the 1772 partition of Poland in which both of his royal correspondents, Catherine and Frederick, participated.[35] In his *Essai historique et critique sur les dissensions des églises de Pologne* (1767), Voltaire tended to make religious divisions within a backward Poland—not Russian expansionism—responsible for an armed Russian intervention. Catherine is depicted, in terms that seem to anticipate Orwellian Newspeak, as benevolently seeking to calm internal Polish dissension: "She sent peace with an army" (26: 465). In literary terms, Voltaire's symbolic elision of Poland, along with his call for the expulsion of the Turks, illustrates to what extent his concept of Europe was linked to the struggle against religious fanaticism, a struggle in which he saw no choice but to ally himself with tyrannical despots.

Europe without Jews

The issue of Voltaire's anti-Semitism remains controversial.[36] Léon Poliakov identified Voltaire as an influential figure in the transition from religious anti-Judaism to a "scientific," race-based rejection of Jews within Europe. For Voltaire, Jews had long been almost universally hated, and deservedly so, for reasons that went beyond traditional religious intolerance: "They were hated, not because they believed in one God, but because they ridiculously hated other nations, because they were barbarians who massacred without pity their defeated enemies, because this vile nation, superstitious, ignorant, deprived of trade and the arts, was contemptuous of more advanced nations" ("Remarques sur les Pensées de Pascal," 22: 45). As Poliakov noted (3: 103), during the German Occupation, Henri Labroue produced an anti-Semitic book consisting mainly of excerpts from Voltaire's works, which were thus instrumentalized for purposes Voltaire could not have imagined.[37]

Given his long-standing hostility toward the "superstitions" of all revealed religions, it is not surprising that Voltaire should have expressed similar contempt for Judaism as he did for Christianity and Islam. However, Judaism as a religion, and the Jews as a people, are present in exceptionally large segments of the Voltairean corpus, as is highlighted in David Lévy's study of Voltaire's exegesis, or rather antiexegesis, of the Pentateuch: "Jews constitute a veritable obsession for the philosophe. The same can be said of the Old Testament" (223). Since there was little risk in attacking them, Jews were particularly useful for polemical purposes. If Jews had not existed, Voltaire would have had to invent them.[38] By purposefully considering the Hebrew Bible as a literal document,

Voltaire was provided with a vast and relatively easy target, one which allowed him to stress its absurd chronology, logical inconsistencies, and lascivious occurrences. He could thus at once condemn the religion of the Jews directly and the basis of Christian revelation indirectly. For him, it was clear that Jews, who incarnated a particularly contemptible form of preposterous and immoral religious dogma, would progressively disappear as a group, along with the more fanatical Christian sects, as a result of the spread of philosophical principles. While Voltaire used praise for China and India in order to censure European institutions, his attempt at undermining the Biblical foundations of Christianity was achieved through attacks on Jews, who consistently exhibited rapacity and barbaric bloodthirstiness in war and peace: "[The tiny Jewish nation] itself boasts of having left Egypt as a horde of thieves, carrying away all it had borrowed from the Egyptians. It finds glory in never having spared the aged, or women, or children, in the villages and the towns it seized. It dares to display irreconcilable hatred towards all other nations. It rises up against all its masters; always superstitious, always greedy for the wealth of others, always barbaric, groveling when defeated, and insolent in times of prosperity" (*Philosophie de l'histoire*, 11: 121–22).[39]

The irredeemably backward Jews are contrasted with their conquerors, who developed from barbarity to a civilizing historical role: "The Romans, who over time became civilized, spread their civilization to the vanquished barbarians, and became the legislators of the West" (11: 146). Voltaire presents the respective historical fortunes of Romans and Jews as an object lesson; while the monotheistic Jews clung to their barbaric superstitions, the pagan—but less fanatical—Romans evolved into the dominant civilizing force of the ancient world. As Arthur Hertzberg argued (299–308), Voltaire cast the classical Roman period as the true European tradition, while he saw Jews and Christians as having introduced an alien, Oriental element that needed to be extirpated. A similar technique is used in Voltaire's *Sermon des cinquante* (1762), which ridicules "the writings of the Hebrews" (24: 439) before moving on to Christianity as an equally mendacious outgrowth of Judaism: "the miserable people from which issued forth the Christian religion, the source of so many divisions, civil wars, and crimes" (24: 449).[40] While Voltaire's anticlericalism led him to situate Christians at the same benighted level as Jews, he could also attack Christians, when it was consistent with his purposes, for persecuting Jews, as in his 1761 *Sermon du Rabbin Akib* (24: 277–85). However, this pamphlet—a call for generalized religious tolerance—was not typical of Voltaire's writings on Jews.

Jews and Jewish history constituted key rhetorical battlegrounds in Voltaire's campaign against "l'Infâme"—an ill-defined term he applied to manifestations of religious fanaticism and intolerance.[41] With few exceptions, he placed Jews, a persecuted minority, within the same category as the powerful Catholic institutions he was indirectly attacking. As a group, Jews probably remained literary abstractions for Voltaire, in the same way that Chinese and Indian sages were polemically useful discursive constructs. He seems to have perceived few distinctions between the Jews of eighteenth-century Europe and the image of the rapacious and bloodthirsty Jews of Biblical times that he had so painstakingly elaborated. However, Jews did constitute a very real minority in France and Europe, a minority that he attacked as harshly as the state and religious power structures he sought to transform. By contrast, Voltaire was never as unremittingly hostile toward another persecuted French religious minority, the Protestants. Graham Gargett concludes his study of Voltaire's views on Protestantism with the notion of a "temporary alliance" (471–79), partly based on a common refusal of the centralizing power of the popes. Voltaire could thus make occasional use of Protestantism in his campaign against *l'Infâme*. The same could be said about Islam, which he sometimes attacked as another descendant of Judaism but which he also utilized as a polemical tool against Christian clerical oppression. Magdy Badir and Djavâd Hadidi have detailed the evolving representation of Islam within Voltaire's works. Badir (151–90) highlights the ways in which Voltaire made use of Islamic faith and history in his battle against Bossuet's view of divinely inspired Christian history. As Hadidi argues (153–73), Voltaire overcame many of his initial prejudices toward Mohammed and Islam, eventually coming to compare them favorably to Jesus and Christianity. While Voltaire did at times praise Protestantism and Islam in order to undermine the Catholic institutions that wielded real power in France, he could make no such use of Judaism, which remained for him the underlying source of Catholic dogma.

Another backward and reviled group that Voltaire designated for exclusion was the Gypsies: "a tiny nation as vagabond, as despised as the Jews, and dedicated to another form of plunder" (*Essai sur les mœurs*, 12: 165). The two stateless, trans-European ethnic groups are unequivocally associated in terms of their level of barbarity and malevolence: chapter 103 is devoted to "l'état des juifs en Europe," and chapter 104 to "ceux qu'on appelait Bohèmes ou Egyptiens" (12: 162–66). Taken together with his urging Catherine II to expel the Turks from Europe, Voltaire's exclusionary attitude toward Jews and Gypsies suggests a mental landscape of a fairly uniform European area made up of distinct nationalities and Christian sects that have achieved mutual tolerance through the gradual adoption of philosophical standards of conduct—and that have clearly identified the groups that cannot be accepted in their midst.

Nonhumans

In *Essai sur les mœurs*, Voltaire described the attitude of the ancient Romans toward Jews, as he understood it: "They were seen as we see Negroes, as an inferior human species" (11: 223). This is the sort of statement that illustrates Voltaire's double legacy: he developed his own form of intolerance and exclusionary logic, grounded on the purported unvarying essence of an ethnic group, which did not prevent him from strongly decrying the effects of crude xenophobia and religious bigotry. While he courageously and often singlehandedly aided the victims of religious persecution, Voltaire also showed signs of the worst kind of racism: that which denies certain groups full membership in the human race. In the 1769 *Lettres d'Amabed*, the title character is forcibly taken from India to Rome in order to be tried as a heretic. On the way, his boat stops off on the African coast. He delivers this comment on "ces animaux," the local inhabitants: "No art form is known among all these populations. They cannot decide if they are descended from apes, or if the apes came from them" (21: 462). Voltaire consistently refused to accept the idea of a common ancestry for humanity. Commenting on the discovery of the inhabitants of Lapland, he categorized them, despite their relative geographic proximity, as radically distinct from the other inhabitants of Europe: "We were thus presented with a new human species, while America, Asia, and Africa had shown us many others" (*Essai sur les mœurs*, 12: 223). The lack of a common origin for humankind is later presented as self-evident, based on its discernible diversity: "Since the African Negro does not originate from among our white peoples, why should those of a red, olive, or ash color come from our lands? And where would the original land be found?" (12: 385). Similarly, chapter 2 of the *Philosophie de l'histoire*, "Des différentes races d'homme," reinforces Voltaire's assertion of the multiplicity, and concomitant inequality, of human races (11: 5). Not surprisingly, the affirmation of different origins for human groups leads to the use of presumed racial characteristics in order to justify intellectual and physical hierarchies among them: "The Negro race is a human species that is different from ours" (*Essai sur les mœurs*, 12: 357). Using the type of pseudoscientific approach that relied on apparently objective comparative anthropological data and that would come to be one of the hallmarks of racist discourse during the next century, Voltaire established varying degrees within his hierarchical classification of races, which of course placed Europeans at one extremity of a biological continuum, animals at the other extremity, and Africans at different levels in between:

> In the middle of Africa lives a race, small in number, of short men as white as snow, with faces shaped like those of Negroes, and whose round eyes closely resemble those of partridges: the Portuguese call them *Albinos*. They are short, weak, and cross-eyed. The wool that covers their head and constitutes their eyebrows is like thin white cotton. They are inferior to the Negroes in terms of strength and reasoning. Nature may have situated them below the Negroes and the Hottentots, but above the apes, as one of the stages in the descent from humans to animals. (12: 367–68)[42]

Voltaire presented his system of racial differences and inequalities as based on the natural order and therefore not subject to change: "There is in each human species, as is the case for plants, a principle that differentiates them" (12: 380). Voltaire's clearly stated racial prejudice generally coexisted with lukewarm or infrequent condemnations of colonialism and slavery. In *Histoire de Jenni* (1775), the wise, deistic character Freind denounces European "barbaric greed" (21: 560) as the root of slavery. Chapter 9 of this *conte philosophique* also includes a denunciation of the massacres committed by the Spaniards in the New World. At times, however, Voltaire stoops to an outright justification of slavery by shifting the responsibility for its existence to the Africans themselves: "We buy domestic slaves only among the Negroes. We incur condemnation because of this trade: a nation that sells off its children is even guiltier than the buyer; these commercial exchanges demonstrate our superiority; those who seek out a master were born to have one" (13: 177–78). Elsewhere, Voltaire does condemn slavery, if only as a means of highlighting European rapacity and religious hypocrisy: "Europeans preached their religion from Chile to Japan only in order to force men to labor, like pack animals, for their insatiable greed" (12: 376).[43] However, with some exceptions, Voltaire did not exhibit the same level of indignation when he was condemning slavery for Africans as when he was fighting against the remnants of serfdom within France.[44] In *Commentaire sur l'esprit des lois*, Voltaire mentioned Montesquieu's denunciation of the enslavement of Africans but mainly called for an end to serfdom within France (30: 445–47).

It is interesting to contrast Voltaire's ambivalent attitudes toward colonialism and slavery—that is, toward very real issues of his day—with his treatment of a long-lived literary topos: cannibalism. In his survey of the image of cannibals since the discovery of the New World, Frank Lestringant (245–49) compares Voltaire's variation to Montaigne's classic formulation of cannibals as dignified, eloquent embodiments of aristocratic virtues who practice violence only against their enemies, unlike the Europeans.[45] In *Candide* (chapter 16), the title character and his servant Cacambo barely escape being cooked and eaten by the Oreillons (who are far removed from the image of the noble savage) by announcing that Candide killed one of their enemies, a Jesuit. Cacambo's speech to the Oreillons, instead of denouncing barbaric alterity, highlights the underlying resemblance in conduct between the Europeans and the cannibals: "Natural law teaches us to kill our neighbor; such is common practice throughout the world" (21: 171). There is no civilized/savage dichotomy here, since Voltaire's Oreillons, like other *anthropophages*, are simply behaving as Europeans would if they lacked food. In *Essai sur les mœurs*, cannibalism is compared to the real horror of war and massacres as routinely practiced within Europe: "What is truly barbarous is to kill, and not to consume flesh that would otherwise be left to crows and worms" (12: 388).[46] In his texts, Voltaire encountered metaphorical cannibals and recognized them as full-fledged members of the human race. It is regrettable that he could not apply the same insight to the real ethnic groups he had relegated to the status of near-animality.

Conclusion

Voltaire's Europe is a relatively unstable political conglomeration linked by a growing level of economic interdependence and cultural affinities. As an economic liberal, Voltaire cogently analyzed the role of free trade as a contributing factor for greater international integration. Although ostensibly an arch-cosmopolitan intent on combating Eurocentric limitations, he tended to construct the rest of the world according to his polemical needs, which revolved around the religious and political order of the countries of Europe. While Voltaire combined sharp criticism of French society with praise for the foreign models he deemed more enlightened, he also labored to justify and to reinforce the then preeminent standing of French literary culture.

In geographical terms, Voltaire's Europe extends to Russia but excludes Turkey. Underlying this conception of where Europe's physical limitations are situated is a vague but exclusionary historical notion of the slow, irregular development of a loose system of strife-ridden European states, which eventually came to aggregate into an interrelated civilizational entity. Having largely evacuated the long-established notion of Europe as the bastion of Christianity, Voltaire nevertheless limited his Europe, in effect, to countries that had long been dominated by a Christian tradition (whether it be Catholic, Protestant, or Orthodox). Among those countries, Voltaire naturally reserved his praise for those that seemed hospitable to the ideals of the philosophes.

Voltaire announces Europe at its best and its worst. On the one hand, he campaigned, often at personal risk, in favor of politically liberal values—tolerance, rule of law, and refusal of provincialism—that tend to accommodate peaceful human diversity. On the other hand, he clearly assumed the superiority of his particular form of civilization, an unambiguous attitude that often translated into open racism and acquiescence in imperialistic conquest, by designating as inferior both internal and external groups. Voltaire was a precursor in that he sought to divorce his conception of Europe from the inherited Christian model. However, he reestablished Eurocentrism on a scientific, civilizational basis by positing the superiority of European technological accomplishments and, by extension, of European societal norms. Voltaire certainly believed in "Civilization" as an abstract value, and Western Europe had developed its most advanced version.

Voltaire was one of the leading lights for the cosmopolitan, largely Francophone, European elite into which Germaine de Staël was born. Although Staël's work is often presented as a forerunner to the Romantic reaction against the anticlericalism, detached irony, and classical esthetic standards that Voltaire incarnated, both of these writers and political activists experienced exile and served as trans-European cultural intermediaries, among other similarities. The next chapter will examine the ways in which Staël's literary work reflects the wrenching changes brought about during the Revolutionary and Napoleonic periods, which contributed to the rise of modern nationalistic movements throughout Europe.

CHAPTER 2

The European Spirit of Germaine de Staël

Nothing is more favorable to the rise of politeness and learning, than a number of neighboring and independent states, connected together by commerce and policy. The emulation which naturally arises among those neighboring states is an obvious source of improvement. But what I would chiefly insist on is the stop which such limited territories give both to power and to authority.
David Hume, *Of the Rise and Progress of the Arts and Sciences*

Born into the intellectual and financial elite of the eighteenth century, Germaine de Staël (1766–1817)[1] became a pivotal literary and political figure during the transitional period of the Revolutionary and Napoleonic regimes. The daughter of the Swiss banker and French government minister Jacques Necker, she married a Swedish diplomat and wrote at length about British, German, and Italian literatures. An innovative novelist, essayist, and literary critic, Staël also played a political role, most famously in her opposition to Bonaparte's dictatorial rule. The multinational literary circle that revolved around her Swiss-Genevan home of Coppet represented the last flowering of the cosmopolitan society of the Enlightenment as well as the emergence of modern European nationalism. Staël's parents are representative of the fluid nature of citizenship during the eighteenth century.[2] Although a foreigner and a Protestant, Necker was assigned the task of reforming the French kingdom's ailing finances by Louis XVI. It was the King's dismissal of Necker on July 11, 1789, that led to the insurrection in Paris three days later. Louis XVI was forced to call back Necker, who enjoyed a triumphant, if short-lived, welcome. Staël's mother, meanwhile, held an influential literary salon in Paris. Due to her family background and to her own activities, Staël was thus in a prominent (albeit dangerous) position during the upheavals of the Revolution.[3] Staël hosted her own literary salon after her marriage in 1786 and would go on to become one of the most important writers of her time during a period of literary history that was generally hostile to women of intellectual stature and accomplishment. As a member of a rich bourgeois family who married into the aristocracy, Staël had the notable advantage of being financially and socially self-sufficient or of having, as Virginia Woolf would later put it, "money and a room of one's own." As had been the case with Voltaire, the list of Staël's social contacts and correspondents extended throughout the European elites of her lifetime.[4] Like her predecessor, Staël made use of her travels and periods of exile, becoming an influential cultural intermediary between France and its European neighbors. Staël certainly traveled more widely than Voltaire and visited several countries he never did: Austria, Italy, Russia, and Sweden.

A precursor in the field of literary history, Staël articulated a theory on the conditions for the rise and expansion of literature. In *De la littérature considérée dans ses rapports avec les institutions sociales* (1800), by stressing the influence of customs and religions, she posited literature as an evolving social and historical institution, linked to a given national and linguistic entity. Along with her literary activities, Staël participated in the development of liberal political thought in the post-Revolutionary era. Not surprisingly for someone of her social class, she defended the principles of private property and enterprise. Like Voltaire, Staël's political model was Great Britain. Unlike him, she did not situate French classicism as the historical culmination of European literary achievement. An inheritor of the enlightened cosmopolitan tradition of the eighteenth century, Staël opposed the enforced uniformity of the Napoleonic Empire, instead championing individual national identities. As a reaction against the excesses of Napoleon's militarized version of "universalism," her Europe is characterized by cultural diversity, which she considered a contributing factor to the development of liberty.

Literary Renewal

In literary and artistic matters, Napoleon's centralized regime emulated the system of monarchical patronage and control that had characterized the reign of Louis XIV. As an officially sanctioned esthetic standard, neoclassicism, which stifled artistic innovation and change, reflected the political conservatism of the Empire. Staël's goals, partly as a reaction to the Napoleonic regime's preference for the seventeenth-century model, were thus to revalorize the literary achievements of the eighteenth century (minus the sort of anticlericalism Voltaire symbolized) and to seek innovative artistic inspiration outside of France.[5] Through her refusal of preestablished standards of taste, no matter how prestigious (Voltaire's generally conservative attitude is again a negative model in this regard), Staël situated herself outside of the court literature that Napoleon was attempting to reestablish. Refusal of imitation and praise for innovation are complementary themes found throughout Staël's work.

As a continuator of the oppositional French literary tradition of the eighteenth century, Staël posited literary progress and innovation as endowed with a socially useful function: "Given the current state of Europe, literary progress should contribute to the development of all generous ideas" (1: 25). Literary progress thus participated in the process of generalized moral *perfectibilité*, a concept which bears a resemblance to Voltairean *méliorisme*—and particularly to Condorcet's vision of human perfectibility in *Esquisse d'un tableau historique des progrès de l'esprit humain* (written shortly before his death in prison in 1794).[6] Despite the widespread sense of disillusionment that resulted from the failings and excesses of the French Revolution, Staël remained faithful to Condorcet's representation and projection of historical progress. Her version of perfectibility linked her to the Enlightenment philosophes, while allowing her to develop a less linear, more dialectical philosophy of history, one that (unlike Voltaire's) integrated the expansion of Christianity in Europe during the Middle Ages, thereby providing the link with Romanticism.

Contrary to Voltaire's harshly negative assessment, Staël saw the Middle Ages as a generally progressive, if uneven, period of moral and intellectual betterment within Europe: "The so-called barbaric centuries contributed, as did the others, first by spreading civilization to more nations, then by improving minds" (1: 146). She associated this progress with the spread of Christianity, which she represented as a contributing factor to the fusion of Europe's north and south. The unifying Christian religion also constituted, during most of the Middle Ages, a source of inquiry and learning, instead of superstition: "I do not believe the human species regressed during this period" (1: 130). Far from opposing Christianity to the Enlightenment, or faith to reason, Staël tended to present one as reinforcing the other.[7] Her efforts at reconciling Christian traditions with Enlightenment values came to shape her representations of Europe.

While she sought to transcend eighteenth-century debates, such as the struggle between scientific inquiry and religious superstition, Staël also developed some of her own binary oppositions, most famously the *Nord/Midi* European literary traditions. However, she tended to find a synthesis or a harmonizing principle that would allow the terms of her oppositions to become conjoined in a relation of complementarity, without losing their specificity. Within the Staëlian dialectic, Christianity, and especially her liberal form of Protestantism, was thus associated with science and philosophy rather than being in conflict with them. Similarly, the figures of Ossian and Homer, and the literary traditions of north and south that they hypostatized, were presented in terms of reciprocal influence, instead of irreducible antithesis. It was in the points of contact between national cultures, or in her updated version of the eighteenth-century cosmopolitan tradition, that Staël's synthetic or associative pattern of thought was most productive. At once distinct and interdependent, individual national cultures participated in a broader process of cultural *perfectibilité*, just as the oppositions between the Classical *Midi* and the Romantic *Nord* and between Enlightenment universalism and Romantic particularism could be transcended. Staël's work was thus solidly grounded in the Enlightenment tradition, which she never renounced, even as she became the principal champion and propagator within Europe of German Romanticism.[8]

European Literatures

One of the most famous quotes from the Staëlian corpus is found in chapter 28 ("Des romans") of the second part of *De l'Allemagne*: "Il faut, dans nos temps modernes, avoir l'esprit européen" [One must think in European terms] (2: 50). Staël addressed this near command to the German novelist Johann Richter (who took the French name "Jean Paul" out of admiration for Rousseau), contending that his excessive originality was preventing him from being read outside of his native land. While Staël's phrase is often quoted within texts and speeches that advocate European unity, its context has been largely forgotten, and perhaps justly so. Staël's invocation of a European *esprit* or mindset constitutes the converse aspect of her better-known contributions to comparative literature and cultural nationalism. In accordance with her opposition to the political and intellectual uniformity enforced by the Napoleonic regime, she extolled individual national cultures, often inveighing against the dangers of fawning imitation of a (French) model perceived as universally valid: "There is nothing natural, nothing alive, in imitation" (1: 97). In general, Staël therefore tended to see value in cultural difference, fragmentation, and originality. In a dialectical movement, the corollary of her praise of cultural difference is the search for a synthesis of cultural expression across linguistic and national borders, a synthesis that, unlike the homogenizing impulse of the Empire, was not designed to merely erase or occlude cultural variance and divergence.

Staël's "European spirit," which characterizes much of her work, is marked by frequent attempts to transcend oppositions and reconcile differences within a broader framework. While she sought to revalorize the Italian and German literary traditions that had been neglected in France, she also advocated—and practiced—a constant flow of reciprocal influence, on equal terms, between national cultures: "Nations should guide one another. All would be mistaken if they chose to do without the guiding lights [*lumières*] they could provide each other" (2: 75). Comparing, associating, and classifying the varied literatures of Europe became one of the main foci of Staël's work as a critic and novelist. She structured her famous categories of the northern and southern literary traditions of Europe not only around Montesquieu's theory of climatic determinism but also around a totemic or originating figure, one of which later became more mythic than she had imagined. Staël's Nord/Midi dichotomy was personalized by two writers she saw as having originated each tradition: Ossian and Homer. Her work therefore participated in a widespread Romantic movement that accepted at face value James Macpherson's 1761 *Ossian* hoax,[9] which would turn out to be one of the most influential instances of forgery in European literary history:

It seems to me that two completely distinct literary traditions exist: one of which comes from the south and the other from the north. Homer is the source of the first, while Ossian is the origin of the second. The Greeks, Latins, Italians, Spaniards, as well as the French during the century of Louis XIV, belong to the tradition I call literature of the south [*littérature du midi*]. Books from England and Germany, along with some texts from Denmark and Sweden, should be classified as part of the literature of the north, a tradition dating back to Scottish bards, Icelandic fables, and Scandinavian poetry. (*De la littérature*, 1: 178)

Along with the influence of the climate and the originating literary figures, Staël posited such societal factors as the political structure, the degree of economic development, the dominant religion and language,[10] and the social and gender norms of conduct as determinants in the development of individual literary traditions. Comparing pre-Revolutionary France and England, for instance, Staël found French writers, because they had no possibility of influencing political events, tempted by purely abstract notions ("jeu d'esprit," 2: 235), while their English counterparts were more realistic, due to their level of influence in a limited monarchy. Similarly, within her category of the North, Staël established distinctions based on societal factors: "la situation politique et religieuse de l'Allemagne" (2: 247). While discussing the lack of political unity in Germany, Staël still finds a "caractère national" reflected in its literature: "The enthusiasm raised by Werther, especially in Germany, is due to the fact that the book is perfectly in tune with the national character. Goethe did not create it, but he knew how to depict it" (2: 248). Staël stated her own "préférence vers la littérature du nord" (1: 181), which she posited as inherently more conducive to innovation, as well as to the introspection and dreaminess that accompanied a poetic sensibility. Seeking literary renewal and political change, Staël increasingly found her inspiration outside of France, with England providing a political model, while German literary innovations would become for her the source that would help rejuvenate French letters.

Against the Empire

Staël's Parisian salon, which brought together personalities of widely differing political opinions (including Napoleon's brothers, Lucien and Joseph), was inherently threatening for Bonaparte, who eventually banished her from the French capital. Michael Polowetzky refers to Staël as "the uncontested leader of the liberal opposition" (121), in part because of the influence of her salon, which she was forced to transfer to Coppet. In *Dix Années d'exil*, Staël refers to her salon, before her exile, as one of the places where the Parisian elite, including foreign diplomats, could meet and converse with relative freedom: "This European atmosphere helped to protect me" (104). Such protection did not last. For her refusal to conform to the propagandistic role assigned to French writers during the Napoleonic regime, Staël was repeatedly punished, most notably after the publication of *De l'Allemagne* in 1810. Her opposition was not limited to the issue of the prescribed societal role of writers, since even her affinity for cross-cultural innovation clashed with Napoleon's neoclassical esthetic choices.

In *Considérations sur la Révolution française*, Staël recounts that she was initially an admirer of Bonaparte, a victorious general who seemed to be attached to the preservation of the Republic. However, she perceived his personal ambitions and unscrupulousness after meeting him in Paris: "He is a skilled chess player seeking to checkmate his opponent, the human race" (338). Despite this realization, Staël generally depicts herself as purely concerned with literary matters, rather than as an opponent to the Napoleonic regime. By downplaying her political activities, Staël accentuated the disproportionality between her supposedly innocuous literary statements and the ferocity of the censorship and repression she endured, a disproportionality she expressed in personal terms as a drawn-out, if unbalanced, duel between Napoleon and herself (or between the embodiments of ruthless power and independent thought): "the long struggle between his omnipotence and my weakness" (218). This personalized and unequal dichotomy had the intentionally paradoxical effect of raising her stature as the political and cultural antithesis of what Napoleon represented.[11] In her dual role of political opposition and national conscience in exile, Staël was partly following in Voltaire's footsteps. In terms of the personal opposition she incarnated against the ruler of the First Empire, Staël prefigured the role of Victor Hugo in exile during the Second Empire, which would be ruled by Napoleon's nephew. For his part (as recounted by Las Cases in *Le Mémorial de Sainte-Hélène*), Napoleon tended to belittle the impact and motivations of Staël's oppositional stance toward his regime, even arguing that it resulted from his rejection of her personal advances (1: 358). However, instead of merely dismissing "la Corinne genevoise" (2: 189), the former emperor discusses Staël and her books at length.

As one of the leaders of the liberal literary and political opposition to Bonaparte's dictatorial rule, Staël applied what she had learned from the excesses of the Revolution: the modern state apparatus can be as dangerous to freedom as traditional religious institutions. The centralized, bureaucratic, militarized governmental system of the Napoleonic Empire constituted the final repressive result of a flawed Revolutionary movement that had strayed far from its initial objectives: "Strange destiny of the French Revolution! It destroyed throughout Europe the very principles of freedom on which it was supposedly founded" (*Dix Années d'exil*, 59). Although Staël was never nostalgic about *l'Ancien Régime* in political terms, she presciently analyzed the increasingly totalitarian nature of Napoleon's regime, which prefigured twentieth-century dictatorships by seeking to concentrate all the instruments of coercion and influence into a single governmental leviathan: "one man with a million soldiers and a billion in revenue, in control of the prisons of Europe . . . and of what is printed" (223). In a letter (October 18, 1804), Staël listed some of Napoleon's military conquests, concluding: "All of Europe, except for England, is controlled by a single man" (5: 443).[12] She saw the continually expanding Napoleonic Empire as a cynical perversion of the universalistic tendencies of the Enlightenment; while Napoleon did contribute to ending feudalism within Europe, he did not use his conquests to spread the liberal principles linked to the French Revolution. Instead, these were the soothing illusions through which he legitimized his conquests and annexations. Implicitly comparing the French emperor to Caligula, Staël noted that conquered nations were forced to adopt French political structures: "Should Europe be reduced to a single concept, as the Roman people to a single head, in order to have the power to control and transform everything in a single day?" (*Dix Années d'exil*, 140). Instead of achieving lasting liberal changes in France and Europe, Napoleon used his power to benefit the French governing caste, thereby contributing to nationalistic reactions against his rule, and against French influence: "Was it necessary to shed rivers of blood . . . so that the Germans could be governed by French administrators, in charge of fiefdoms whose names they could barely pronounce, but whose income they enjoyed in every language?" (*Considérations*, 401).

Opposed to the rigid uniformity imposed by Bonaparte throughout Europe, Staël, who coined the word "nationalité,"[13] was led to affirm the value of national specificities and particularisms as a means of counterbalancing the perverse effects of forcibly imposed universalism. The revalorization of literary diversity was associated with the need for political autonomy for each national group within Europe. Staël's "European spirit" thus rested on the rejection of the unchecked transnational regime that the Napoleonic perversion of universalism had brought about. While understandable in the context of Bonaparte's repressive Empire, Staël's concept of Europeans associated mainly by shared cross-cultural affinities would soon find its limits with the rise of jingoistic nationalism during the nineteenth century. That the cult of nationalistic pride would itself later become a vehicle for aggressive totalitarianism was a development she did not foresee. At the start of the century, marked by the seemingly continual victories of Revolutionary and Imperial French armies, Staël offered a defense of national diversity, and therefore the cultivation of pride in individual national literatures and cultures—"national patriotism must be selfish" (*De l'Allemagne*, 1: 56)—as a contributing factor to European opposition against despotic rule.[14]

In political terms, Staël's liberal model was Great Britain, a coherent national entity ruled by a hereditary monarchy wielding only limited political power, with mechanisms that balanced aristocratic rule and popular representation.[15] Of course, the reality of Staël's model was problematic, to say the least, within Europe (the case of Ireland) and throughout its colonial empire. While she did provide measured criticism of the "abus affreux" (*Considérations*, 566) of the colonial administration in India and of British "dédain" (568) for the United States, Staël saw Great Britain as uncommonly resistant to the temptation of despotism, praising its political system, as had Voltaire, for its relative stability and degree of individual (particularly economic) freedom. In chapter 3 ("De la prospérité de l'Angleterre") of *Considérations*, she attributes a large part of Great Britain's eventual victory over Napoleon's regime to its economic strength, which rested on guaranteed property rights, budgetary transparency, and freedom of the press.

Staël's sympathies with the British constitutional system naturally led her to hope for the defeat of Bonaparte. However, one of the paradoxical consequences of Staël's opposition to the Napoleonic Empire was her grudging support for another multinational empire ruled by an absolutist despot. While Staël harbored few illusions about the Russian Empire, which "could hardly have been considered the freest state in Europe" (*Dix Années d'exil*, 255), it constituted the last continental bulwark against French expansionism. She was thus apparently willing to suspend disbelief when encountering the Russian emperor and his talk of reforms, such as "alleviating the plight of peasants still subjected to serfdom" (291). Although Staël was aware of the eighteenth-century debates among the French philosophes over the nature of the increasingly powerful Russian Empire, she had not planned a lengthy stay (her real destination was England), and she was thus unprepared for the social and political realities of Russian life, unlike her preplanned explorations of Italian or German culture.[16]

Staël's perceptions of other countries she visited were similarly influenced by their relative degree of cooperation with, or opposition against, the French Empire. In *Dix Années d'exil*, Staël finds support for Napoleon within a resurrected Polish state (under French influence), which was previously divided between Austria, Prussia, and Russia: "the Poles are the only Europeans who can serve without shame under the command of Bonaparte" (240). A similar comment, concerning Italy, is found in *Considérations* (402). In particular, Staël attributed much of the success of Napoleon's military campaigns in Italy to support from the local elites: "he was welcomed by the Italians because of their hope for independence" (328). Staël understood that the popularity of Bonaparte among Polish or Italian intellectuals was largely based upon the absence of national unity in these two countries within pre-Revolutionary Europe.[17]

Exile and Travels

One of the similarities between Staël's biography and that of Voltaire is the repeated experience of involuntary exile, whether internal (from Paris) or external (from France). An early supporter of the Revolution, Staël opposed its radicalization during the Terror. In 1792, she was forced to flee Paris at the start of the infamous September massacres. While this was largely due to her status as an aristocrat, later periods of exile would result from her political and literary activities. Although she was able to return at the start of the *Directoire* in 1795, she had to leave again a few months later. After he seized power, Napoleon first banned Staël from Paris in 1803, thereby cutting her off from the social and literary life she had known. In 1810, after halting the publication of *De l'Allemagne*, he effectively consigned her to Coppet and Geneva. In 1812, Staël was forced to flee to England, by way of Russia and Sweden, in the middle of Napoleon's campaign against Russia.[18] Staël stayed in Sweden, where the French general Bernadotte had become king, from September 1812 to May 1813. She then moved to Great Britain, where she was at last able to publish *De l'Allemagne*, returning to France after Napoleon's abdication in 1814. Overall, as had been the case for Voltaire, many of Staël's travels were not undertaken primarily out of choice. Her 1803–4 stay in Germany, for instance, followed unsuccessful attempts to persuade Napoleon to lift his order banning her from the capital.

While Staël devoted much time to learning the languages of Germany, Italy, and Great Britain, she visited and wrote about other European countries with varying degrees of interest or accuracy. Her comments on Russia, while necessarily diplomatic, would find echoes a generation later in Astolphe de Custine's characterization of the vast country as still largely "Asiatic"—that is, backward and despotic (*Dix Années d'exil*, 269). She depicts Moscow, where she briefly stopped before its occupation by Napoleon's invading *Grande Armée*, as the eastern limit of European influence: "Asia and Europe were combined in this city" (272). She also takes notice of French cultural influence, some of which she finds excessive: "Russians, as in so many other countries of the continent, unfortunately imitate French literature" (279). During her trip across Central and Eastern Europe, Staël established comparisons between national cultures, attitudes, and behaviors, just as she had long been doing with the more familiar countries of Western Europe. Unlike Voltaire, Staël wrote (and seemed to know) relatively little about the rest of the world: "The vast lands of Asia are lost to despotism. For centuries, what remains of civilization has been static" (*Considérations*, 64). With the partial exception of the United States, her novels, essays, and correspondence are definitely centered on Europe. Perhaps because she never crossed the Atlantic, Staël tended to represent the United States as having solved many of the political and social problems that continued to bedevil most European countries: "Its citizens are happy and free" (*De la littérature*, 2: 376). While decrying the persistence of slavery, she anticipated Tocqueville's prediction of the rise of the United States as a world power: "The Americans will one day be a great nation" (*Considérations*, 568).

Staël's writings, unlike those of Voltaire, contain only infrequent comments concerning Jews. What few comments she does make, however, are clearly hostile, reflecting the traditional religious prejudices of her privileged milieu.[19] In *Considérations*, she sadly recounts having noticed during her trip in 1812 that in Poland "all trade is controlled by Jews" (247). Upon entering Russia, she remarks that the first province she crosses is "inondée [*flooded*] de juifs" (256). French Jews had been conferred citizenship in 1791. This was not one of the accomplishments of the Revolution that Staël lauded. Her call for religious tolerance and cross-cultural influence stopped short of including non-Christians within Europe. Likewise, her frequent characterization of Napoleon as radically alien to France, due to his geographical origin—"un Corse africain"—carries an overtone of racism, in spite of her campaign for the abolition of slavery.[20]

North and South

In *De l'esprit des lois* (books 14 to 18), published in 1748, Montesquieu developed his influential *théorie des climats*, the long-lived theory of climatic determinism, seeking to explain Europe's relative degree of political freedom by its mostly temperate climate. To these favorable meteorological conditions he opposed the extremes of heat and cold he saw in countries that adjoined one another in Asia, where absolute despotism reigned, unchecked by any separation of powers. Staël adapted this theory in order to explain the differences in terms of political regimes, and especially in terms of literary development, among the countries of Europe. By stressing her Nord/Midi dichotomy, structured around the iconic literary figures of Ossian and Homer, Staël was generally able to systematize her observations on the culture and social mores of the societies that she visited. These observations, while present throughout most of her work, are most clearly found in her second novel, *Corinne ou l'Italie* (1807), and in her 1810 essay devoted to German society and culture.

In *Corinne* (which was even more successful than her first novel, *Delphine*),[21] Staël blends themes and techniques from the seventeenth and eighteenth centuries with those that would dominate during the Romantic period. It is often associated with Chateaubriand's *René* (1802) as one of the two most influential novels of the Napoleonic period. Through the identification of the title character with her native land, Staël extolled not only Italian literature, but also the spontaneity she perceived in its vibrant, if anarchic culture: "a nation so vividly expressive of its feelings" (2, 1).[22] Along with praise for Italian artistic achievements, there are calls for national unity and independence, which would allow the divided country to emulate the politically advanced countries of the north. Most infuriatingly for Napoleon—who crowned himself "King of Italy" in 1805—there is no mention in the novel of the French military and political domination in Italy, which was already established during the latter part of the period narrated in the novel (1795–1803) and which, at its height, reduced Rome to the status of *Préfecture du Département du Tibre*. Staël achieved popular success with a novel that was set outside of France, that did not praise all things French, and that provided both subtle criticism of military dictatorship and a call for Italian national unity.

In her second novel, Staël most clearly developed the opposition she perceived between the cultures of northern and southern Europe. The main characters Corinne and Oswald, as well as d'Erfeuil, represent national types: the vivacious, exuberant Italian (her brooding side is attributed to England), the restrained, melancholic Englishman, and the witty but frivolous Frenchman. In terms of national culture, Corinne is a hybrid character, situated between the Staëlian categories of the *Nord* and *Midi* of Europe; born and raised in Italy by her British father and Italian mother, Corinne also lived in Britain with her father and British stepmother after her mother's death. She eventually becomes an independent cultural intermediary, not unlike Staël's real-life role. As an autonomous woman, the character of Corinne constitutes an audacious rarity in French fiction of the period, defining herself by her literary talent, rather than by her social background or conjugal status: "the most famous woman in Italy, a poet and writer" (2, 1). She is also independently wealthy, a crucially important condition for a female artist. Due to her forthright claim to artistic eminence, the fictional character of Corinne, and of course the well-known female writer who created her, automatically elicited negative reactions.[23]

The most important secondary character in the novel, d'Erfeuil, a social gadfly seeking conversation but no real intellectual exchange, represents the French elite as generous but superficial. Concerned with keeping up appearances, he seeks pleasure, but only in conformity with the strictures of his aristocratic milieu. As the embodiment of the frivolity Staël sees as common among French elites, d'Erfeuil's attitude is one of fleeting, inconsequential curiosity when encountering any form of esthetic stimulus: "The comte d'Erfeuil, after having spent some time in Switzerland, and having tired of nature in the Alps, as he had of art in Rome, suddenly felt he should go to England where, so he had been made to believe, intellectual profundity was to be found" (18, 1). Napoleon would rail against Staël for her depiction of d'Erfeuil and other French characters in *Corinne*: "I cannot forgive Mme de Staël for having demeaned the French in her novel" (Las Cases, 2: 187).

In an illustration of Staël's long-standing cross-cultural interests, *Corinne* includes comparative discussions of English, French, and Italian literatures. In the course of these discussions, d'Erfeuil, a neo-Voltairean figure, haughtily upholds classical French theater against the "monstruosités" of Shakespeare: "Our theater is a model of refinement and elegance" (7, 2). Predictably, he is similarly dismissive about Italian or, for that matter, any theatrical tradition that deviates from the French model. While the main nexus of Staël's novel remains the Nord/Midi opposition she had elaborated in *De la littérature*, an opposition here incarnated respectively by Oswald and Corinne, a recurring theme is the tendency of the male characters to project their national model onto the countries they visit, thereby seeking imitation instead of cultural exchange. For these characters, traveling abroad thus becomes, instead of a learning experience, simply a means of reinforcing one's notion of national superiority and universal validity. In *Corinne*, the French character d'Erfeuil, who is willfully superficial and oblivious of other cultures, incarnates a specifically cultural form of hegemony.

The advantages of the orderly and efficient British political and economic model that Staël admired, as compared to both Italy and France, are stressed in *Corinne*. Oswald, its representative in the novel, is dismayed by much of what he sees within the politically fragmented and relatively less developed Italy, whose "institutions and society generally reflected confusion, weakness and ignorance" (16, 4). His often peremptory judgments on the countries he visits make no allowances for historical contingencies: "I believe that [nations] always deserve their fate, whatever it may be" (4, 2). It is Corinne who defends her country's reputation, pointing out its artistic heritage and attributing its ills to the lack of national independence and unity: "Italians are far more remarkable for what they once were and for what they could be" (1, 5).[24] A character shaped by rigorous English norms of conduct (13, 3), Oswald also exhibits both sensitivity and physical courage. He is twice called upon to show his bravery, while the Italian characters appear all the more helpless by comparison. Oswald takes the lead in putting out the fire in Ancona (1, 4) and in saving a drowning man in Naples (13, 6). By contrast, the Italian inhabitants ask Oswald not to open the gates of the Jewish ghetto during the fire in Ancona. They would also prefer to let the insane asylum burn down with its patients. Similarly, in Naples, no Italian character attempts to rescue the man who is about to drown. In both cases, Oswald's bravery and self-abnegation serve to highlight, by contrast, Italian passivity and complacency. The representative of *le Nord* thus has ample opportunities to show his strength and virility, while the Italian characters, who are embodiments of *le Midi*, exhibit varying degrees of weakness and feminization.

The causes of the clearly feminized representation of Italy in Staël's novel are prominent among the topics of discussion and disagreement between the two main characters.[25] In "La Société italienne dans *Corinne*" (*Madame de Staël: écrire, lutter, vivre*, 199–211), Simone Balayé argued that the distinctions between the characters of Corinne and Oswald are more vividly highlighted by their disagreements over Italian society than over its literature. Corinne's defense of her nation, in response to Oswald's associated accusations of generalized decadence and lack of virility, is based on Italy's subjugated status as a conquered and divided country, lacking the stable, representative political institutions from which Great Britain derives its strength and stability. The Staëlian vision of Italy as politically and socially—but, significantly, not artistically—degraded was already present in *De la littérature*, where she also found climate and religion to be causal factors: "fanatical prejudice, various governments that are not united around the common love and defence of a single country, a burning sun that exacerbates the senses" (1: 163).

Although Staël praised Great Britain as a political and economic model, she sharply highlighted its social conservatism in *Corinne*, particularly in terms of the constraints imposed on women's roles and conduct. Meanwhile, Italy, a divided nation with little political freedom, is presented as allowing relatively more autonomy for individuals, particularly for women. Staël's novel thus juxtaposes the twin paradoxes of a "free" British society that severely restricts women's freedom and of a conquered Italian society that allows them comparatively more freedom. Through the interplay of the multiple dichotomies represented by the two gendered national entities—freedom/servility, self-restraint/passion, order/imagination, power/sensitivity, politics/art—male achievements and self-realization are portrayed as dependent on female submissiveness. Outside of the political domain, *Corinne* partly reverses the terms of Staël's "Nord/Midi" opposition, holding up the south of Europe as a more beneficial environment for artistic and personal development. As Madelyn Gutwirth put it, "England becomes normalcy, continuity, immanence; Italy stands boldly for art and its triumphant victory beyond personal mortality" (208). The foregrounding of the artistic and personal freedom incarnated by "Corinne ou l'Italie" highlights Staël's critique of the politically and economically advanced, but socially retrograde, British model—a critique that, with relatively few changes, could also be directed at the norms of social and esthetic conformity enforced within Napoleonic France.

While *Delphine* highlighted the deleterious effects of class-based social determinism on women's lives, *Corinne* transposes the weight of assigned gender roles to a form of national determinism, opposing Italian passion and spontaneity to the closed-in, regimented world of English domestic life. The character of Corinne changes radically according to her national setting. While she is triumphant in Italy, she becomes nearly invisible during her trip to England; the recurring device of her hiding (while surreptitiously observing Oswald) becomes a metaphor for the social and emotional death she experiences when she leaves her invigorating Italian environment for the androcentric British social norms. The nationally determined patriarchal law is spelled out in a letter written by Oswald's father to Corinne's father explaining why their children would make a mismatched couple: "In countries whose political institutions allow men honorable opportunities to act and be seen, women must remain in the shadows" (16, 8). Corinne is thus radically unsuited for England: "only Italy suits her" (16, 8). Similarly, Oswald's inability to adapt to the different values and attitudes Corinne represents is due to his national background: "the English, who are accustomed to living among themselves and who do not adapt easily to the manners of other nations" (1, 5).

Staël contrasts the restrictive standards of British society for women with those for men, who are encouraged to participate in public affairs: "[men] always have dignified means of occupying themselves; women's lives, on the isolated plot of earth where I lived, were exceedingly bland" (14, 1). In the same chapter, when Corinne's stepmother invites her neighbors for tea, the deadening impact of rigid gender roles in Britain is illustrated through dialogue that is so absurdly empty that it recalls the opening lines of Eugène Ionesco's 1950 "antiplay," *La Cantatrice chauve*. While Great Britain may be Staël's political model, it does not constitute an exemplar in terms of the limitations imposed on women. It is, however, the British model of constrained feminine behavior that Oswald asks the independent Corinne to accept, even though he admires her talent: "I hope that love will make you cherish it, and that you will value domestic happiness, natural and practical virtues, even over the brilliance of your genius" (15, 1). As his masculinized country's representative within the novel, Oswald asks a gifted female character who is in between national cultures (and outside of fixed class identities and gender roles) to conform to her proper familial and domestic role, as defined by his society.

As several critics have noted, *Corinne* is at once a tragic story of star-crossed lovers and an Italian travel guide. Book 4, for instance, includes long descriptions of what would later become a common Romantic topos, the ruins of Roman monuments. In an illustrative variant of what John Ruskin would call the pathetic fallacy, the landscape, architecture, and monuments of Italy are used to symbolize the evolution of the unlikely relationship between the lively Italian artist and the brooding British aristocrat.[26] During their travels through the Italian cities and countryside, the contrasting moods and feelings of Corinne and Oswald are reflected in the natural settings, varying from such extremes as Corinne's illuminated triumph in Rome to the ominously foreboding Mount Vesuvius. In Staël's novel, parts of Italy and, to a lesser extent, Britain and France become the hypostatized manifestations of emotional states and intellectual outlooks.

Imagining Germany

One of the consequences of the publication of Voltaire's *Lettres philosophiques* in 1734 was to make English literature better known in France, where it had been largely ignored. The publication of Staël's *De l'Allemagne* had a similar effect for German letters—with the difference that Voltaire was referring to a politically unified country, while "Germany" did not exist in any constitutional or political sense. Staël's lengthy essay also met with a comparable level of censorship as had Voltaire's (it was banned shortly after its initial publication in 1810, and almost all copies were destroyed),[27] and it eventually led to her fleeing across Central and Eastern Europe—an unavoidably roundabout means of reaching the haven of Great Britain (where she was finally able to publish her book). French readers would have to wait until the fall of the Empire to discover *De l'Allemagne*. As she had done with *Corinne*, Staël mixed different genres—travel literature, literary criticism, philosophic considerations, implied political critique, the only exception being romantic intrigue—within her account of what she had discovered, through her travels and texts, about France's little-known neighbor.

Practicing an early form of cultural relativism, Staël advocated an examination by French readers, without preconceptions, of German literary achievements: "If foreigners have a different conception of the theater, it is due neither to ignorance, nor to barbarity, but to profound considerations that merit examination" (1: 257). Alongside novelists, poets, and playwrights, Staël introduced German philosophers such as Immanuel Kant and Johann Fichte. Providing highly personal presentations of her German literary sources, in order to render them consonant with her polemical purposes,[28] Staël implicitly compared the unregulated development of German thought and imagination to the debilitating effects of despotism on French intellectual expression. As had been the case in *Corinne*, there is no mention of French influence or domination in Germany and not a (direct) word about Napoleon—an eloquent silence on the part of the most famous living French writer.[29] Staël presented an idealized foreign culture, as had Voltaire, with the aim of indirectly criticizing French institutions—a literary undertaking that, in the context of the Napoleonic regime, nevertheless bordered on treason. By highlighting the virtues she perceived in German literature—enthusiasm, dreaminess, imagination, and sentiment—she undermined the "universal" or preeminent model of seventeenth-century classical French literature favored by the Empire. Through her introduction of German culture, Staël therefore went further than Voltaire had done with his praise of an English model, which did not question established French esthetic standards.

For Staël, Germany became in the esthetic domain what Great Britain represented politically. Together, the two countries constituted most of the "Nord" of her famous European duality. Just as Voltaire exaggerated the advantages of the enlightened political, economic, and religious model he found in Great Britain, Staël amplified the contrast she perceived between "the two extremities of the moral spectrum" (*De l'Allemagne*, 1: 46), as represented by France and Germany. Staël's dichotomy sets up a relationship of complementarity between the literary traditions of the two nations, at the cost of simplifying each one.[30] With some exceptions, Staël's method tends to assign an unvarying, homogeneous character to each of the poles of her "deux extrémités," thereby essentializing not only their literary traditions but also their culture in general. The emphasis on the contrast between classical French taste and German enthusiasm led to presenting the two nations as largely devoid of internal variation. The dangers of such a method would only become evident later in the century. There is not a very large discursive step from the essentialized representation of a national culture to the myth of an ethnic or national essence in biological or genetic terms, a step that racist propagandists of various stripes would enthusiastically take.

When *De l'Allemagne* was published, Napoleon had already dissolved the last remnant of the Holy Roman Empire. During the Revolutionary period, France had annexed the left bank of the Rhine as early as 1795, to which Napoleon added a section of what is now northern Germany, which briefly stretched the French border to the Baltic Sea. French troops had occupied and politically reorganized much of the rest of German territory. The traditional system of semi-independent German states had therefore been totally transformed through the force of French arms, a situation that is ignored in Staël's book, which deals with her vision of "Germany" in both a past and future sense. Staël's Germany was a personal discursive construct that corresponded to her polemical intents, rather than a consistent attempt at providing an accurate description of the cities and states she visited.[31] Within an imprecisely defined territory, she discerned a long-divided cultural and national entity without a state.

As had been the case with Italy, Staël emphasized the political and cultural fragmentation of Germany. Both of these yet-to-be-established countries stood in stark contrast to the highly centralized French model, which had reached its culminating point with Napoleon's militaristic regime. While Staël praised the varied artistic achievements of the two nations that lacked unifying state structures, she also lamented their continuing political weakness, which left them vulnerable to Napoleon's hegemonic aims. As part of her intellectual opposition against the Empire, Staël generally sought to defend individual national cultures against the tide of forced "universalism" embodied by Napoleon's troops. Ironically, by the end of the nineteenth century, Maurice Barrès, who would condemn Staël's Germanophilia (as would other French writers after the Franco-Prussian War), adopted a similar, if inverted, method by defending the specificity of French culture against what he considered to be the universalistic pretensions and the intellectual encroachments of the then-dominant German model. Unlike Staël, Barrès would champion the individuality of his national culture without situating it within a future context of equal and reciprocal influence with its German counterpart.

In *De l'Allemagne*, Staël returns to the theme of perfectibility, which she had previously developed in *De la littérature*: "One can glimpse a consistent design, always continuous, always progressive in human history" (2: 230). The constant forward movement of progress, if not always linear and direct, is for Staël the characteristic trait of the development of study and learning throughout Europe, her version of the *République des lettres*. Within this continual development, she saw contemporary German thinkers and writers as being in the forefront, as opposed to the French, who had lost their way during the second half of the eighteenth century: "Germans deserve special recognition in this regard" (2: 233). In a curiously militaristic metaphor, Staël insists on the inventiveness and originality of German intellectuals: "Germans are like the scouts of the army of the human mind; they explore new paths" (1: 166). As had been the case with Voltaire, Staël's praise of innovative foreign achievements implied parallel condemnation of French conservatism. The Staëlian topos of Germany as the contemporary fountainhead of literary and philosophical innovation is spelled out in a letter to Charles de Villers (August 1, 1802), a French *émigré* who had written a book on Kant's philosophy: "I believe, as you do, that human intelligence, which seems to travel from one country to another, is currently in Germany" (4: 541).

In her investigations into German culture and society, Staël was influenced by the literary critic August-Wilhelm von Schlegel, who along with his brother Friedrich provided information on the writers discussed in *De l'Allemagne*. Staël met Schlegel during her 1803–4 trip to Germany, after Napoleon banned her from Paris.[32] Schlegel, who would become an active member of the Coppet group, served as the tutor of Staël's children and assisted Staël in her efforts to learn the German language. In the course of her ten-week stay in Weimar, Staël met several other writers, most notably Goethe and Schiller. She later described her enthusiastic reactions to her encounters with German writers and texts in her unfinished memoir, *Dix Années d'exil*: "I reached Weimar where I was heartened to find, despite the difficulty of the language, immense intellectual resources outside of France. I learned to read German. I listened to men who could comfortably express themselves in French, Goethe and Wieland. I came to understand the soul and the genius of Schiller, in spite of his lack of fluency in French" (159).

In *De l'Allemagne*, which was to become crucially important for the development of Romanticism outside of Germany, Staël develops an opposition between Classical French literature, characterized by clarity and regularity of form, and Romantic German literary inspiration, distinguished by spontaneous enthusiasm and feeling. Staël's version of Romanticism was centered on vital, expansive themes such as the exaltation of artistic genius and a lyrical form of religiosity. She did not discern or foresee the dark, Gothic incarnations of the Romantic movement, which would become dominant during the nineteenth century. Staël's Romanticism is thus, paradoxically, optimistic and forward-looking; it is a continuation of the Enlightenment rather than its negation. In "De la poésie classique et de la poésie romantique" (part 2, chapter 11), she contrasts the long-dominant Classical literature of Italy and France with the emerging Romantic literature of Great Britain and especially Germany. The former is traceable to Greek and Roman antiquity, while the latter derives from the Germanic chivalric tradition of the Middle Ages. Staël's religious and historical dichotomy (Pagan Antiquity/Christian Middle Ages) is thus associated with her established geographical opposition (Nord/Midi). She posited the Classical tradition of the south as having reached an enviable but sterile plateau of perfection, while the still-evolving Romantic tradition of the north, closer in religious and historical terms, remained vital, innovative, and progressive: "Only Romantic literature can still be perfected . . . it expresses our religion; it recalls our history: its origins, while ancient, are not to be found in Antiquity" (1: 214).

Instead of John Locke, the guiding light of most eighteenth-century philosophes, Staël chose Immanuel Kant as a philosophical model. Once again, her contrasting presentations of these two philosophers are in large part determined by her polemical intent, in the twin historical contexts of the excesses of the Revolution and of the Napoleonic conquests. In particular, Staël rejected Locke's theory of ideas as deriving purely from sensations, a theory that she saw as contributing to the atheism and materialism of the Revolutionary period.[33] She therefore presented Kantian philosophy in terms antithetical to what she considered to be a destructive strain of French thought that dominated the second half of the eighteenth century, when "the Enlightenment became an inferno" (2: 108). She found in Kant's work the reconciliation between religion and reason, between belief and critical thought, which was consonant with her version of liberal Protestantism—and with her Romantic sensibility: "What is needed is a philosophy of belief, of enthusiasm; a philosophy that confirms through reason what emotion reveals to us" (2: 138). Staël described the philosopher from Königsberg as having not only dismantled the intellectual foundations of atheism and materialism, but as also having laid the rational basis for the harmonization of thought and feeling (2: 139). This portrayal of Kantian philosophy as a revalorization of spontaneous feeling and enthusiasm, within the framework of rigorous reasoning, was long influential in France—although it was in fact closer to Staël's own synthetic, reconciliatory pattern of thought. In another example of Staël's tendency to seek harmony between the terms of her oppositions, while maintaining them, she sees no contradiction between religiosity and philosophical inquiry: "Philosophy consists in finding reasonable interpretations of divine truths" (2: 105).

While Staël praised German literary and philosophical accomplishments, she presented no German political model, nor did she portray Germans as concerned with political liberty: "The love of freedom is not developed among Germans; they have not learned, either through joy or suffering, the value it represents" (1: 62). German intellectuality, like Italian artistry, was for Staël a form of compensation, a way to make up for the lack of national unity and independent political structures. In this respect, she tends to provide a feminized representation of Germany, as she had in the case of Italy. In a letter written after her arrival in Germany (December 10, 1803), she insisted on the lack of national sentiment or strength among the Germans she had thus far encountered: "Germans do not constitute a nation, and the *Premier Consul* [Napoleon] can treat them as he pleases" (5: 134). While she did not foresee or explicitly advocate German national unity, Staël posited German political independence as crucial to the emergence of a Europe free of domination by one country: "Germany, in geographical terms, can be considered the heart of Europe, and the great continental association could only recover its independence if that country were to recover its own" (1: 41).

In what would later become a source of much derision, Staël depicted Germans as generally disinclined toward militarism. For instance, she used the differences in climate to try to explain why a German soldier living in a relatively moderate climate would be less inured to wartime suffering in comparison to the Russian soldier who was hardened by his country's more bitter cold (1: 60).[34] Needless to say, many French writers would take a different view after 1870 and after the subsequent wars between France and Germany, which would lead to the long-held stereotype of Germans as aggressively regimented and militaristic. Since the publication of Staël's book in France coincided with the fall of the Empire and the presence on French soil of foreign—including Prussian— troops, her lenitive characterization of German dreaminess and introspection, which had been written during the high point of Napoleon's domination over much of Europe, was not well received in many French circles. Eve Sourian detailed the response to *De l'Allemagne* elaborated by the poet Heinrich Heine, who wrote a polemical book on the topic of Staël's representation of Germany in 1835—in French and with the same title. Heine's critique of Staël's idealized representation of Germany became highly influential in France, especially after the 1870 Franco-Prussian War. In particular, Staël was portrayed as having been oblivious to the rising tide of aggressive nationalism among German intellectuals (the forerunner of which was Fichte's 1807–8 *Addresses to the German Nation*), a portrayal which accounts for many of the often vicious attacks directed at her work and influence.[35] According to this discourse, Staël, blinded by Romantic illusions about German idealism and by her systematic opposition to Napoleon's regime, lulled the French public into a dangerously false appreciation of what would later become expansionist German militarism. The author of *De l'Allemagne* was thus faulted for having foreseen neither the aggressive form of German nationalism that developed as a reaction against Napoleonic expansionism, nor the French defeat that occurred sixty years after the initial publication of her book. As Sourian noted (105), Heine sounded a prophetic note in his own *De l'Allemagne* when he announced the renewal of an age-old Germanic lust for war, of the awakening of "les vieilles divinités guerrières" (1: 182). That Staël did not foresee this awakening led to her being represented as somehow complicit with the long-term consequences of jingoistic German nationalism.

Among all of Staël's texts, *De l'Allemagne* produced the harshest reaction from Napoleon's regime, which not only banned her from France but effectively consigned her to Coppet and Geneva and prevented most of her friends from visiting her (even sending into internal exile some of those who did). While in Coppet, she was constantly watched by the French police; her letters were also opened and read. This situation led to her escape to England, via Russia and Sweden, in 1812. In the preface, written in London in 1813, to *De l'Allemagne*, Staël includes the infamous letter from Napoleon's Minister of Police, General Savary (September 24, 1810), which notified her to leave France within a week: "We are not yet reduced to seeking models among the nations you admire. Your latest work is not French" (1: 39).[36] As Staël indicates in a note to her 1813 edition, the following passage, which concludes her book, was particularly irksome to Napoleon's censors: "France! Land of Glory and love! If enthusiasm should one day vanish from your land, if caculations governed all and if reason alone inspired fearlessness, of what use would be your beautiful sky, your so brilliant minds, your so productive fields? An active intelligence, an impetuous skill would make you the masters of the world; but you would leave behind only the trace of torrentially flowing sand, as terrifying as a stormy ocean, as arid as a desert!" (2: 316).

In her preface, Staël adopts a technique that had been familiar to Voltaire: disingenuously disclaiming any political intent, stating that her book was merely concerned with literary matters, that she noncommittally maintained "the same silence on the current French government as in my previous texts" (1: 37), and that she avoided "any comment on the political status of Germany" (1: 38). Had *De l'Allemagne* truly lacked political relevance, Napoleon's censors would not have delivered the sort of inverted praise that dictatorships typically give to important, dangerous books: seizing and destroying all the copies they could find. In fact, Staël's book is of course profoundly political, an indirect but far-reaching indictment of the repressive, rigidly conservative social and political system in France (as Voltaire's *Lettres philosophiques* had been). It is also political in the sense that it depicts the development of German literature and philosophy within the broader historical context of a German societal entity that had yet to achieve national unity.

Ernest Renan posited a degree of historical inaccuracy as necessary for the establishment of shared emotional connections, forged upon a selectively remembered past, among the generally disparate members of an emerging national entity: "Forgetting, and I would even say historical error, are essential to the creation of a nation" (*Qu'est-ce qu'une nation?* 227). Benedict Anderson built on Renan's insight to elaborate on the processes leading to the formation of modern nation-states, based on a largely imagined or creatively misremembered past. This common emphasis on the cultural dimension of nationalism (especially in its early stages) is particularly relevant to Staël's discourse of revalorization of individual national cultures within the context of intellectual resistance to Napoleon's ever-expanding transnational Empire. In the cases of Italy and especially of Germany, Staël provides a unique instance of a foreign intellectual actively participating in the process of national formation. The errors and omissions of her representations of foreign cultures, which several critics have pointed out, were in fact coherent within the polemical purposes of her rhetorical model. While inaccurate or exaggerated, her portrayals of Germans as introspective and Italians as feminized provided myths, or common discursive sources of pride or shame, which were applicable to an entire "imagined community," to use Anderson's term. In *De la littérature*, Staël had already linked the creation of an emotional sense of national commonality or interconnections to the development of literature and the arts: "Eloquence, a love for literature and the arts, philosophy: only they can transform a territory into a common homeland, by providing similar tastes, habits and feelings to the nation that inhabits it" (1: 36). Her presentation of the culture of what was not yet "Germany" was enormously influential (in both positive and negative terms) not just in France but also, as the example of Heine indicates, among German writers. By implicitly calling for the unity and independence of both Italy and Germany and basing the coherence of these two future national entities on their internal cultural links (whether real or imagined), Staël, the multilingual cosmopolitan with no fixed national identity, became one of the initiators of nationalism as an intellectual discourse and a political movement.

Coppet: A European Literary Retreat

Shortly after Staël's death, Stendhal—who was otherwise critical of Staël's opposition to Napoleon's regime[37]—referred to Coppet as the "Etats Généraux de l'opinion européenne," and praised "the illustrious woman that France mourns" (364). As a result of Staël's forced exile, her home in Switzerland had become a multinational meeting place for writers from several European countries. Some members of the group also followed her during her travels. A unique literary circle, Coppet did not revolve around a review or a clear political or esthetic manifesto. It was in many ways a European extension of Staël's Parisian literary salon and thus an indication of the degree of her influence. The only female writer in the group, Staël was its pivot. Representing a combination of political liberalism and multilingual artistic diversity, Coppet became, geographically and metaphorically, a European cultural hub. In terms of multicultural exchange, Staël's Swiss home was more influential than had been a neighboring "lieu de mémoire" (to use Pierre Nora's term), Voltaire's Ferney. Instead of being dominated by a single figure, Coppet, with its constant stream of guests and visitors from several countries, became one of the relatively few places in which the intellectual elites of Europe could meet and converse freely, a situation that facilitated the propagation of new ideas and movements.[38]

The intellectual pursuits and activities among the participants of the Coppet circle were varied. Some common thematic strands, however, emerge from the lists of their publications, both before and after Staël's death. A shared topic of interest was comparative cultural history, an example of which is found in Simonde de Sismondi's *De la littérature du Midi de l'Europe*.[39] The complementary themes of European diversity and unity, sometimes based on climatic determinism (as illustrated by Charles-Victor de Bonstetten's *L'Homme du midi et l'homme du nord, ou l'influence du climat*), were articulated by several members of the group.[40] One of the other important aspects of the cross-cultural role of the Coppet group was the practice of translation as a means of disseminating literary productions across national and linguistic borders. Translation constitutes an important element of the plot in Staël's *Corinne*. The title character, who embodies two national cultural traditions, has translated Shakespeare's

Romeo and Juliet into Italian and wants to play Juliet, with Oswald among the audience (7, 3). Staël also made use of her home, as had the "Patriarche" of Ferney, in order to indulge and promote her interest in the theater, by staging and acting in her own plays—and those of Voltaire, among others.

The diffuse but palpable political dimension of the Coppet circle should not be overlooked. Since it became an unofficial meeting place for some of the leading representatives of the liberal opposition (particularly, of course, Staël and Constant),[41] Coppet, with its multilingual milieu of unorthodox writers and political figures, was viewed with suspicion—and quite rightly so—by Napoleon's regime, which increasingly sought to isolate Staël from her friends and correspondents after having exiled her from Paris. In the preface to his 1830 play *Hernani*, Victor Hugo defined Romanticism as "le libéralisme en littérature" (8: 539) and linked political change to artistic innovation in the context of the repressive monarchy of Charles X. It is a definition and a program that, a generation and a political regime earlier, could well apply to Staël and to the literary circle that revolved around her home.

Conclusion

Through her continuing interest in the literary productions of neighboring countries, Staël gradually developed a vision, or "spirit," of Europe within the context of the domination of much of the continent by one country, which extended the presumed universalistic principles of its Revolution by force of arms. As a reaction to both the stifling legacy of traditional French cultural preeminence and the enforced political uniformity of the Napoleonic period, she sought to revalorize individual national cultural traditions and modes of expression. In the ongoing historical dialectic of European unity and fragmentation, Staël's work therefore represents a renewed level of appreciation of the value and fruitfulness of diversity in terms of cultural expression and political structures.

Staël could not have foreseen that the revalorization of individual national cultures could also contribute, via the organic model of cultural nationalism, to enduring nationalistic hatreds and wars. Ironically, by the end of the century, Maurice Barrès, who would severely upbraid Staël for her literary Germanophilia, would claim the legacy of cultural nationalism for France, arguing that it was German philosophers who incarnated a pernicious form of domineering intellectual universalism. Staël's framework of resistance against the reductively homogenizing effects of an allegedly universal cultural model was thus adopted by some of her most severe critics, who would simply invert the national poles of her universalism/particularism continuum. Barrès's inversion of the terms of this perceived cultural opposition reflected the historical shift in the balance of military and political power between France and Germany during the nineteenth century.

Staël's pro-European legacy is today more relevant than her praise of individual national cultures. By stressing the need for continuous exchange on an equal and reciprocal basis, Staël envisioned a peaceful, multipolar European cultural field, a vision that Victor Hugo would later draw upon. Due to her background and interests, Staël was well suited for the role of cultural intermediary that she increasingly undertook. Through her work, she rejected the widely accepted notion of cultural preeminence or leadership by any one national tradition, while constantly seeking points of contact and interpenetration between cultures. In so doing, she straddled a fine line between illusory universalism and reductive particularism, between aggressive cultural imperialism and reactionary forms of cultural obscurantism, a line that remains relevant nearly two centuries later.

A literary innovator, Staël was the first exponent of what would later become the French Romantic movement, a literary and political movement of which Victor Hugo would become the undisputed leader. As had Staël, Hugo would be fascinated by, and involved in, transnational cultural and political issues throughout his life. In 1842, he would also produce the most influential book on Germany published in France since Staël's *De l'Allemagne*: *Le Rhin*. The next chapter will explore the European theme that is present in much of Hugo's work—a theme within which the issue of future European unity is explicitly addressed and enthusiastically promoted—against the backdrop of increasing rivalry between France and Germany.

CHAPTER 3

Victor Hugo's European Utopia

Hugo (Victor): Such a shame he dabbled in politics.
                                                    Gustave Flaubert, *Dictionnaire des idées reçues*

Victor Hugo's life (1802–85) spanned every French regime and revolution of his century: the Napoleonic Consulat (1799–1804) and Empire (1804–15); the royalist restoration that followed Napoleon's defeat (with the interlude of the "Cent Jours"); the revolutionary "Trois Glorieuses" of 1830, which produced the July Monarchy;[1] the two revolutions of 1848, leading to the Second Republic, which was cut short in 1851 by the second military coup organized by a Bonaparte, who would in turn establish the Second Empire; the Franco-Prussian War and the ill-fated Paris Commune in 1870–71, which were followed by the Third Republic, whose patron saint Hugo would, perhaps unwittingly, become. These transformations at the national level are reflected in Hugo's personal conversions. The youthful ultraroyalist first became fascinated with the myth of the usurper, Napoleon; the admirer of the conquering Emperor later became a liberal republican, with pacifist tendencies.[2]

A Child of the Century

Hugo identified himself with his century and with the historically providential role he saw being accomplished by the people of Paris through the continuation, in various forms, of the 1789 Revolution. The prophetic function of Hugo, the people's visionary poet, found a logical outlet in his political role, which allowed him to exalt the splendors of the future he foresaw at the same rhetorical level he used to denounce the injustices of his own era. He was not the only major French writer of his century seeking to interpret the course of universal history and to influence it through his literary and political activities.[3] What his writings indicate is that Hugo came to identify historical progress with the utopian goal of a peaceful, united Europe. This goal constitutes the intersecting point of several Hugolian themes and polemical stances, the point at which his literary and his political roles, or self-appointed missions, connect: "I would like to sign my life by a great action, before dying. Hence, the founding of the United States of Europe" (*Océan* 15: 294). With the telling phrase, "signer ma vie," Hugo likened his own existence to one of his works and linked his life's work to a goal that he endowed with almost eschatological import. His faith in future universal redemption was largely unaffected by the numerous setbacks inflicted to his ideals during his own lifetime. While Marcel Proust, in a famous passage, would later nostalgically seek to reconstruct "l'édifice immense du souvenir" (47), Hugo never stopped looking ahead, toward the European utopia he referred to in an 1851 speech at the National Assembly as "cet édifice immense de l'avenir" (10: 275).[4]

In Hugo's passionate vision—"For God wishes this sublime purpose!" (10: 302)—which he first delivered, fittingly enough, at an 1849 peace conference in Paris, the diverse peoples inhabiting the European states would peacefully coalesce into a multinational unit, just as the provinces had earlier combined to form French unity. Combining practicality with prophecy, he pointed out that European unity would allow its inhabitants to enjoy the fruits of peace: "elimination of domestic poverty, elimination of foreign wars" (10: 304). During his speech at the conference, of which he was the president, Hugo called for, among other things, the transfer of military budgets to civilian purposes, the development of education, technology, and commerce—and the continuation of colonial expansion as a means of alleviating "la misère" within Europe. He figuratively placed France at the political center of a European federal structure whose implicit institutional model was the United States of America. Hugo's conception of a united Europe, built along the lines of the French cultural model and with Paris as a common capital, was based on the French people's historical role since the Revolution.

Although he lived through several revolutions and participated in crushing one in 1848,[5] Hugo, as both a pacifistic idealist and a practical-minded property owner, did not advocate societal transformation through violent means: "Neither despotism nor terrorism. We seek a steady pace of progress" (*Les Misérables*, 2: 675). Since 1789, however, French history had been characterized not by incremental, peaceful evolution, but by bloody fratricidal struggles, such as those depicted in his last novel, *Quatrevingt-treize*. Especially after the hopes raised by the 1848 revolutions were dashed throughout Europe, the concept of historical progress was not easily integrated into Hugo's providential vision, hence the leap into a prophecy of a European future. In *Les Misérables*, Enjolras's speech to his fellow revolutionaries, before the final assault on the doomed barricade they are defending, offers a consoling perspective: "Civilization will meet at the summit of Europe, and later at the center of the continents, in a great parliament of intelligence" (2: 940). The redemptive culmination of history invoked by Enjolras represents nothing less than Hugo's secularized version of Christian eschatology, a transposition of messianic beliefs into the political upheavals of the nineteenth century. This fervent Hugolian wish to discern an overarching design within human history shares a common teleological objective with the Marxist fallacy that was born during the same period. While Enjolras's impassioned speech does not envision the final transcendence of class struggles, it does propound a future—the twentieth century—that radically breaks with the suffering and injustice that characterized previous centuries: "One could almost say: there will be no more events, only happiness" (2: 941).[6]

Revolution thus coincides with revelation. Far from succumbing to despair, the revolutionaries who are about to die on the barricades imagine a historical unfolding that will conclude with happiness becoming synonymous with serenity, with future generations living uneventfully ever after. Along with a meaningful end to history, Hugo is constructing a heartening outcome for the plot of his novel: "Universal well-being is divinely fated" (2: 791). In Hugo's reading (literally and metaphorically) of historical development, the centuries progress from violent absurdity to peaceful harmony, as they become chapters of a divinely inspired narrative, leading toward an ineluctably triumphant, redemptive *dénouement* of the plot, albeit not in linear fashion. The Hegelian concept of the "end of history" increasingly came to be embodied by what Hugo famously called the United States of Europe, with the age of peace and tranquility that such an ideal seemed to promise, and with its concomitant technical and social advancements. Hugo's Europe should not, however, be simply reduced to a political ideal. At a personal level, it allowed him to synthesize his yearnings toward statesmanship (thereby following in the footsteps of his Romantic forebears, Chateaubriand and Lamartine) and his well-established role as a literary visionary, the herald of a bright future. As both a literary theme and a utopian political goal, European unification also allowed Hugo to reconcile or transcend many of his own previous positions. In particular, through his espousal of the European cause, Hugo was better able to subsume his traditional French nationalism into his version of universalism, and to proceed with his rhetorical shift from the "Great Man" to the "People" as the agent of historical change. Over time, Hugo devised a variety of designations for his evolving European topos: "la République d'Europe," "les Peuples-Unis d'Europe," "la Communauté européenne," and of course, "les Etats-Unis d'Europe," which he first proclaimed, to great acclaim, at the 1849 Peace Conference in Paris (10: 301) and which drew mostly jeers two years later at the National Assembly. As Angelo Metzidakis pointed out (72), the ideal of bringing peace and progress, through unity, to the European continent was renewed after the wave of democratic and nationalistic revolutions in 1848. Although the insurrections were eventually crushed, they contributed to the feeling of anxious anticipation that Hugo's speech reflects.

Since there was continuity, not conflict, between Hugo's visions of Christianity and of the 1789 Revolution, and since the practical historical goal of a European federation derived from the ideals of the French Revolution, Hugo's Europe was endowed with religious symbolism and value. In his early revalorization of religion against part of the revolutionary legacy, Hugo was close to Staël.

He would gradually become more direct in his linkage of religious sentiment with popular progress. His belief in an overarching divine plan remained compatible with his confidence in the eventual triumph of republican principles. Although he became increasingly anticlerical, in the Voltairean tradition, in his later years—"Crush fanaticism and venerate the infinite" (*Les Misérables*, 2: 409)—Hugo never abandoned his deistic faith, and he never contemplated any authentic contradictions between his faith and his political ideals: "What the Revolution wants, God wants" (*Paris*, 10: 24). In *Les Misérables*, Bishop Myriel reluctantly calls on a dying old man who had been a member of the Convention and who had voted for the death of Louis XVI. The dialogue between the two characters allows Hugo to cross-examine the mixed legacy of the Revolution, including the Terror. The former "conventionnel," who is depicted as at least equal in saintliness to the Bishop, affirms, in unmistakably Hugolian terms: "the French Revolution is the most powerful step taken by the human race since the advent of Christ" (2: 34).[7]

L'Homme Qui Écrit

Hugo's childhood was marked by trips to Italy and Spain with his mother and brothers, in quest of his father, a Napoleonic army officer who would rise to the rank of general and baron (as part of the *noblesse d'Empire*).[8] Despite his early exposure to Mediterranean countries, or to Staël's category of "le Midi de l'Europe," Hugo's principal literary influences and political writings would derive from "le Nord." Through his phenomenal literary production and constant political activity, Hugo achieved a unique historical status in France and Europe, which can only be compared to that of Voltaire a century earlier.[9] Like his predecessor, Hugo became one of the most famous individuals in the continent during his lifetime, and he also managed to amass a tidy fortune. As had Voltaire, Hugo became the self-appointed conscience of his age, to which he added an oracular function, an evolving blend of humanism and mysticism. Hugo's successive literary transformations are even more complex than the stages of his political evolution. While his poetic output was relatively continuous, it underwent substantial thematic and formal changes, such as his incorporation of popular speech. He continued to write innovative plays even after his career as a playwright ended with the lack of success of *Les Burgraves* in 1843. His novels—in which he famously sought to achieve at total work blending history, philosophy, and epic—varied greatly in terms of setting and narrative technique. As for his speeches, essays, and polemical texts, they seem to cover almost every aspect of French literary and political life in the nineteenth century.

As a playwright, Hugo achieved celebrity by claiming the right to transgress the elaborate rules of French theater and poetry, rules that Voltaire had staunchly defended against the incursions of Shakespearean "barbarity." The influence of Shakespeare on Hugo's plays is visible in the variations in level of language, in the instances of comic relief, and in the grotesque characters who complement the hero. Through his pairing of the grotesque and the sublime and his attacks on two of the theatrical *Unités* (time and place), Hugo epitomized the artistic revolt of the French Romantics, a revolt that would spill over into the political domain, despite the partly reactionary origins of the movement. Roughly coinciding with the political revolution of 1830, Hugo's celebration of artistic innovation and renewal was influenced by Staël's contrasted presentations of Classical and Romantic poetry, which she had found best illustrated by the cases of France and Germany, respectively.

Hugo's first two novels are set on the fringes of Europe, in geographic or colonial terms. The 1823 *Han d'Islande* is a paroxysmal Gothic novel, horrific to the point of parody. It includes Mephistophelean laughter echoing through damp caves littered with human remains, while the fiendish title character drinks blood from a skull. Set in the most distant part of Staël's literary "Nord," with its extremes of cold and desolation, Hugo's satanic tale, which nevertheless includes a romantic subplot, bears traces of his readings of Goethe and Schiller.[10] *Bug-Jargal* (the second version was published in 1825) also contains elements of Gothic horror and cruelty, but it already includes such Hugolian thematic elements as universal brotherhood and the possibility of redemption through friendship or love. Set in Saint-Domingue, which is now Haiti, it depicts the slave revolt of 1791 against the French colonists, with atrocities committed by both sides. While Hugo takes note of the abolition of slavery during the French Revolution, there is no mention of its reestablishment by Bonaparte (which reignited the struggles that led to Haitian independence).[11]

A Popular Epic

Especially in such later novels as *Les Travailleurs de la mer*, Hugo's innovative treatment of the epic genre reverses the traditional perspective of the conquering warrior-hero, embarking on a perilous journey or accomplishing mighty tasks. His Christlike, self-sacrificing characters, Jean Valjean and Gilliatt, who are lowly embodiments of the people, nevertheless achieve a form of greatness, indeed an apotheosis, not through conquest or victories, but through renunciation and acceptance. The topos of *Les Travailleurs*—an isolated man on a barren rock, struggling against the *ananké* of the hostile ocean—derives from Hugo's years as an exiled resident of the Channel Islands, a *proscrit*, patiently waiting for the ignominious end of Bonaparte's regime. This reflects the evolution of Hugo's representation of the historical "Grand Homme"—the best example of which is found in his fascination with Napoleon I.[12] One of the main characteristics of the early Hugolian Great Man is the capacity to disregard national borders, to extend his power or influence across Europe: "ce grand bûcheron de l'Europe qu'on appelait Napoléon" (*Les Misérables*, 2: 242). Aside from Napoleon, the characters of Cromwell, Charles V, and especially Charlemagne are depicted as lengthening their reach beyond the borders of the lands they rule. In *Hernani*, the soliloquy of Don Carlos (Charles V) in front of Charlemagne's tomb, associates across the centuries two emperors who sought to achieve a universal monarchy (Napoleon is also implicitly associated):

> Such a beautiful spectacle, a delightful thought
> Europe thus made, as he left it! (8: 626)

The experience of exile led to a shift in Hugo's work, away from his previous exaltation of the exceptional individual and toward a new central role for the people and their symbolic representatives. For Hugo, a practitioner of the epic genre, the representation of exceptional achievement or heroic grandeur became situated either among lowly outcasts or within the collective genius of the people of Paris. His choices in terms of characterization thus mirrored his own political evolution, which in turn accompanied the successive political changes of French society during the nineteenth century. Hugo's writing while in exile, and especially his concept of the historical role of "le Grand Homme," was influenced by the less than glorious reality of the Second Empire, an inverted mirror image of the literary mythology that had accumulated (in no small part because of Hugo himself) around the First Empire. The Great Man, especially the warrior and conqueror, was supplanted in the Hugolian pantheon by the People and the Genius—which represented different kinds of myths: "The swordwielders are finished; time for the thinkers" (*Les Misérables*, 2: 277). In the new Hugolian concept of historical progress (which recalls Voltaire's concept), historians and poets would no longer emphasize royal successions, such as "how François II came after Henri II, Charles IX after François II, and Henri III after Charles IX," but would instead trace the progress of the "mysterious dynasty of geniuses," of those whose inventions improved the lives of the people, or "how Watt came after Papin, and Fulton after Watt" (*William Shakespeare*, 12: 449). The ideal of a United States of Europe was the logical extension of Hugo's political and esthetic evolution. Having evolved from a Royalist to a Bonapartist and finally to a liberal Republican, he gradually developed an aversion for the destructive conquerors and "sabreurs" exemplified by Napoleon. Meanwhile, Hugo's celebration of scientists and inventors derived from and contributed to his championing a European federation that seemed to promise a limitless potential of commercial and artistic development.

The chapter entitled "Ceci tuera cela" of *Notre-Dame de Paris* (1: 618–28) presents the technical evolution of art forms as the adumbration of societal transformation. Easily duplicated print will thus supersede unique architectural achievements and democracy will similarly replace monarchy/theocracy. Hugo, an admirer of Gothic architecture, was torn between his love for the enduring relics of the past and his exaltation of future progress. One can only wonder how he would have characterized the expanding audiovisual culture of our own day and the concomitant displacement of literary production from its previously central role. Another form of "Ceci tuera cela" is found in the reiterated Hugolian prediction of an end to wars and to the glorification of warriors. Linked to the topos of European peace and unification, Hugo's affirmation of the future disappearance of conquerors, whom the people obeyed out of fear, was accompanied by an exaltation of the role of writers who would serve as guides, not masters. Hugo's notion of the poet's "mission" in his century derived from his vision of the people's historical role in the aftermath of the Revolution. Few writers have so eloquently prophesied a new age, the reality of which could not possibly keep up with his vision.

A Republican Saint

Hugo was one of the main speakers and symbols during the 1878 commemorations of the centennials of the deaths of Voltaire and Rousseau. Hugo inaugurated the institutionalized republican "culte des grands hommes"—which would allow the still-fragile regime to impose its own ostentatiously ceremonial values by replacing the traditional veneration for kings and saints with its corresponding secular pageant of writers and scientists. In 1885, Hugo himself would spectacularly join that pageant. His death became a moment of triumph for the Third Republic, whose bourgeois, secular values he had come to incarnate. In a lengthy ceremony, his body was transferred from the Arc de Triomphe to the Panthéon—a former church that had been, once again, recommissioned as the final resting place of republican symbols. The event drew an unprecedented crowd of mourners and onlookers, which was greater in numbers than the entire population of Paris.[13]

Even before his death, Hugo would become the principal secular patron saint of the Third Republic, although he was temporarily marginalized for calling for amnesty for the Communards after the savage repression by the Versaillais troops. As Graham Robb details (511–16), Hugo allowed himself to be appropriated by a regime that had been born in a bloodbath. It was in part his status as a living statue, as the deified embodiment of the Third Republic, that contributed to Hugo's decline, in terms of critical appreciation, during much of the twentieth century. The age of peace, brotherhood, and progress, which he had so eloquently predicted for the century that followed his own, failed to materialize, leaving him with the retrospective image of yet another naïve and pompous dreamer of a bygone positivistic period.[14] The official adulation that accompanied his later years, and only increased with his death, had the effect of occluding the dark, sardonic elements of his work, while highlighting his iconic representation as the prophet of uncritical scientism and maudlin morality.

Europe as an Extension of France

There is a natural progression within Hugo's epic of human progress, from the French Revolution to European unity, and onward toward Humanity: "What happens to France happens to the whole world" (*Choses vues*, 11: 1327). Throughout these stages, the French people, as initiators of the Revolution, are presented as playing a leading role: "The law of Europe is to evolve as does France" (11: 1313). The centrality of French characters in Hugo's fiction reflected his often expressed political and historical Francocentrism, an expansive form of ideologically motivated patriotism that he projected onto the rest of the continent: "France is already Europe" (11: 1336). In "Souvenir d'enfance," Hugo depicts his father, glowingly describing Napoleon's intentions for the future of the continent: "Europe is now only a vast France" (4: 637).

Seeking to exert influence within France, even while in exile, Hugo wrote an introduction to a "guide" to Paris published for the 1867 World's Fair, in which he suggested that the main exhibition hall should house the statues of a short list of European artists, each representing the best of their respective nations: Homer, Dante, Shakespeare, and Beethoven. However, the last statue, that of Voltaire, was to be physically and figuratively set apart. In Hugo's ideal exhibit, Voltaire is not simply the representative of France, but of humanity (*Paris*, 10: 38).[15] To paraphrase the last remaining, and altered, Commandment in George Orwell's *Animal Farm*—without seeking to ascribe any totalitarian intention to Hugo—all geniuses are apparently equal, but some are more historically equal than others. Hugo's Francocentrism was more than simply a presentation of the French civilizational model as *primus inter pares*. The sequence France-Europe-Humanity, each term successively conditioning the next, and which might be preceded by "Paris," reflected both the established centralization of French society and Hugo's view of the fundamental importance of the French Revolution for world history. From his exile in Guernsey, Hugo begins his long introduction to *Paris* with a prophecy; combining lyricism with concern for property rights, he explains how war, poverty, and ignorance will be eliminated through European unity. He also highlights the role of Paris—"the human Jerusalem" (10: 26)—as the focal point of Europe: "This nation will have Paris as its capital, and will not be called France: it will be called Europe" (10: 6). Just as Voltaire represents all of humanity, Paris represents all of Europe. In Hugo's prophecy, Paris is the natural capital of a European federation, for that is where human history was decisively transformed: "What does Paris have? The Revolution" (10: 19).

The peaceful universalism that Hugo saw as incarnated by Paris and France turned out to be quite compatible with the violent enterprise of colonization carried out by its successive regimes. In particular, the Third Republic, which sought to figuratively annex the Hugolian heritage through its public celebrations, would ruthlessly expand the French colonial empire, in the name of its civilizing mission. For his part, Hugo approved the principle of French colonialism, particularly in Africa, while deploring the brutality of its methods.[16]

European Evangelism

In his first speech at the *Chambre des Pairs* in 1846, Hugo denounced Austrian oppression within what had once been Poland (10: 125). In an interesting choice of words, Hugo's sympathy for Polish nationalists was motivated by the former country's service to "la communauté européenne" (10: 124).[17] In 1856, in a letter of support for Greek independence, when he was already calling for European unity, he still saw the goals of national independence movements as worthy intermediate steps (10: 510). Through his calls for a European federation, Hugo integrated his support for oppressed nationalities, his view of the French Revolution as inaugurating a new age, and his vision of the people's redemptive historical role. Focused on the need to finish the work of the Revolution by abolishing the reactionary kingdoms that had cynically divided up ethnic and linguistic groups, Hugo, like Staël, did not anticipate that movements of national independence and unity could in turn become aggressive, imperialistic forces. Hugo's European utopia represented the main objective of historical development, if not the final culmination, which was its extension to the rest of humanity: "the social and democratic republic, the immense good news, the supreme form and definitive idea of progress" (*Choses vues*, 11: 1313). Establishing a stylistic parallel between the slogan of the Revolution and its extension to the rest of the world, Hugo succinctly linked "Liberté-Egalité-Fraternité" and "France-Europe-Humanité." For Hugo, the goal of European unification represented more than the sort of sentimental idealism of which he has often been accused. It was an essential element of his eschatological vision of technical and social progress.

In 1869, one year before the Franco-Prussian War, Hugo began a letter to the participants of a peace congress in Lausanne with: "Fellow Citizens of the United States of Europe" (10: 623). As in his 1854 speech, he was not optimistic for the near term, foreseeing the inevitability of a "dernière guerre," which would be the fault of kings who wished to "divide and conquer" (10: 624). Although a war remained likely, its aftermath—in a prefiguration of the slogan, "la Der des Ders," used during the First World War—would be lasting peace, which Hugo described, blending visionary millenarianism with very practical economic liberalism: "Peace once and for all" (10: 623). In 1874, Hugo sent to the participants of a peace congress in Geneva a letter of support that began in a similar fashion: "Dear Fellow Citizens of the European republic" (10: 882). After the French defeat and the annexation of Alsace-Lorraine, the author of *L'Année terrible* did not show the same level of enthusiasm for the future: "There is currently nothing but dark, repressed hatred" (10: 882). He predicted that the humiliating terms imposed on France would lead to another war—from which would nevertheless result in the United States of Europe.[18] Hugo was not blindly idealistic, and he did not predict an unbroken and peaceful linear path toward his goal of European unity, but he never lost sight of it. Along with the completion of the ideals of the French Revolution, it had become the central element of his vision of a redemptive historical finality.

Europe, Within and Without

For a committed European, Hugo wrote relatively little about other European countries, with the major exception of Germany. Despite his stays in Italy and Spain during his childhood, he did not make Mediterranean countries the focus of his travels as an adult. While he wrote three plays set in Spain (*Hernani*, *Ruy Blas*, and *Torquemada*), the first two were interpreted by audiences as projections of French issues. He attempted no equivalent to *Le Rhin* for Spain, Italy, or Great Britain. As will be discussed, the conclusion to that book, based on trips to the region, essentially limited Europe to the Franco-German alliance Hugo called for, while hardly mentioning the smaller neighboring countries (an eloquent silence which even includes Italy). Spain, classified as largely African, was symbolically distanced from Europe and associated with the representative of Asia, Turkey.[19] As for Great Britain, it constituted a looming foreign presence, allied with an even more menacing Russia.

During his long period of exile in the Channel Islands, Hugo, the admirer of Shakespeare, did not take the opportunity to travel extensively through Great Britain, or even to become proficient in English.[20] He simply used British ports as way stations on his trips to French-speaking Belgium. Sheila Gaudon has detailed the largely negative Hugolian representation of France's British neighbor, which had been the enemy of Napoleon I and had become the ally of Napoleon III. Hugo's notion of geographic determinism (which he would apply, by contrast, in order to figuratively unite France and Germany) tended to symbolically separate Britain from Europe: "Selfishness is an island. I have just written the history of England" (*Choses vues*, 11: 1288). Paired with Russia in *Le Rhin*, Britain was for Hugo similarly inimical to national independence movements: "England, which condemns Russia for its occupation of Poland, does not see its own occupation of Ireland" (*Choses vues*, 11: 1324). The prophet of European unity would only fully integrate the country into his vision by distinguishing between the British people and their monarchical form of government. Unlike Voltaire, Hugo did not systematically posit Great Britain as a model of tolerance and progress. In the century that followed Voltaire's, these values had in Hugo's work largely crossed the Channel (with such major exceptions as the Second Empire). In *L'Homme qui rit*, Hugo provides an account of the absurd ceremony at the House of Lords in scathing detail (3: 705–14), an account which can be compared to Voltaire's focus on what he considered progressive British institutions.

One of the consistent aspects of Hugo's social and political thought, as has been mentioned, was his support for movements seeking national independence, unity, or both, particularly in Greece, Italy, Poland, and Germany. In the tradition of Romantic activism best illustrated by Byron, he repeatedly attacked, in political speeches as well as in fictional texts, the empires that had carved up, and were oppressing, national entities, particularly Turkey, Austria, and Russia. The plight of divided Poland figures prominently, in *Les Travailleurs de la mer*, among a list of what Hugo considers as crimes committed by despotic rulers: "[Czar] Nicolas assassinating Poland in full view of the civilized world" (3: 171–72). The distant Russian empire itself is for Hugo a vast mechanism for repression: "Every year, 14,000 prisoners, most of them political, are sent to Siberia" (*Choses vues*, 11: 1336).[21]

While Hugo often expressed his support for national entities that lacked democratic state institutions, he displayed, until the latter part of his career, clear signs of traditional religious prejudice in the case of Jews, a minority with no fixed national home in Europe. The historical figure of Manassé Ben-Israël is turned into an utterly dehumanized version of Shylock in *Cromwell*: "The disgusting Jew should be hung between two dogs!" (8: 86). *Marie Tudor* (8: 1079–185) also includes the typical caricature of a Jewish usurer. In *Les Burgraves*, the character of Job tells of his long-lost son, apparently the victim of a "ritual murder" committed by Jews: "He was taken from me . . . to be slaughtered during their Sabbath" (9: 208). Aside from Hugo's historical plays, the poem, "A l'homme qui a livré une femme" (4: 719–21) provides a portrait of a nineteenth-century Jew who is grasping, cowardly, and treacherous. Ironically, for an ultraroyalist, Hugo, in his early "Journal d'un jeune jacobite de 1819," appears Voltairean in terms of his derogatory characterization of Jews: "A strange book could be written on the Jews during the Middle Ages. They were hated, but they were odious; they were treated with contempt, but they were vile" (12: 66). With the experience of exile and the crystallization of his ideology of a European republic, however, Hugo began to include Jews in his humanitarian appeals. His condemnation of religious intolerance is vividly articulated in the play he wrote in 1869, *Torquemada* (9: 263–377). It was published in 1882 as part of one of Hugo's last public appeals (10: 1070–71), in which he called for an end to the wave of pogroms that had been encouraged by Russian authorities after the assassination of Czar Alexander II.

While the development of Hugo's Europeanism was a major factor in the evolution of his attitudes toward internal minorities, it did not transform his view of what Rudyard Kipling infamously called the "white man's burden" abroad. In the conclusion to *Le Rhin*, Hugo had already predicted that the worldwide civilizing mission of Europe would ultimately be completed by France: "To educate the human race, such is Europe's mission . . . France will civilize the colonies" (13: 432). In his 1879 "Discours sur l'Afrique" (10: 1008–12), Hugo praised his friend and fellow former *proscrit*, Victor Schœlcher,[22] for his leading role in the campaign to abolish slavery. Hugo then proceeded to contrast Europe and Africa: "On one side all is civilization, on the other all is barbarity" (10: 1010). Unabashedly exalting the ongoing colonial enterprise, he depicted Europeans as acting generously in order to regenerate the African continent: "How to make the old Africa fit for civilization, such is the problem. Europe will solve it" (10: 1012). As an added benefit, through the presumably peaceful economic development of Africa, Europe could also alleviate its own social problems: "Pour your overflowing population into Africa, and thereby solve your social issues: turn your proletarians into owners" (10: 1012).

Hugo's paternalistic presentation of Europe peacefully bringing the benefits of civilization to a benighted Africa illustrates the political contradictions in France after the Franco-Prussian War. While much of the political right wanted the country to remain focused on the eastern borderline ("la ligne bleue des Vosges"), the republican left—whose icon Hugo had become—spearheaded a massive colonial effort as a means of strengthening the still fragile Third Republic. Somewhat fittingly, Hugo died shortly after the close of the 1884–85 Berlin Conference, which sealed the final division of Africa between the European colonial powers.

Along the Rhine

As a young Romantic, Hugo followed in Staël's footsteps by privileging, among his literary influences, German and British works, the principal incarnations of her category of the Romantic "Nord." Staël's *De l'Allemagne*, as has been mentioned, was for Hugo a major reference in terms of what might be called comparative literary theory, as well as an introduction to German Romantic literature. In his 1824 preface to *Odes et ballades* (4: 56–62), Hugo, referring to Staël's famous book, praised her as "une femme de génie, qui, la première, a prononcé le mot de littérature romantique en France" (4: 57). However, Hugo found that her definitions of the categories of "Classicism" and "Romanticism," representing respectively the sensibilities of the eras before and after the establishment of Christianity, were no longer applicable. Charles Dédéyan has detailed the evolution of German literary influences on Hugo and of the representation of Germany in his works, a representation that, predictably, became distinctly negative after the Franco-Prussian War.

The result of trips he made with Juliette Drouet, *Le Rhin* is an exception within the Hugolian corpus, his only major publication that derived from voluntary travels outside of France.[23] It should be noted that Hugo did not travel as widely as Staël had. Aside from his childhood, his travels were limited (as had been the case for Voltaire) to northern Europe. Part travel literature, part political essay, *Le Rhin* allowed Hugo to discuss France's contested eastern border, a border that during the Revolutionary period had been along the Rhine until Napoleon's second abdication in 1815. Most of the book is devoted to Hugo's reactions as a visitor to the region, to his descriptions of its cities, its ruins, and its monuments, as well as of its legendary past.[24] In the long conclusion, he delves into European history and geopolitics. Unlike Staël, who had crossed the Rhine to further her study of German literature, Hugo seems to have had few contacts with German writers. Another difference between Hugo and Staël was that the military and political balance between France and Germany (which would not become a fully unified country until the Franco-Prussian War) had been transformed after the fall of the Napoleonic Empire. An increasingly powerful Germany was replacing Great Britain as the geopolitical archrival, the "ennemi héréditaire" of France.

The publication in 1842 of Hugo's writings on the Rhine as the "natural border," as well as the uniting, not dividing line between France and Germany, occurred within the context of an already raging debate. Alfred de Musset's poem, "Le Rhin allemand," was a sardonic reply to a bombastic 1840 song by Nicholas Becker, whose *Rheinlied* (translated in Musset, 187) had affirmed the disputed river to be strictly, and forever, German. Musset recalled sarcastically that both the left and right banks of the river had been French possessions during the Revolutionary and Napoleonic periods: "We had your German Rhine" (187). Aside from the retrospective saber-rattling, Musset's defiant 1841 poem was also partly a rebuke, directed at Alphonse de Lamartine, for his far more irenic poem of the same year, "La Marseillaise de la paix" (1173–77), which, as did most of Hugo's writings, posited the Rhine—"the Nile of the West"—as a site of peaceful exchange, instead of nationalistic struggle: "Only selfishness and hatred have a fatherland; brotherhood does not" (1174). Musset was not the only French writer to criticize Lamartine (to whom Becker had originally sent his *Rheinlied*) for what was widely perceived in France as an overly conciliatory reply to an aggressive taunt.[25] The same year, Edgar Quinet, a historian who, like Hugo, would later be exiled during the Second Empire, also weighed in with his "Le Rhin. A M. de Lamartine" (149–52). Quinet's avian metaphors, likening Germany to an aggressive vulture ("Au premier coup de bec du vautour germanique") and Lamartine's France to a graceful but timorous swan ("Noble cygne de France, à la langue de miel"), implicitly recalled the fallen Napoleonic eagle (149). Apostrophizing Lamartine, Quinet reasserted French claims to the left bank of the Rhine: "Du Nil de l'Occident nous ne voulons qu'un bord" (151).

The elegant phrasing of the poems notwithstanding, the aggressive posturing, on either side of the disputed river, of the "Querelle du Rhin" in the early 1840s reflects the nationalistic tensions of post-Napoleonic Europe, tensions that would culminate in the long-sought completion of German unity—through a war with France in 1870–71.[26] Hugo was obviously conscious of these tensions, and of the importance of the issue of Franco-German relations, the crux of which he saw along the Rhine. At once mirror and window, the river became integrated into Hugo's vision: "This admirable river provides a poetic glimpse . . . into Europe's past and future" (*Le Rhin*, 13: 3). In spite of the emotionally charged nationalistic context of the "Querelle du Rhin," Hugo presented himself as an admirer of Germany, "the homeland of all thinkers" (13: 9). However, emotional affinities did not cancel out historical disputes. Even before the concluding section of his book, which is devoted to political issues, Hugo was very clear on the question of where the border between France and Germany should lie: "Geography gives the left bank of the Rhine to France" (13: 108). His typically Romantic fascination with tombs, ruined castles, and Gothic legends was thus intermingled with the political considerations of his day. Even in his most lyrical passages, he reminded his readers of his view that the long-disputed river should be equally and peacefully shared by the two countries: "It is a noble river, feudal, republican, imperial, worthy of being both French and German" (13: 99).[27] Germany and France are also linked through their greatest imperial rulers and through the related numerological analogies that Hugo finds significant. Describing his visit to Charlemagne's tomb, Hugo draws a parallel, across the centuries, between two empires: "In 814 Charlemagne died; a thousand years later . . . in 1814, Napoleon fell" (13: 68). Hugo returns to the parallel in his conclusion, presenting Charlemagne and Napoleon as having both tried to constitute a version of the Europe he calls for, structured around the alliance of France and Germany.[28]

Hugo's positions on Franco-German relations and on the issue of the Rhine as a border between the two countries did not lack originality. Based on a traditional notion of a static balance of power, the limited alliance that Hugo advocated was essentially defensive and lacked the expansiveness his European topos would later acquire. In the conclusion to *Le Rhin*, he provided a curious historical and geopolitical review, presenting Europe in the seventeenth century as besieged from the east and the west by two external empires, Spain and Turkey. The nucleus of Europe, meanwhile, was in fact limited to France and Germany, which he saw as natural partners, united by the Rhine (whose left bank should logically revert to France), against the twin external dangers. In Hugo's historical model, therefore, Europe had been, and remained, threatened by two neighboring but foreign empires, one on either side of the continent. In the seventeenth century, "Through Turkey, the mindset of Asia was spread over Europe; through Spain, it was the mindset of Africa" (13: 378). In the nineteenth century, new empires had arisen, but in the Hugolian schema, Europe was still hemmed in from the east and west, the twin threats having shifted toward the north: "Turkey has been replaced by Russia, and Spain by England" (13: 387). After supplying a list of smaller European states that had either disappeared or been diminished by the middle of the nineteenth century, Hugo identifies most of the Europe of his day as the French-German partnership—which he correspondingly calls for—and he proceeds to assign roles for each country based on their established traits (which recall Staël's formulation): "France and Germany essentially constitute Europe. Germany is the heart; France the head. France and Germany essentially constitute civilization. Germany feels; France thinks . . . They have similar origins. They are not insular, nor invaders. They are the true sons of the land of Europe" (13: 403).

The Hugolian division of roles and qualities between France and Germany, expressed as a linked set of anatomical metaphors (the mind and the heart of the European body), is marked by the influence of Staël's depiction of Germans as generally oriented toward dreams and sentiments. In this schema, Hugo correspondingly ascribes logic and rationalism to the French. Once the national dichotomies are in place—France/head/thought versus Germany/heart/feeling—an apparently symmetrical division of civilizational labor can be assigned. Aside from Hugo's previously discussed Francocentrism, which undergirds the obvious hierarchy of this complementary set, the Franco-German alliance he advocates has an unmistakably modern ring, even if its dual defensive purpose seems farfetched: "The union of Germany and France would provide protection against England and Russia, would save Europe, would promote worldwide peace" (13: 406). Hugo saw whatever antagonism existed between the natural allies, France and Germany, as resulting from the Machiavellian power politics of the two external empires, after the fall of the Napoleonic Empire. Due to British and Russian pressure at the Congress of Vienna in 1815, the left bank of the Rhine had been detached from France and given to Prussia, precisely as a means of sowing discord between France and Germany (13: 411). In order to counteract the effects of the British and Russian attempt to drive a wedge between France and Germany, it was therefore in Germany's own interest to renounce its claim on the left bank of the Rhine: "Discord between France and Germany means the dislocation of Europe" (13: 427).

The Hugolian analysis of history and geopolitics led to a clear conclusion; in order to redress the balance within Europe, Germany would have to accept ceding the left bank of the Rhine to France, which would be content at having reached its "natural border" to the east. However, this transfer should be accomplished peacefully, through a realization of the common interests of the two countries. Furthermore, according to Hugo, there would be no real prejudice for Germany, which, secure along the Rhine, could concentrate on completing its process of unification and expansion toward the Danube. Great rivers thus conditioned a form of geographic determinism for the Franco-German duopoly, with each country unified within natural borders and allied against external threats. The perspective of German unification was for Hugo linked to a mutually beneficial alliance with France, which would make the Franco-Prussian War, or the achievement of German unity *against* France, all the more traumatic. Overall, his detailed plan for a Franco-German alliance, based on the concept of an equally shared Rhine river, was of course less than realistic. It did, however, posit the two countries as the nucleus of a future united Europe.

In the 1843 preface to what would be his last staged play, *Les Burgraves*, Hugo returned to a broader concept of Europe. Comparing individual nations within nineteenth-century Europe to the city-states of ancient Greece, he found more factors of commonality than of differentiation: "There is today a European nationality" (9: 156). Referring to the "Querelle du Rhin," he stressed the historical and cultural links that transcended national borders (9: 156). The central theme of the conclusion to *Le Rhin* had been the need for a defensive alliance between France (with its eastern border on the Rhine) and a united Germany occupying most of central Europe. The twin central nations would thus be in a position to counter the aggressive ambitions of the two external powers, Russia and Great Britain. With the preface to *Les Burgraves*, however, the practical notion of a European equilibrium built around competing alliances is replaced by a vision of wholeness, with the continent's various nationalities intrinsically linked and subsumed into a European collectivity. In this perspective, German national unity simply constituted one prefiguration, along with Italian or Polish unity, of the future European political entity. For Hugo, the original model remained France, which had already successfully (if not altogether peacefully) aggregated its various provinces into a coherent whole.

As was previously stated, the European topos became in Hugo's writings an essential aspect of his prophetic vision of a peaceful, prosperous future, in which the seemingly absurd vicissitudes of history would be decisively brought to a close. His efforts to integrate the apparent chaos of human events into a wider meaning or finality were sorely tested by the French defeat of 1870, the siege of Paris, and the forcible annexation of Alsace-Lorraine. Immediately upon his arrival in France, after nineteen years of exile, Hugo fruitlessly attempted to call for an end to the fighting. His 1870 "Lettre aux Allemands" (10: 725–28), published in French and German, was written shortly after the fall of the Second Empire, when Prussian troops were closing in on Paris. Using the familiar thesis that Paris belonged to all of humanity, Hugo argued that the fall of Bonaparte's regime had removed any justification for the continuation of a war he characterized as an absurd fratricidal conflict. As is visible in *L'Année terrible*, this most sorrowful of historical junctures was exceedingly difficult to inscribe within a providential design. While the alliance of France and Germany had been central to his conception of Europe, Hugo could no longer foresee its occurrence before another bout of warfare. Although he had previously supported the concept of German national unity, he could not accept that it had been achieved against France (and not just against Napoleon III). The grand design of the Hugolian vision, the redemptive power of his poetic discourse, had been confronted with precisely the sort of bloody, meaningless historical events whose end he had been prophesying. France's putative friend and ally had become its pitiless archenemy. In a bitter 1871 poem entitled "A ceux qui reparlent de fraternité," written in the aftermath of the Franco-Prussian War, Hugo shelved his calls for reconciliation, which he could not envision before another war. This poem provides an early literary example of the use of the term "revanche," which would occupy a prominent place in the French political lexicon until the First World War:

> A declaration of peace is never frank
> Coming from those who, knocked down, seek revenge (6: 81)

In February 1871, Hugo was elected to the National Assembly that would have to negotiate the terms of surrender with the Prussian occupiers.[29] He resigned a few days later, after having vainly opposed the humiliating treaty worked out between Bismarck and the future president who would crush the Paris Commune, Adolphe Thiers. In an astonishing section of this speech (March 1, 1871) that anticipates Barrès's revanchist discourse, Hugo called for all-out war against the new German Empire, apparently hoping the defeated French army, bolstered by the sort of mass conscription that had fueled Revolutionary victories, could somehow reconquer not just Alsace and Lorraine, but the entire left bank of the Rhine (10:756). In the aftermath of this highly imaginative Hugolian epic, Germany would become a republic, France would willingly return its occupied territory, and the borders between the two countries would be abolished in an outbreak of generalized brotherhood. A call for total war, to be immediately followed by wholehearted and everlasting reconciliation, all couched in lofty Hugolian rhetoric: "No more borders! The Rhine belongs to us all! Let us be a single Republic, let us be the United States of Europe . . . let us be worldwide peace!" (10: 756). It is not without reason that Hugo's biographer refers to him in this instance as a "megalomaniac" (Robb 461). Hugo's fierce call to arms, in the context of the French defeat, can be compared to the sort of bellicose rhetoric Barrès would later specialize in. Hugo would not, however, consistently deny any possibility of future reconciliation with Germany. In 1872, he sent a message from Guernsey to the participants at a peace congress in Lugano. Beginning with "Mes compatriotes européens," this short text (10: 858–59) shows that, despite the annexation of Alsace-Lorraine, he had not lost his vision of a peaceful, united Europe. Nevertheless, he predicted another war or revolution before it could occur.

Against the Second Empire

In his 1852 pamphlet, *Napoléon-le-petit*, Hugo used animal metaphors to contemptuously compare Napoleon III to the historical stature of his uncle, Napoleon I: "Look at the slime-coated pig sprawling on a lionskin" (11: 86). Hugo had first used the derisive epithet in a speech at the National Assembly (July 17, 1851) that drew continuous jeering from the right-wing majority: "Because we had Napoleon the Great, must we have the little Napoleon?" (10: 290). This was the same speech in which Hugo first spoke of "les Etats-Unis d'Europe" at the Assembly. Hugo was objecting to attempts at revising the constitution, which would have allowed the single-term President of the Republic to run for reelection and which, Hugo implied, betrayed Bonaparte's ambitions of unlimited personal power. The constitutional issue was rendered moot by the military coup (December 2, 1851) organized by Bonaparte and by the ensuing bloody crackdown on his political opponents. The Second Empire would soon follow. With this coup, the Romantic myth that accumulated around "le 18 brumaire" was shattered; this time it was the elected President of the Republic who had cynically broken his oath of office, while France was not threatened by any reactionary army.

Hugo exhibited a high level of personal courage in his unsuccessful attempts to rally popular opposition to the coup, but he was forced to flee the country. As had Staël, Hugo, although never a real threat, would remain a symbolic thorn in the side of the Bonapartist regime. His long period of exile in the Channel Islands turned the former royalist and admirer of Napoleon I into the embodiment of republican opposition to the new regime, and hastened the evolution of his utopianism toward political objectives at the European level. France was now fully part of the reactionary coalition of monarchs that rolled back the revolutionary tide, which swept Europe in 1848. Hugo would thus tend to foresee any future revolutionary shift to a republic in France as spreading to its neighbors. The experience of forced exile led Hugo to reenact the roles played by Voltaire in Ferney and Staël in Coppet. Living outside of France, while remaining close to it, Hugo the artist sought to embody the conscience of a society that had lost its way and was not fulfilling its historical mission.

A masterpiece of oppositional literature, *Napoléon-le-petit* announces (in unallegorical form), as Robb pointed out (309), Orwell's depiction of totalitarian practice and propaganda in *Animal Farm*, in which facts would be cynically and endlessly manipulated to suit the dictator's needs of the moment: "This man lies as other men breathe" (*Napoléon-le-petit*, 11: 16). Unlike *Napoléon-le-petit*, which had a huge clandestine success during the early years of the Second Empire, the even more scathing *Histoire d'un crime* was not published, for reasons that remain unclear, until 1877. However, in his response to Bonaparte's bloody coup and restoration of the Empire, Hugo was in a logical, and self-inflicted, bind. It was mainly due to his kinship with Napoleon I that the new Bonaparte had been democratically elected President of the Second Republic in 1848. Even before he orchestrated the official constitutional switch to the Second Empire, Napoleon III relied on the symbols and mythology of the original Napoleonic epic in order to prop up his regime and whatever legitimacy it could muster. The myth of "Napoléon le Grand" had precisely been nurtured and expanded by Romantic artists, of whom the most prominent was none other than Victor Hugo. It could in fact be argued that Hugo indirectly contributed to the fall of the Republic by glorifying the figure of the uncle, without whom the nephew would not have gained power. Even when insisting on the contemptible nature of the Second Empire, Hugo was still magnifying the First by contrast.

In *The Eighteenth Brumaire of Louis Bonaparte*, Karl Marx disparaged the superficial nature of Hugo's attacks on the new Bonapartist regime, which in

Marx's view merely tended to personalize the broader historical shifts he saw as resulting from class struggles: "[Hugo] sees in [the coup d'état] only the violent act of a single individual. He does not notice that he makes this individual great instead of little by ascribing to him a personal power of initiative such as would be without parallel in world history" (8).[30] The personified Hugolian rhetoric, however, produced a polemical effect that echoed what Staël had accomplished; by focusing on the dictator he was combatting, Hugo ultimately magnified his own stature, as the irreducible opponent of an illegal regime. The representative of the declining Romantic movement thus became the incarnation—all the more so in light of his isolation—of the values of the Republic: "And if only one remains, I shall be that one" ("Ultima Verba," 5: 198).

Hugo, whose lifetime spanned a bewildering series of political transformations in France, tended to privilege the importance of the country's constitutional transition from monarchy to republic, which corresponded well to his providential vision of history. In this perspective, the forced transition from republic to empire, by contrast, constituted a historical regression, a crime against the march of political and moral progress. Hugo remained largely oblivious to the degree of social, economic, and even institutional continuity that persisted in France throughout the variations in constitutional regimes during the nineteenth century. It is telling that he did not display similar levels of moral outrage when the workers' uprising of June 1848 was crushed (indeed, Hugo took part in the repression) or when the *Communards* were systematically executed in 1871, as he did in the case of Bonaparte's coup d'état.

For Hugo, the bitter historical irony of the new political situation was overwhelming; the grotesque reality of the Second Empire had caught up with the sublime fiction of the First. Other ironies abounded. The technical, scientific, and economic advancements lauded by Hugo were among the hallmarks of the new regime, during which France began industrializing at a rapid pace, although it was still decades behind Great Britain.[31] The railway system, which Hugo saw as leading to peace and reconciliation through the abolition of national borders, was greatly expanded—and would of course also be used for military purposes. In a ruthless campaign of urban destruction and renewal waged by Bonaparte's prefect, Baron Haussmann, the city of Paris that Hugo posited as the center of Europe was radically transformed and modernized (with some of its famously narrow streets being widened and thereby made safer for cavalry charges).

From Technical to Social Progress

Although Hugo never simply equated the two, nor naïvely posited one as deriving in a direct and unimpeded fashion from the other, he did present scientific progress as facilitating and reinforcing social progress. His fascination for technical innovation reflected the social changes brought about during the nineteenth century by some of its most spectacular examples, particularly in the domains of transportation and communication. For Hugo, the political revolution of 1789 would be completed by the industrial revolution, which was abolishing borders and linking regions and nations. The train, steamship, and telegraph would thus participate in facilitating contacts and reducing suspicions and hatreds. Hugo makes this argument in the conclusion to *Le Rhin*, apparently unwilling to consider that technological progress can also facilitate wars and make them more efficiently murderous: "Perpetual peace remained a dream until railways spread out, creating a solid, tenacious, living network. Watt is the complement to the Abbé de Saint-Pierre" (13: 429).

Along with quicker, more efficient means of transportation, a common language would facilitate the peaceful exchange of ideas: "These two vehicles, which tend to erase the borders between empires and of intelligences, today the world has them: the first is the railway; the second is the French language" (13: 429). Hugo was following an established tradition when he posited the French language as the logical and efficient vehicle for intercommunication within Europe. He added to this topos his vision of a United States of Europe, patterned after France, with Paris as its capital. The former ultraroyalist traditionalist, who had campaigned for the preservation of medieval monuments, quickly became the herald of the onrushing process of modernization that characterized the bourgeois age. In Hugo's linkage of the scientific and the moral domains, economic and technical progress will combine to free humans from long and backbreaking toil, thereby allowing them to devote more time and energy to higher pursuits. It is this linkage that is, to say the least, difficult to accept in our day: "a less tired body allowing for more wide-ranging intellect, a vast appetite for thought will awaken in every brain; humanity will increasingly be possessed of an insatiable thirst for knowledge and reflection" (*William Shakespeare*, 12: 292).

The ingenuity of Gilliatt in *Les Travailleurs de la mer* illustrates Hugo's interrelated notions of technical progress and social amelioration. The modern steamship is part of a pioneering enterprise of settlement or colonization, a taming and organizing of the brutish wilderness. In Hugo's epic of work and ingenuity, the innovative steam engine that Gilliatt labors so long and hard to free from the grasp of the ocean and its reefs is endowed with a symbolic ethical function of struggle against, and ultimate triumph over, the chaos of harsh natural forces. As David Charles notes (109), the technical creative imagination exhibited by Gilliatt, coupled with his sheer tenacity, eventually translates into social achievements. A modern Prometheus, Gilliatt is made to suffer for having wrested progress from the blind *ananké* of the ocean. As a partial outcast in the small, close-knit island community, he represents the universalism of progress against local conservatism and resistance. At the beginning of the nineteenth century, Staël had contrasted the more recent Romantic literature of "le Nord" to the Classical tradition of "le Midi." In his later years, Hugo would link Romanticism with technical and social progress, and later with the ideal of a transnational Europe (as opposed to the local specificity of Classicism). In an 1846 fragment, Hugo links technical innovation, again particularly in the domains of transportation and communication, to social advancement in international terms, and even to literary progress. In the process, he occludes the violence by which linguistic and national unity was achieved within France: "Railways tend to blend populations, to erase borders, to link today's nations along the lines of the former provinces, to effect within a century, for example, that Germany will be to France what Burgundy is to Normandy, to create European unity . . . The current literary revolution is thus nothing less than the struggle of the European spirit, known as Romantic, against the local, known as Classical" (*Choses vues*, 11: 937).[32]

In the section entitled "Le Beau serviteur du vrai" of *William Shakespeare* (1864), Hugo propounded his view of the mission of the poet and of artists in general: "Be useful! Serve a purpose. Do not act disgusted when the goal is to be efficient and good. Art for art's sake can be beautiful, but art for progress is even more beautiful. It is good to dream a daydream; it is better to dream a utopia" (12: 399). By this time, he was defending the usefulness of artistic expression— "le Beau Utile"—against the various versions of Art for Art's sake, represented by such younger poets as Leconte de Lisle, Baudelaire, or Gautier: "Art must support science. These two wheels of progress must turn together" (12: 400). For Hugo, the conjoined efforts of artists and scientists would contribute to greater mutual tolerance and peace: "No more borders; this is almost achieved; the railway traffic punctures and dislocates the barriers that separate populations; trains connect people to others; the shared life of humanity is dawning; poets, writers, and philosophers have preached the sublime crusade of peace" ("La Civilisation," 12: 608).

Hugo detailed his linkage of technical and social progress, which can be described as a virtuous circle of reinforcing causes and effects. Just as more advanced systems of transportation and communication would eliminate borders and contribute to peace and unity, these lasting benefits would in turn encourage (with the added bonus of reduced military expenditures) the sort of economic growth necessary to bridge the growing gap between rich and poor. Unity at the European level would thus ease tensions between social classes. In an 1855 speech commemorating the revolution of February 1848, Hugo illustrated the advantages of a common currency, which would facilitate transnational economic exchanges and growth, thereby reinforcing European unity: "In the matter of currency, as in all others, circulation leads to union" (10: 484). Scientific and technical progress, economic growth, reconciliation between nations and social classes, and the elimination of war all contributed to, and were in turn reinforced by, European unification. The oracular and hortatory functions of artists in this Hugolian pattern of progress have already been mentioned. Hugo set an example through his constant calls for reconciliation at both the vertical (across social classes) and horizontal (across national borders) levels. In a fragment written after the savage repression of the Commune, he attempted to lenitively characterize the opposition between workers and the bourgeoisie as a mere "misunderstanding" between family members (*Choses vues*, 11: 1335), which could be bridged through mutual tolerance.

Hugo's liberal pronouncements, such as calls for integration of workers into the propertied classes, made him a highly visible target for attacks from both the right and left. He thus acquired complementary political images, on one hand as an irresponsible demagogue verging on anarchism and as a muddled idealist on the other, providing ideological cover for a bourgeois system that was pursuing imperialism abroad and repression at home. These dual lines of political criticism reflect the inherent contradictions, not just of Hugo, but also of the republican left during the Third Republic. Hugo's social ideal is exemplified by Jean Valjean, the proletarian and former convict who starts a rigidly paternalistic company that brings jobs, prosperity, and bourgeois morality to a poverty-stricken town. When he is forced to leave, the company folds, and the social ills Hugo often decried, such as crime and prostitution, quickly return. The workers, who were not owners and who lacked the guiding hand of their providential innovator, leader, and father figure—"He was called *le père Madeleine*" (2: 128)—were unwilling or unable to run the company on their own, and they let it go bankrupt: "Nothing remained for the poor. All was lost" (2: 287). Although Marxist critics would later attempt to classify Hugo as sharing ideological affinities with communism,[33] there is no doubt that he differed fundamentally from Marx and other nineteenth-century secular prophets on the issue of private property and enterprise: "Property and society are two identical terms. In a perfect society, everyone would be a property-owner" ("La Civilisation," 12: 606). In *Choses vues*, denying any legitimacy to communism as a historical continuation or achievement of the French Revolution, Hugo provided the following definition: "Communism: a dream for some, a nightmare for all" (11: 1242).

Hugo's paternalism applied across social classes (the bourgeois guiding the workers) and across continents (Europe civilizing Africa). The role of the propertied classes was to assist workers in climbing the economic ladder, just as Europe would help Africa climb the rungs of civilization. And just as the people looked to a visionary poet to guide them toward the future, workers needed a capable, devoted manager to direct them. Hugo's faith in economic and historical progress, while glowingly advocated, was neither simple nor self-fulfilling. In a secularized transposition of priestly service to a deserving congregation, it predicated well-intentioned leaders who would willingly provide guidance and assistance to followers, who would in turn accept the higher ethical or civilizational standards exemplified by their leaders. In the conclusion to *Le Rhin*, Hugo's political liberalism was combined with his version of the Staëlian Nord/Midi dichotomy: "The north resorts to invasions and the people to revolutions" (13: 433). The Hugolian solution to the twin problems of war and social injustice was to willingly integrate, politically and economically, the northern countries and the lower classes: "For Europe as for society, the key to peace may be simply stated: give the north its share of the south and the people their share of power" (13: 434). The geographical axis of Hugo's recommendations could be extended, for example, in order to justify the colonization of Africa by Europe. Throughout most of his work, Hugo would reaffirm his pattern of reconciliation between classes and nations—in the idealized form of selfless assistance—through material and moral progress. The accelerating rate and increased visibility of technological transformations in his century would only reinforce what for Hugo seemed to be a historical predestination.

Conclusion

The vision of a united, peaceful, and prosperous Europe gradually became central to Hugo's providential projection of historical finality, his secularized version of Christian eschatology. Unity would bring peace to the often warring continent, which would allow new resources and energies to be devoted to economically useful endeavors, which would in turn end the vicious generational cycle of endemic misery endured by a large part of the population. Among all the prophets of European unity, Hugo delivered the most vivid and eloquent pronouncements, thereby producing impossibly high expectations in terms of its potential value. Outside of Hugo's demiurgic discourse, no form of political organization could embody such an auspicious vision of historical finality.

Although it was sometimes shaken by catastrophic historical events, particularly during and immediately after the Franco-Prussian War, Hugo's abiding faith in the future reconciliation of often warring European nations remained intact throughout his life. His uninterrupted belief in the necessity and inevitability of European union coexisted, quite openly and candidly, with a Francocentric orientation that made the future organization of Europe appear in clear terms; it would have Paris as its capital, the Declaration of the Rights of Man as its political basis, and French as its common language. This particular combination of opposites, a utopian vision of Europe and a latent form of nationalism, reflected other clashing Hugolian juxtapositions, such as triumphant rationalism and lingering mysticism, or nostalgic medievalism allied with forward-looking liberal republicanism.

In the aftermath of the Franco-Prussian War, the unified German Empire became the dominant political and economic power in continental Europe. Instead of the alliance between France and Germany that Hugo envisioned, the smoldering rivalry between the two countries—with the issue of the annexed regions of Alsace-Lorraine as a catalyst—would obviate any possibility of a European union for decades to come. For a significant cross-section of French intellectuals, the dream of *la Revanche* would displace revolutionary and constitutional disputes as the crucial issue bequeathed by history. The next chapter will examine the work of the author who best exemplified that dream and who was also largely responsible for popularizing the term "les intellectuels"—which he meant as an insult. While an admirer of part of Hugo's legacy, Maurice Barrès came to represent in his literary and political activities the negation of the Hugolian vision of a united Europe.

CHAPTER 4

The Shrunken Europe of Maurice Barrès

> War! The word has suddenly become prestigious once again. It is a young, newly-coined word, adorned with a seductiveness that the eternal fighting instinct has brought back to life in the hearts of men.
> Agathon, *Les Jeunes Gens d'aujourd'hui*

Published in 1913, *The Young Men of Today* celebrated the bellicose rhetoric of Maurice Barrès (1862–1923), who called for another round of fighting (literally, *la revanche*) against Germany in order to recover the lost provinces of Alsace and Lorraine: "Thanks to the bold, strong vision of Barrès, *la revanche* has acquired a new intellectual and moral dimension" (81). Not content with being one of the most influential French writers of his day, Barrès was also an active politician. Born in the Lorraine region eight years before the Franco-Prussian War, Barrès devoted much of his literary talent to the exacerbation of the nationalistic fervor that flourished in turn-of-the-century France, urging the defeated nation to focus its moral and military energies on its eastern border, "la ligne bleue des Vosges."[1] While he lived to see the French recapture of Alsace and Lorraine with the end of World War I, he was less successful in the other political causes he championed as an anti-Dreyfusard and in his calls for an authoritarian republic with a strong, Napoleonic leader.

Literature and Politics

Barrès's immense stature as a writer during the Belle Epoque, including among those who opposed him politically, is indicated by texts included as prefatory material in *L'Œuvre*. Aragon combined praise for Barrès as a literary stylist— whose ideas had become irrelevant—with contempt for André Gide's work (2: xii–xiii). Referring to his generation, François Mauriac stated: "For us, Barrès remained the leader" (1: xi). Other admirers included Léon Blum, Jean Cocteau, André Malraux, Henry de Montherlant, and Marcel Proust.[2] Even those who reviled his influence in French letters and politics negatively confirmed Barrès's crucial role.

As the most relentlessly enthusiastic supporter of the French war effort, Barrès was a natural target for the postwar Dadaists, who staged his "trial" in 1921 for "crimes contre la sûreté de l'esprit."[3] Another famously negative portrayal of Barrès's influence is found in Jean-Paul Sartre's *L'Enfance d'un chef* (1939). More recent critical evaluations of Barrès's work have generally dealt less with his undeniable talent as a stylist than with the issue of his political significance as a precursor of European fascism. Contrary to the assessment of Aragon, the former surrealist who converted to communism, Barrès is read today precisely for his ideas.[4] Stewart Doty defines him as a "counterrevolutionary;" Robert Soucy presents the "case" of Barrès in *Fascism in France*; while David Carroll lists him as one of the "fathers of literary fascism." The most thorough examination of Barrès's work has come from Zeev Sternhell, who situates Barrès as a prefascist intellectual.[5]

Aragon's comparison of Barrès and Gide recalls the controversy over the nationalistic "rootedness" that Barrès championed, starting with his second trilogy, *Le Roman de l'énergie nationale*. Gide's *Les Nourritures terrestres* was published in 1897, the same year as Barrès's *Les Déracinés* (followed by *L'Appel au soldat* in 1900 and *Leurs Figures* in 1902). With this novel, Barrès began stressing an unswerving adherence to a fixed personal identity grounded, or subsumed, in a larger, all-encompassing collective entity. Gide's work, meanwhile, shared common traits with the individualistic *Culte du Moi* of Barrès's first trilogy— *Sous l'œil des barbares* (1888), *Un Homme libre* (1889), and *Le Jardin de Bérénice* (1891). Gide found cultural enrichment precisely in the pluralistic cosmopolitanism or "uprootedness" that Barrès had come to despise. This opposition, which is linked to the theme of Europe, led Gide to provide a sarcastic rejoinder to Barrès's botanical metaphor: "Since I was born in Paris, my father being from Uzès and my mother from Normandy, where do you expect me, Monsieur Barrès, to set down roots?" (4). Of course, a similarly absurd rhetorical question could have been formulated for Barrès, who lived in Paris and whose ancestors came from Auvergne as well as Lorraine.

Through his restrictive, jingoistic form of nationalism, Barrès represents a break with "l'esprit européen" of Germaine de Staël and with the pan-European humanism of Victor Hugo (notwithstanding his frequent praise for Hugo as a poet). Despite his early enthusiasm for the cultural influence of Spain and Italy, Barrès's theory of rootedness led him to an increasingly reductive view of a timeless, unchanging French national identity. After Barrès systematized his nationalism, he was less given to praising the influence of other countries. The only exceptions were a few "hommes de génie." Ridiculing the Nietzschean concept of the "good European,"[6] Barrès represented individual national cultures as inherently self-contained and largely impenetrable for most outsiders, thereby limiting his Europe to a select group of Great Men who transcended their national origin: "What rubbish! There are no European creative minds.

Each writer is French, English, Italian, or German, and difficult to understand outside of his own country" (*Mes Cahiers*, 20: 48).

Barrès and Charles Maurras, despite their obvious differences,[7] were the most influential French writers whose revanchist rallying cries preceded and prefigured a grotesque mutation of the European topos: fascist Europe. Later represented by younger authors such as Robert Brasillach and Pierre Drieu la Rochelle, as well as by the special case of Louis-Ferdinand Céline, this form of literary ultranationalism paradoxically veered into the tacit acceptance of a "new European order" built around a dominant Nazi Germany—and a shared hatred of Jews. The epigones of the most vitriolic advocates of war against Germany before World War I consequently descended into collaboration with the German occupiers during World War II, thus transcending their ultrapatriotism through ideological convergence with their Nazi counterparts.

A defender of French traditionalism, Barrès hated the parliamentary republic that followed the humiliating defeat of 1870—and that he considered hopelessly weak and corrupt. However, he refused to participate in the "nationalisme intégral" of Maurras's royalist *Action française* because he believed that the principle of republican (albeit not parliamentary) governmental institutions had become an inescapable part of French traditions: "France is the consequence of these events" (*Scènes et doctrines du nationalisme*, 5: 78). Barrès's embrace of Catholicism derived less from deeply held religious faith than from a similar principle: upholding established French traditions (*La Grande Pitié des églises de France*, 8: 158–59). He expressed his nationalism in quasi-religious terms, thus endowing his political views with a metaphysical, absolute aura: "I transferred my piety from the sky to the land, the land of my dead compatriots" (*Scènes*, 5: 25).[8] Conversely, he tended to nationalize his religious faith and to downplay the universalistic aspect of Catholicism.

Barrès was an early follower of General Georges Boulanger, the former Defense Minister who made an unsuccessful attempt at turning the parliament-centered Third Republic into an authoritarian regime with a dominant executive branch. He saw in Boulanger the sort of strong leader who could reverse previous French setbacks (*L'Appel au soldat*, 3: 459). Elected Député from Nancy in 1889 as a member of the Boulangist movement,[9] Barrès was, at the age of twenty-six, the youngest member of the National Assembly (as well as an already famous novelist). His electoral platform, predictably enough, included a protectionist call to "protect French workers against competition from foreigners" (Girardet 137). Boulangism constituted for him an innovative approach to the historical cycle of seemingly perennial constitutional crises and alternating political regimes in France since the 1789 Revolution, one that promised to privilege a newfound sense of national cohesion over inherited partisan quarrels: "Why should our generation care about the old rivalries: republicans, royalists, or bonapartists?" ("Boulangisme. Notes d'un lettré," 1: 512). After Boulanger's suicide in 1891 and the subsequent collapse of his movement, Barrès found another political home in Paul Déroulède's *Ligue des Patriotes*, becoming its leader after Déroulède's death in 1914. Barrès's literary and political career covered some of the most turbulent events of recent French history. Aside from the tragicomic episode of the Boulangist movement, there was the scandal over the financing of the Panama Canal (during which Barrès honed his antiparliamentary rhetoric), the traumatic Dreyfus Affair, the ensuing battle over the separation of Church and State, colonial entanglements (including French rivalries with Great Britain at Fachoda and with Germany over Morocco), and World War I and its aftermath (when Barrès sought to separate the Rhineland from Prussia).

Barrès's hatred of the parliamentary regime, which he expressed often and virulently—especially in *Leurs Figures, Une Journée parlementaire*,[10] and *Dans le cloaque*—rested on a paradox; it was precisely the sort of strong, populist leader he called for who had lost the regions of Alsace and Lorraine during the Franco-Prussian War, while it was the "weak," "corrupt" parliamentary Third Republic that eventually waged a long and very bloody war to recover them. Of course, by the beginning of the First World War, Barrès had already been reelected as a Député after a long absence from the National Assembly, and he had largely muted his revolutionary rhetoric and activities.[11] After the war, he would even form a temporary electoral alliance with members of that embodiment of the parliamentary regime he had sought to overthrow, the Parti Radical.[12] Although he initially represented a district of Lorraine, Barrès lost his seat in 1893. His subsequent campaigns for parliamentary office in Nancy were unsuccessful. It was not until 1906, the year he was elected to the Académie française, that he managed to return to the Palais-Bourbon—as a representative, ironically, of Paris, a seat he held until his death.

Like most writers, Barrès embodied his share of contradictions. He opposed the parliamentary regime of the Third Republic while repeatedly running for parliamentary office; he mythologized his self-proclaimed "rootedness" in his native Lorraine but spent most of his life in cosmopolitan Paris; and he promoted rigorous intellectual elitism alongside ostensibly classless nationalism. He was also capable of forming temporary alliances with a wide range of political friends and adversaries, as when he directed *La Cocarde*, the newspaper Sternhell identifies (*La Droite révolutionnaire*, 62–64) as a forerunner of the ideological alliance of nationalism and socialism.[13] However, Barrès was extremely consistent, even predictable, once his nationalist doctrine had become established. It colored nearly all his texts, whether journalistic or more purely literary, and was expressed throughout his political life. He applied his exclusionary form of nationalism to culture and economics as well as politics, both at home and abroad. Barrès thus defined the "violentes passions nationalistes" of his generation: "It is anti-Semitism, it is anti-Protestantism, it is opposition to foreigners gaining access to governmental positions; it is also a provincialist movement. These movements, these passions must be justified and elevated to the dignity of French truths" (*Scènes*, 5: 109). Just as he sought French—not universal—truths, he strove to find harmony with all forms of thought and action that were specific to his country: "the point at which all things are organized to suit a Frenchman" (5: 27). It comes as no surprise that Barrès did not trust the post-World War I Society of Nations (which was based in Geneva), seeing little usefulness for it in terms of the interests of his country. The concept of a multinational organization was opposed to his politics, and its symbolism went against his esthetic of rootedness: "Decisions must always be made by the French, taking into consideration French interests first and foremost" (20: 83).

Barrès's life overlapped the half century between the Franco-Prussian War and the Treaty of Versailles that formally ended the First World War. Starting in 1914, sensing the possibility of seeing Alsace and Lorraine liberated at last, he unswervingly praised the French war effort in a monumental series of newspaper articles, which were later collected in *Chronique de la Grande Guerre*. Several French writers participated in the war: Charles Péguy and Alain-Fournier were killed at the front, and Guillaume Apollinaire was wounded. However, in his triple role as politician, journalist, and celebrated novelist, Barrès was the most visible and perhaps the most enthusiastic proponent of "la Revanche," in spite of the unprecedented cost in human lives: "This war in the trenches is holy; it is saturated with blood, it is saturated with souls" (*Les Traits éternels de la France*, 8: 301). Other evaluations of the war were less sanguine. Paul Valéry's "La Crise de l'esprit" begins with a new realization of Europe's fragility: "As civilizations, we now know that we are mortal" (988). Published shortly after the war, this text reflects a collective shudder at the extent of the carnage, and its effects on Europeans' self-perceptions: "Not all was lost, but all felt the presence of death" (989). During the conflict, Romain Rolland, one of the few openly pacifist writers (and thus an enemy of Barrès), put it more directly: "European civilization smells of corpses" ("Aux Peuples assassinés," 153). In part, the postwar Dada and Surrealist movements constituted an expression of revulsion with this "European civilization," which, despite its professed values, had culminated in such a methodical and senseless bloodbath.

European Nationalisms

Surprisingly, the concept of Europe looms large in Barrès's work, although its representation is, on balance, mostly negative. This ultranationalist had a lifelong fascination with the cultures of several European countries, a fascination demonstrated in the intertwined skein of his travels, writings, and political activities. Thus, while looking inward for renewed national strength in his political activities, Barrès was also looking outward as a writer of lyrical fiction and essays, particularly toward Spain and Italy, in which he saw natural sources of the sort of moral and instinctual vitality that an excessive degree of Germanic intellectual influence had weakened in France. The Europe of Barrès was first and foremost an extension of his view of nationalism as the driving force of the modern world. His work represents a significant reaction against the universalistic tendencies that he linked to a misreading of the Enlightenment and the French Revolution. For Barrès, the Revolutionary and, in particular, Napoleonic legacy was mainly the reorganization of Europe according to national groupings, instead of outmoded multiethnic states. The modern nation-state, not a political ideology with universalistic pretensions, was the real result of the Revolution: "Europe organized itself in accordance with the principle of nationalities" (*Scènes*, 5: 421).

In this reading of post-Revolutionary history, the torch of nationalism, ignited in France, had been passed on to other peoples by armies united under a strong, purposeful leader (the sort of protofascist leader Barrès called for in his day) at a time when France was not lacking in "énergie nationale." Ignoring the fact that Napoleon had attempted to establish a multinational empire dominated by France, Barrès confused the emperor's presumed intent with the series of nationalistic reactions that resulted from his policies of conquest, occupation, and annexation. Europe has only twice been "united" by military means in the course of modern history: under Napoleon and under Hitler. An unabashed admirer of the Emperor, Barrès offered in *Les Déracinés* a veritable panegyric of his historical role: "French, Germans, Italians, Poles, Russians—all believed Napoleon was destined to jolt them, since he actually did awaken nationalities from their lethargy" (3: 166). The brave new nationalistic world ushered in by the Revolution and by the Napoleonic epic was not one of peace and prosperity and especially not one of interethnic *fraternité*. The corollary of each national group's self-affirmation was hostility toward competing nation-states. Strangely prescient—in light of the recent bloody disintegration of multiethnic Yugoslavia—Barrès foresaw lasting hatreds and struggles between established or emerging nationalities that would affirm their internal identity through violent rejection of others: "The principle of nationalities, such is the direct result of the French Revolution . . . A single language and shared legends are what constitute nationalities. The Czech and Irish nationalities, among others, reappeared. And how do they manifest themselves? Through hatred for their neighbors. Examine all the nations freed from Turkish oppression: what is the first thing they do? Serbs, Greeks, Bulgarians: they persecute each other" (*Scènes*, 5: 420).

Barrès saw the turn of the century as a period of national regression, when the literature and language of France were not as dominant in Europe as they had been during the eighteenth century, when the aftermath of the Franco-Prussian War seemed to coincide with a deterioration in the traditional cultural influence of the French nation on its neighbors. Hence an obsession with the perceived decline or decadence of the country that had once dominated Europe—what Barrès called in *Les Déracinés* "la France dissociée et décérébrée" (3: 179)—and the need for a renewed "énergie nationale" to reverse the trend. This moral and spiritual energy would be found in "la vieille âme française, militaire et rurale" (*Colette Baudoche*, 6: 169). To his regret, Barrès viewed the French nation-state as mainly a historical construct, not a racially homogeneous group having naturally evolved its own social and political system: "There is unfortunately no French race, but a French people, a French nation" (*Scènes*, 5: 86). Viewing this French specificity as a potential weakness, he envied the "organic," instinctual unity that he perceived in the adversaries of France: England and Germany.

The Land and the Dead—"la doctrine de la Terre et des Morts"—are for Barrès the inescapable, concrete embodiments of French nationhood. The organic attachment, the individual acquiescence to the immutable legacy bequeathed by history (territory, ancestors, and the values they represent), defines the relationships between French citizens, their leadership, and their collective societal entity. It is useful to compare this historical but nevertheless essentialist definition of national identity with what has slowly evolved into the European Union since the end of World War II. The step-by-step approach toward a multinational entity initiated by Jean Monnet in 1950 was predicated on premises of mutual tolerance and commonality of interests—rational premises that are totally incompatible with the mystical form of patriotism espoused by Barrès. To a great extent, the postwar movement toward European unity resulted from the previous excesses of competing nationalisms and from the increasingly urgent need to integrate existing nation-states into a more peaceful and stable European institutional framework. Barrès often expressed his version of nationalism in terms so extreme as to verge on fascism. Nonetheless, his exaltation of the role of the modern nation-state prefigured much of the current opposition to the progressive formation of supranational institutions within Europe.[14]

North and South

In some respects, Barrès tended to invert the preestablished theory of climatic determinism—developed by Montesquieu and later reformulated by Staël—as shaping national character. The more southerly nations of Europe, and in particular France, were, in Barrès's view, more capable of striking a balance between relativistic emotion and absolutist reason. Germany and Great Britain, the dominant—and northerly—economic and military powers of his day, could only achieve a sterile form of mechanical, domineering strength based on a coldly abstract, universalistic pattern of logic. The author of such lyrical works as *Du Sang, de la volupté et de la mort* (1894), *Amori et dolori sacrum* (1903), and *Gréco ou le secret de Tolède* (1912) thus sought personal, spiritual, and esthetic regeneration in the southerly cities of Spain and Italy. Since Germany, the representative of modern rationalist values such as organization and efficiency,[15] had triumphed militarily, Barrès affirmed the superiority of instinctual, nonlogical forces, which he found in Latin, Catholic countries that were less economically developed. In valuing instinctive emotion over abstract reason, he applied a *fin de siècle* form of romantic sensibility—"le Culte du Moi"—to his political writings. His subsequent conversion from individualism to nationalism can be compared to the conversion of Joris-Karl Huysmans to Catholicism after *A rebours* (1884). Barrès quickly evolved from the ego-driven "Culte du Moi" of his first trilogy to a quest for immutable roots, which led to a veneration for the land and for the dead ancestors buried therein—"le Culte de la Terre et des Morts"—and to a particularly rigid form of intellectual determinism: "We are not the masters of the thoughts that generate within us. They do not come from our intelligence; they constitute behavior patterns, shaped by very old physiological predispositions" (*Amori et dolori sacrum*, 7: 127).

The individualistic revolt of *Un Homme libre*, the antisocial connotations of *L'Ennemi des lois* thus faded into an acceptance of nationalistic determinism, into an identification with the sort of pretotalitarian collective ego that Gustave Le Bon announced in *Psychologie des foules* (1895). "Barbarians," who in the first trilogy had been the embodiment of cultural mediocrity and of all that stifled the development of the Self, became simply identified with foreigners, with all those who had different roots. Barrès came to provide a distinctly nationalistic interpretation of his early work: "*The Free Man* encouraged many young people to distinguish themselves from the *Barbarians*—that is, from foreigners" (*Scènes*, 5: 29). In his 1904 preface to a new edition of *Un Homme libre*, he was also clear about his personal evolution and its political consequences: "The free man had discerned and accepted his determinism" (1: 139). Roots were by definition hereditary and exclusive, and southern, Latin nations, united by traditional Catholicism, were more apt to have an intuitive grasp of them. Opposed to what he considered to be the post-Enlightenment model of rational, voluntary adherence to a nation-state based on universalistic values, Barrès stressed a prelogical, deterministic link between individuals and the ancestral traditions that shaped them, relegating the entire issue of personal freedom to the single, momentous decision of whether to accept the organic solidarity with the Land and the Dead: "Nationalism means accepting determinism" (*Scènes*, 5: 25). From this decision emerges a comprehensive world view based on strict adherence to societal discipline as the logical culmination of the process of self-affirmation, in a seamless, harmonious amalgamation (apparently devoid, that is, of internal conflicts of interest) of individuals with the inherited social institutions that link them.

Rootedness

Once his nationalism was firmly in place, there could be no Deleuzean *rhizome*, no multiplicity or horizontal network of roots for Barrès. In a departure from his previous quest for cultural stimuli abroad, he defined his metaphorical rootedness as strictly vertical, limited to one land, one culture—hence his consistently negative use of such words as "cosmopolite" or "apatride." As Barrès repeats endlessly, his roots are in the Lorraine region; the preliminary phrase "Je suis lorrain," for instance, keeps reappearing as a causative determinant in *Scènes et doctrines du nationalisme*.[16] In *Mes Cahiers*, he specifies that his roots condition, indeed govern, his thought: "Lorraine is fundamental to my thinking" (14: 174). Barrès's Lorraine, however, is as highly personal a construct as his presentation of the cities of Venice or Toledo.[17] Barrès also proclaims himself attached to Alsace, despite the differences between the two regions. The motivation for this last attachment probably has more to do with opposition to German occupation than with cultural roots. Barrès assigns, in book after book, a timeless mission to these twinned "Marches de l'Est:" "The Romanization of the Germans is the constant goal of Alsace-Lorraine" (*Au Service de l'Allemagne*, 6: 64). These border regions, instead of encouraging cultural osmosis, should act as barriers or shields: "It was the constant destiny of our Lorraine to sacrifice itself in order to keep 'Germanism'—already filtered by our Alsatian neighbors—from disfiguring Latin civilization" (*Amori et dolori sacrum*, 7: 133). If Barrès felt any meaningful attachment to a wider entity than his native Lorraine and the French nation, it was not to some vague notion of Europe, which he disdained, but to the historical idea—which is at least as vague—of a Latin civilization: "As a Lorrain, I am predestined towards classical Latin civilization" (*Mes Cahiers*, 14: 174).

Barrès's land-based determinism reflected his literary influences, particularly Hippolyte Taine's famous triptych of causal factors for artistic production— "la race, le milieu, le moment"—and Ernest Renan's emphasis on the role of common ancestors.[18] Starting from the domain of esthetic appreciation, Barrès extended his own determinism to all forms of individual thought and emotion, reifying local (or religious/racial) identities into monolithic, mutually exclusive essences: "You are shaped to feel as Lorrains, as Alsatians, as Bretons, as Belgians, as Jews" (*Un Homme libre*, 1: 270). Sternhell has shown the political consequences of Barrès's conversion to exclusive, immutable rootedness; the author of such dogmatic texts as *Scènes et doctrines du nationalisme* went far beyond traditional religious and political conservatism, providing ample intellectual fodder for twentieth-century fascism and racism. The individualistic cultural rebellion of his early years, which to a great extent flowed from the romantic literary tradition, was transformed into a broader, politically oriented revolt against the bourgeois values of the Third Republic. The traditional conservative opposition to a rationalist concept of society posits preexisting social ties that transcend individual choice. As expressed in texts written against the heritage of the French Revolution by authors such as Joseph de Maistre or Hippolyte Taine, established social institutions such as religion or family are not freely chosen, and their willful modification can lead to disastrous consequences. The notion that a society can be reshaped according to new principles—however meritorious those principles might seem when considered abstractly—thus represents nothing less than dangerous hubris. Barrès also opposed the concept that society could be the product of rationality and of logical choices, a concept he attributed to the Enlightenment, particularly to Rousseau. He praised, and even identified with, the "Romantic" Rousseau in his first trilogy (*Le Jardin de Bérénice*, 1: 347). However, he rejected the Rousseau of *Le Contrat social* and attempted to prevent the transfer of his remains to the Panthéon: "the man who posited that the social order is wholly artificial, that its basis is conventional" (*Les Maîtres*, 12: 92).[19]

The organic concept of societal organization (as opposed to the "rootless" individualism and rationalism of liberal democracy) that Barrès came to espouse rested on a long intellectual tradition, one that had direct—and highly negative—consequences on the evolution of the conceptions of Europe. The pan-European ideal that Hugo had promoted was an extension of the humanistic, universalistic principles of the Enlightenment and the Revolution as he saw them. Barrès also perceived abstract rationalism and individualism as partly deriving from the Enlightenment, which led to the destructive illusion of universalistic principles applicable at all times to all peoples. Among these principles were reason, truth, and justice, which for him could have no absolute definitions, only contingent applications within specific historical and national contexts: "Does reason lead to truth? . . . A truth remains true only so long as it is thought to be so" (*Mes Cahiers*, 13: 99). He most clearly applied this generalized relativistic ethos during the Dreyfus affair, unswervingly defending his version of "French truth and justice" (*Scènes*, 5: 27).

As a follow-up to his rhetorical question—"Qu'est-ce qu'un intellectuel?"— Barrès supplied this deprecatory definition: "An individual who holds that society must be based on logic and who disregards the fact that it is conditioned by imperatives that precede, and are perhaps foreign to, individualistic reasoning" (5: 56). He also tended to link abstract rationalism specifically to Immanuel Kant, a foreign, German thinker whose philosophy of universalism had permeated, or infected, French intellectual elites.[20] Any overt form of Europeanism was thus doubly suspect as foreign and based on purely intellectual abstractions. National identity and patriotism remained for Barrès a matter of instinctive emotion, shared by a specific organic societal group, which far outweighed individual logic or intellect: "Intelligence, what a small thing at the surface of our being!" (*Les Déracinés*, 3: 239). A supranational organization, based on rationally examined common interests, constituted a negation of the prelogical determinism of the Land and the Dead, since foreigners, no matter how close they might be in geographical or cultural terms, were themselves by definition determined by ties to another land and different ancestors.

Jews as the Embodiment of Alterity

From an absolutist form of nationalistic determinism, it was only a short logical and discursive step for Barrès to xenophobia and anti-Semitism since the most dangerous *déracinés* would necessarily be foreigners living in France, in particular, Jews, who have "no homeland as we understand it. For us, it means land and ancestors, the land of our dead. For them, it is where they find the highest profit" (*Scènes*, 5: 72). Through his characterization of Jews as lacking any fixed ancestral and national roots, Barrès designated them as the ultimate outsiders in a Europe built around national identities. As the most well known of the trans-European minorities, they constituted a living contradiction to Barrès's organic concept of societal development, thereby evoking the dreaded specter of generalized uprootedness [*déracinement*]. With no natural attachment to any country, Jews were inherently prone to play off one national interest against another, according to their needs at any given moment. Barrès was thus predisposed to believe that "the little Jew," "the traitor Dreyfus" (5: 46) was guilty on the basis of his origins: "That Dreyfus is capable of treason, I can conclude from his race" (5: 149). Barrès remained one of the most articulate and vituperative anti-Dreyfusards throughout what came to be known simply as *l'Affaire*.

A modern, racialist anti-Semite, Barrès used physical descriptions of Jews (just as he did for Germans) as a metonymic device to convey their alterity. Drawing on the opposition between Semites and Aryans, which had already become a well-known topos through Arthur de Gobineau's *Essai sur l'inégalité des races humaines* (1855) and Edouard Drumont's bestseller *La France Juive* (1886),[21] Barrès pointed out Dreyfus's "ethnic nose," and his "face of a foreign race" (*Scènes*, 5: 134) in order to explain why it should hardly be surprising for "this descendant of Sem," who lacked "the handsome characteristics of the Indo-European race," to commit treason against France: "He is immune to everything we find stimulating in our land, our ancestors, our flag, the word 'honor'" (5: 142). Barrès was also capable of stooping to the more traditional form of religious anti-Semitism. Comparing Dreyfus to Judas (5: 133), he then describes a prayer in church for "the treacherous Jews" (5: 139) before returning to Dreyfus: "Lord, clear the darkness brought on by this perfidious Jew" (5: 141). In order to provide a contrast with his radical distanciation from Dreyfus, Barrès describes his feelings toward a criminal who was about to be guillotined but who was (presumably) authentically French: "In my heart, I felt only sincere brotherhood towards an unfortunate man of my race. But what have I in common with a man named Dreyfus?" (5: 134–35).[22]

Barrès's work epitomizes what Girard calls "le mécanisme victimaire." In this analysis, societies, like most (if not all) human groups, constitute themselves through a process that is inseparable from a mechanism of exclusion. It is the establishment of an us-versus-them perspective that negatively provides at least part of the definition of "us." Barrès not only applied this mechanism to his nationalism (Dreyfus, Jews, and foreigners in general), but also to his own being ("le moi" against "les barbares"). Unlike such rabid Jew-baiters as Maurras or Drumont, Barrès did not systematically describe all Jews as inherently degenerate and malevolent. He was able to praise individuals and to admit that some assimilated Jews had become part of France. His anti-Semitism derived quite logically from the exclusionary logic of his brand of nationalism.[23] Most Jews simply could not experience the emotional links that Barrès valued above pure intellect. Indeed, when praising Jews for their intelligence, Barrès was merely emphasizing their rootlessness: "Jews are consummately logical. Their reasoning is clear and impersonal, like a bank account" (*L'Ennemi des lois*, 2: 256). With the possible exception of Germans, Jews as a group were clearly the most effective target for differentiation and exclusion: "You cannot deny that a Jew is a different being" (*Scènes*, 5: 72). During World War I, it should be noted that, due to the pressing need for a nationwide *union sacrée* to defeat Germany, Barrès shelved his anti-Semitism and accepted French Jews (along with Protestants and socialists) as full participants in the war effort. In 1917, one of his contributions to maintaining national morale, when the war was already in its fourth year, was *Les Diverses Familles spirituelles de la France*, in which he celebrated the suspension of internal divisions: "Our differences disappear on August 4, 1914" (8: 325).

Economic Nationalism

The electoral platform of economic protectionism that Barrès developed, during and after his Boulangist phase, was initially presented as a form of socialism, designed to shield French workers, farmers, and shopkeepers against unfair competition from immigrant labor and imported products. Barrès's "Programme de Nancy," written for his unsuccessful 1898 legislative campaign, begins with nationalism, then proceeds to protectionism by way of anti-Semitism.[24] Reminding voters that the "opportunistic" economic system of the Third Republic was unfairly tilted in favor of "le juif, l'étranger, le cosmopolite," Barrès identifies the socioeconomic purpose of his nationalist program: "Nationalism necessarily leads to socialism. We define socialism as 'the moral and material improvement of the largest and poorest social class.' It took centuries for the French nation to provide political security. It must now protect the people against economic insecurity" (*Scènes*, 5: 387). He then defines insecurity as it applies to workers, shopkeepers, and farmers, before proposing a list of measures designed to counteract the role of foreign products, foreign workers, and "the international financial aristocracy" (5: 387–90). The causal link between the two lists is only tenuously established, Barrès being more concerned with directing attention toward the malignant consequences of an often fantastical foreign influence. Predictably, Barrès's version of socialism has little to do with Marxist concepts, such as the collectivization of the means of production. It is instead a smokescreen for such populist and paternalistic notions as the protection of French workers, farmers, and shopkeepers from the effects of industrial dislocation, the source of which is generally linked to foreign interests.

Barrès's forays into economics, especially for the purpose of electioneering, provide examples of some of his weakest writing as well as of his most simplistic logic. Having brought up the highly controversial and ambiguous question of socialism, he then proceeds to skirt the issue of economic inequality, attributing it to what has become an increasingly obvious straw man, pervasive foreign influence. The solution thus lies in preferential treatment for French workers, which would involve greater regulation of the economy by the state (5: 412). Eclectic in its sources, Barrès's right-wing anticapitalism allows for xenophobia, anti-Semitism, and an early version of what would become a widely shared political myth, from the communists to the extreme right, of the "two hundred families" who surreptitiously run the French economy: "List the names of all those sitting on boards of directors: fewer than fifteen hundred . . . First, the Protestant bankers who came from the Republic of Geneva during the Orleanist Monarchy [1830–48]. Then the Kingdom of Israel which has so flourished during our Third Republic" (5: 403–04).[25]

Barrès envisioned a French economy built on the predominance of small, locally owned farms and businesses and on a policy of outright protectionism. Internal decentralization was thus allied with external economic barriers, designed to achieve a degree of national economic autarchy. In an attempt to reconcile socialist equality with local free enterprise, the Barrésian economic vision reflected a nostalgic yearning for supposedly simpler times, when the jobs and livelihoods of French workers were not dependent on decisions made by foreign capitalists, when a larger proportion of the active population was self-employed, and when working the land was still a noble calling. As Robert Paxton detailed, the enduring notion of "France as a peasant nation" (174–86) has reappeared in various guises during different phases of French political history. In particular, the Vichy regime would later draw on similar fantasies of a largely self-sufficient national economy dominated by agricultural production and by sturdy peasant values. For Barrès, economic decentralization called for more local political control, including the possibility of federalism. Ever mindful of his literary sources, he invoked Taine's work in support of the need to loosen centralized state control (5: 434). Another source of inspiration was Pierre-Joseph Proudhon, who had the distinct advantage of offering a French alternative to foreign socialist theory (5: 460).

After World War I, Barrès renewed his interest in economic issues. As the increasingly mechanized conflict (which included the first systematic uses of tanks, aerial bombardment, and poison gas) had highlighted the importance of industrial development, he campaigned for a greater national effort in favor of scientific research. As always, he was motivated by nationalist concerns, seeking to emulate and go beyond the German model of scientific research linked to industrial development, particularly in terms of military applications. By rhetorical association with the French soldiers who had fought and won the war, science and technology were enlisted into the continuing struggle against foreign foes: "The scientific and spiritual supremacy of a nation is a function of its exceptional men" (*Pour la haute intelligence française*, 9: 330).

Masculine and Feminine

Jean Foyard has inventoried the (mostly condescending) images of women in Barrès's texts: "precious object, small animal, bird, insect, butterfly, tiger, young mare, rose, plant, vine . . . " (89). In this context, it is interesting to note that the masculine-feminine dichotomy constitutes another tropological organizing principle, in addition to the previously outlined north-south partition, of the Europe of Barrès. Some cities and countries are thus masculinized (Germany being the most obvious example), while others, such as Spain and Italy, are generally feminized: "For centuries, men have obtained from Italy all forms of intoxicating pleasures, and rightly consider her their mistress" (*Du Sang, de la Volupté et de la Mort*, 2: 167). Italian cities are the locales that Barrès most clearly eroticizes, presenting them as objects for his sensual conquest. Describing "Les Beaux Contrastes de Sienne" (2: 148–52), he associates the entire region with the image of a sexual encounter: "It is characteristic of all of Tuscany. Nowhere is youthfulness more attractive than in these Florentine lands; indeed, nowhere is youthfulness more of a pretty young thing to take to one's bed" (2:149). Venice is similarly endowed with an inescapable erotic charge: "This sleepy, adorned city whose intoxicating touch keeps us in a state of unfulfilled and yet exhausting desire" (*L'Ennemi des lois*, 2:243). The process of feminization and eroticization also applies to the "Oriental" cities visited by Barrès: "I see all these cities of the Orient as a circle of young women, among whom I was invited to choose" (*Une Enquête aux pays du Levant*, 11: 364).

Alongside obvious sexual connotations, the Barrésian pattern of feminization of cities or countries is highly correlated with images of decadence, stasis, and death. The visibly aging city of Venice, in particular, is endowed with a mortiferous aura, which is reminiscent of the deadly contagion silently plaguing the city in Thomas Mann's *Death in Venice* (1912). In the section of *Amori et dolori sacrum* aptly titled "La Mort de Venise" (7: 11–59), Barrès dwells on the city's "atmosphere of irremediable failure" (7: 54). He compares its languid allure to "the song of a beauty bound for death" (7: 55). Its picturesque, decaying architecture—"crumbling churches, vast dilapidated palaces" (7: 57)—is the perfect environment for his "feverish" imagination: "This city has always made me feel feverish" (7: 12); "feverish thoughts of the evening" (7: 56); "misery and fever woo each other" (7: 57); "the fever was in Venice" (7: 59). The decrepit city seems to be largely uninhabited, serving only as a vast mausoleum of strangely fascinating sensations: "I tried to decypher this lingering memory, this voluptuous sadness that Venice perpetually revels in" (7: 14). With its "palais d'Orient" (7: 55), Venice is also Orientalized, associated with an evocation of women dancing in the Indian city of Bénarès, each dancer personifying a Barrésian motto: "One whispers: 'to desire all'; the other replies: 'to disdain all'" (7: 58). Venice's tarnished beauty provides Barrès with the darkly romantic motif of "death through excessive love of life" (7: 59). As is consistent with his sexual esthetic, the city is all the more precious to him precisely because of its ruinous state, which prefigures the intensity that inevitable aging and death bring to the possession of the object of his love: "Mortality is an exquisite quality. The sight of our mistress slowly decaying while in our embrace, adds a perfecting touch of supreme melancholy to the pleasure she brings us. There is no true intensity that does not incorporate the idea of death" (*Du Sang*, 2: 101).

In *Le Voyage de Sparte*, Barrès contrasts Venice with the strength and "virility" of Sparta, which is not "like Venice, a note of tenderness that sounds in the midst of pleasure" (7: 275). He at last finds cause for identification and personal "enthusiasm" in the course of his visit to the archeological site of Sparta, as opposed to the distanced "dismay" (7: 187) he felt during most of his travels within Greece. Admiring the famous self-discipline of the ancient Spartans, he is inspired by their sense of purpose: "Here is one of the corners of the earth where an attempt was made to build a superior human race" (7: 273). Instead of languid charm or feverish eroticism, he finds in the masculinity of Sparta a call to glory: "A heart consumed by poetry . . . seeks to die for an ideal cause. The blissful wish to be heroic shines forth" (7: 275). It is not necessary to indulge in Derridean deconstruction to see a degree of contextualized overlapping between the two forms of hierarchical binary oppositions that Barrès uses in his writings. With some exceptions, it is northern countries or cities that tend to be masculinized. They are characterized by efficiency, strength, and aggression. They are to be respected or feared. Southern countries, meanwhile, are generally feminized. They are economically backward, but they have romantic ruins and a rich artistic heritage. They are endowed with a highly estheticized, somewhat morbid allure, procuring violent, contrasting sensations that often invite attempts at symbolic sexual conquest. The gendered geographical divisions elaborated by Barrès roughly correlate with the traditional "théorie des climats."

Dissociating Germany

Mme de Staël becomes enthusiastic within the sentimental atmosphere of Germany, without considering the positive accomplishments of the Revolutionary armies and the Napoleonic administration. In contrast with a French moral life reduced to a narrow civic domain, to a regimented spirit and body, Mme de Staël would like the Rhine to lead to enthusiasm and to the invigorating power of intuition. For her and for her Romantic successors, the river will become a gateway to music and mysteries, an introduction to idealism and reverie.

Le Génie du Rhin, 10: 48–49

Barrès's version of nationalism required both internal and external enemies. Positioning his work against the multicultural or *cosmopolite* outlook that Staël incarnated, he posited the French view of German culture and society as having been clouded by the delusions of the Romantics, whose perceptions in turn derived in large part from the idealized images in Staël's *De l'Allemagne* (1810).[26] Endeavoring to correct this view, Barrès wrote at length about the German national character as he saw it, both before and after World War I, when French troops occupied much of the Rhineland. Sensing a possibility of durably shifting the balance of power between France and its longtime adversary, he sought to separate the Rhineland, in which he saw the fruits of a long period of French cultural influence, from Prussia, the despised embodiment of "le teutonisme." In his zeal to see most of Germany purged of its Eastern European background, Barrès had grandiose dreams of redirecting its culture under French tutelage: "Germans have distorted their own greatness. It is up to us to restore its proper meaning" (10: 40).

Early in his career, Barrès had been able to acknowledge that he was influenced by German writers, and he had even been able to criticize the "chauvinism" of those who would reject all aspects of German culture: "The best among us owe much to Kant, Goethe, and Hegel" ("Un Mauvais Français: M. Victor Tissot," 1: 405). While he already advocated war to recover Alsace-Lorraine, he did not yet show the unyielding hostility that would soon come to dominate his writing on Germany. He instead stated his admiration for the country and its role in the world: "Three nations guide civilization during this century: France, England, and Germany" (1: 404). Barrès would not long cling to such views, soon identifying his native Lorraine as the most exposed bulwark of French resistance against the invaders from the East: "a race that for centuries has fought on the frontline against German power" (*Amori et dolori sacrum*, 7: 12). As Jacques Portes emphasized (194), as of 1896–97, the clear designation of Germany as an irreconcilable enemy constituted the catalyst of the Barrèsian version of nationalism. Barrès's Germany became less a country than an aggressive force, a relentless mindset based on brute strength and its glorification, which he referred to by the essentializing terms of "le germanisme" or "le teutonisme" (as opposed to "la latinité"). Barrès usually characterized this force in esthetic terms, rendering it as the negation of the grace and harmony exemplified by France. "Germanicity" is thus unfailingly heavy, awkward, and domineering. In *L'Appel au soldat*, Sturel and Saint-Phlin meet a "typical" German during a trip to occupied Lorraine: "Powerfully but crudely built, his potbelly made him seem wider and lower" (4: 91).

Another set of descriptions of such Germans is found in *Au service de l'Allemagne*, where the same sort of terms, connoting mechanical and aggressive propensities, are used: "stiff and arrogant," "trained and disciplined," "a brutal soul," "Germanic-Slavic barbarity," "aggressive warrior," etc. As opposed to French "culture héréditaire," Germans are characterized by cold, unwavering determination: "Their willpower never slackens" (6: 100). The individuals described by Barrès reflect the eternal essence, in the Herderian tradition, of their collective cultural and national entity. Instead of a specific militarized regime with expansionist tendencies, France was, in his view, facing what had always been, and always would be, its hereditary enemy. He would thus see little difference between the domineering German Empire and the weakened postwar Weimar Republic: "Goodwill among men has no more resolute enemy than an unmistakably German conception of *the struggle for life*, of *the survival of the fittest*, of *might makes right*" (*Les Grands Problèmes du Rhin*, 10: 261).

In *Au service de l'Allemagne* (1905), Barrès considers the plight of the inhabitants of occupied Alsace-Lorraine, particularly the young men who are faced with a choice between being drafted into the German army or crossing into France, never to return to their hometowns. The hero of this book is Paul Ehrmann, a medical student from Strasbourg, whom Barrès praises for remaining in Alsace and enduring the rigors of German military service while maintaining pride in his French identity. By not fleeing to France, Ehrmann is keeping faith with his roots and fulfilling a timeless mission of resistance against the invaders from the East. This view of the French-German antagonism had also been elaborated in Barrès's second trilogy. During their trip through Lorraine, Sturel and Saint-Phlin go by military fortifications in which Barrès sees the concrete embodiments of a seemingly endless struggle between eternal enemies: "They are not about to disarm, the two ethnic forces that confront each other here, and with no historical end in sight" (*L'Appel au soldat*, 4: 46). Germans are usually referred to as "Prussians," a way to emphasize their Eastern European origin, or more benevolently as "Rhinelanders." The two are not simply used as geographically neutral terms. In the writings of Maurice Barrès, the degree of civilization improves among Germans in relation to their geographical proximity to France. Barrès thus adds an internal east-west dichotomy to his established opposition between northern and southern countries. True to form, he uses physical descriptions to distinguish the two groups, to the point of using putative racial characteristics to link Rhinelanders to France and separate them from Prussia (*Problèmes du Rhin*, 10: 509).

In *Colette Baudoche*, published in 1909, Hermann Asmus, a well-read, well-meaning, and somewhat naïve professor from the eastern part of the Empire, is sent to spread Germanic culture in occupied Lorraine. The uneasy contact that ensues between the German occupier and the occupied French can be compared to Vercors's *Le Silence de la mer* (1942), despite obvious differences in style and historical context. As the suitor of a young French woman whose family remained in the city of Metz after it was annexed by Germany, Asmus, initially a "typically" uncouth Prussian, progressively discovers, through Colette, the innate richness of French culture: "He raises himself to a higher level of civilization" (6: 218). Now that he is living in the westernmost part of the Empire, Asmus is increasingly drawn to Colette's balanced, serene self-assurance, which he finds lacking in his own national background. His Prussian friends, however, warn him that in seeking to absorb presumed French virtues, he is only losing his Germanic soul, thereby using arguments that, ironically, harmonize well with the Barrésian ethic of rootedness: "Belong to France or Germany: you must choose" (6: 222). In spite of his love for Colette and his efforts to learn about her French heritage, Asmus cannot bridge the ethnic and civilizational gap that separates them. Colette, although initially drawn to him, ultimately heeds the voice of the Land and the Dead, which she most clearly hears during a Church ceremony honoring French soldiers who had died defending Metz. In a blending of the religious and national traditions exalted by Barrès, Colette is decisively moved to turn down Asmus's marriage proposal after a reading of "the story of the Maccabees . . . where is found the origin of Church doctrine on the dead" (6: 245).

The weight of nationalistic determinism obviates any other possible outcome. Colette does not formulate any arguments against the ancestral forces that are making the decision for her: "She does not use logic to resist" (6: 247). In the presence of the dead, she is not alone in her decision, nor, as the inheritor of an eternal tradition, is she a free agent. While the voices she hears are not necessarily of divine origin, Colette evokes another strong-willed young woman from Lorraine, Joan of Arc, who personifies the spirit of French resistance against foreign occupiers. Barrès has thus created a heroine who illustrates by her actions the doctrine of rootedness, which he had previously elaborated: "There is not even freedom of thought. I can only live in accordance with my dead. They and my land compel my choices" (*Scènes*, 5: 26). The impossibility of Asmus ever winning the love of Colette, the living symbol of the enduring French presence in Lorraine, had therefore been foretold. The scholarly Prussian, in spite of all his intellectual efforts to understand her spiritual and national heritage, lacked the organic link with the Land and the Dead that the less educated French woman intuitively felt. When viewing a landscape in Lorraine, Asmus's ineradicable alterity is emphasized when the narrator switches to the first person: "He negates and seeks to destroy, this son of conquerors, everything that enobles this land, that can make it productive. Where I find stability and fulfillment, he is out of place" (6: 182).

Barrès was of course not the only writer to give literary expression to the Franco-Prussian War and its consequences. The traumatic French defeat, the forcible annexation of Alsace-Lorraine, and the brutalities of the invaders are vividly captured in such texts as Alphonse Daudet's "La Dernière Classe," Zola's *La Débâcle*, and several of Maupassant's short stories.[27] In an influential, polemical article written in 1870 ("L'Alsace est-elle allemande ou française? Réponse à M. Mommsen"), the French historian Fustel de Coulanges assailed an eminent German historian's attempt, through rationalizations based on preexisting racial and linguistic ties, to justify the conquest and annexation of Alsace: "Alsace may be German by race and language; but by nationality and patriotic sentiment, it is French" (509).²⁸ As François Hartog noted (51), Renan would later provide, in his 1882 lecture ("Qu'est-ce qu'une nation?"), a definition of "nationality as volition" (236), which was similar to Fustel de Coulanges's formulation of national formation through voluntary association.²⁹

However, no writer did more than Barrès, through his journalistic and political activities as well as through his novels, to keep the issue of the eventual liberation of the occupied eastern regions alive. In what would later become a monumental understatement as to the cost in human lives, he called for war in order to recover them: "It will only take a little blood and a resolute soul" (1: 404). Typically, Barrès did not cast the issue of Alsace and Lorraine in terms of self-determination for their inhabitants (as had Fustel de Coulanges and Renan); his nationalistic determinism had settled the question of their identity. What he was concerned with was the danger of permanent encroachment within the occupied regions by foreign, Germanic elements: "The German race is supplanting the indigenous throughout eastern France" (*Les Déracinés*, 3: 238). No less dangerous was the possibility of intellectual conquest. The problem lay in deciding what to keep and what to reject among German cultural production or, as Barrès put it, "Quelles limites poser au germanisme intellectuel?" (*Problèmes du Rhin*, 10: 398).

The balance of power between France and Germany having been inverted by the Franco-Prussian War, Barrès became (in a comparison that he would not have appreciated) the most consistent French counterpart to the German philosopher Johann Fichte,³⁰ who had elaborated an early form of ultranationalism, directed against Napoleonic imperialism, in *Addresses to the German Nation* (1807–08). Barrès's German predecessor also developed his xenophobic theory in the historical context of his country's perceived weakness. Fichte delivered his *Addresses* at the Berlin Academy of Sciences after the defeat of the Prussian army at Jena. Since the city was occupied by French troops, the author resorted to allusions, denouncing the ambitions of the "new universal monarch" (233) and making bitter but indirect references to the conquerors: "As for us, we are defeated, and they are the victors" (238). As Barrès would later do, Fichte called for a revival—indeed, an exacerbation—of the national spirit as a means of expelling the foreign occupier and restoring his country's tarnished glory. Each author sought to exclude Jews from his purified national community. Their ultranationalism also led both authors to advocate economic protectionism.³¹

For all his saber-rattling, Barrès had an ambiguous relationship with the German model he decried. He praised its economic organization, its methodical pursuit of scientific research, and its social welfare system. He professed admiration for the tireless efficiency and discipline of Germans in general, and for German civil servants in particular. Perversely, the sort of changes he wanted to see occur in France mirrored to a great extent the situation of the German adversary as he described it. If there was a recent prototype for the sort of strong, decisive leader Barrès wanted for France, it was none other than the German

Chancellor, Otto von Bismarck. To achieve revanchist aims, France would have to submit, paradoxically, to the sort of regimentation and mechanization Barrès condemned in Germany.

After World War I, Barrès continued writing about Germany and its future relations with France. In an echo of "la querelle du Rhin" of the early 1840s (which was discussed in the previous chapter), Barrès provided his variant of the recurring issue of the Rhine as the "natural border" between France and Germany. Concerned with national boundaries as a way of preserving limits between cultures, he dreamed of resurrecting a semiautonomous Rhineland that, under continued French influence, could become a buffer against the threat of a resurgent Germany. His fairly detailed economic proposal would have linked the region to France "through trade, means of communication, railways and canals, public works . . . through banking and cooperative institutions, through common social legislation" (*Problèmes du Rhin*, 10: 190–91). Interestingly enough, this Barrésian program of transnational cooperation seems quite compatible with more recent attempts to establish common European institutions, with one crucial distinction: it was designed to isolate, not integrate, most of Germany.

The degree of economic and political interdependence that Barrès sought to establish between France and the Rhineland derived from his perception of their cultural contiguity. In *Le Génie du Rhin* (1921), he inventoried the historical and cultural links, real or imagined, between "les Rhénans" and France. Pointing out that the Rhine is closer to the French border than to Eastern Prussia, he decried "Pangermanist" attempts to reclaim control of the Rhineland, to make the Rhine into "not the border, but the spiritual center, the holy ground of Germany" (10: 68). Ironically, Barrès himself waged a long literary and political campaign to make Lorraine—which is after all a border region with long-standing cultural links to Germany as well as France—the spiritual heart of the French nation. In the preface of this curious book, which includes rapturous accounts of folk legends of the Rhine, Barrès gives his interpretation of the cultural meshing between France and the Rhineland that occurred before the rise of Pangermanism, citing no less a figure than Goethe as an example (10: 40). Meanwhile, on the French side, Barrès also invoked a major literary figure as an example in favor of his perceived Franco-Rhinelander cultural continuum, linking Victor Hugo—"a man from the Rhine valley"—to an increasingly imaginary Rhineland: "On his father's side, his origins sink deep into Lorraine" (10: 78). True to Barrésian logic, by defending "eastern France against the German invasion" (12: 143), Hugo was only following the determinism of his origins. While Barrès's hopes for a lasting political and cultural French guardianship over the Rhineland never materialized, they constitute a revealing example of his particular European outlook, which puts France at the center of a fairly stable system of partners and adversaries, a system based on shared, long-standing cultural affinities, instead of temporary political alliances. As previously mentioned, the natural partners of France were for Barrès to the South: Spain and Italy.

Latin Affinities

For Barrès, culture precedes and conditions politics. His inventory of French writers who owed a debt to Spanish culture—Corneille, Hugo, Mérimée, Gautier (*Mes Cahiers*, 20: 54)—is thus followed by a proposal of a political association with Spain in order to balance the influence of France's more northerly neighbors. While his repeated travels to Spain led him to write two books, his vision of France's southern neighbor, like that of the Rhineland, remained an intensely personal construct, based on highly selective literary and artistic images. In this Catholic country steeped in traditions, Barrès perceived a legacy of violent, instinctual passion, of sensual beauty, and of an estheticized form of worship for the Dead (which in turn fed into his own "cult of the Land and the Dead"). Barrès's Spain, like Germany, was less an actual country than the embodiment of an idea, that of a passionate, perhaps overdeveloped version of the Bergsonian *élan vital*: "Spain is the most unbridled country in the world" (*Du Sang, de la Volupté et de la Mort*, 2: 33).[32]

In Spain, as in Italy, Barrès enjoyed visiting cities rich in history, including Cordoba, Toledo, Venice, and Sienna. As befits a novelist with a romantic sensitivity, he made use of the views of these cities, and of the descriptions of their history in order to trigger subjective, fiercely emotional sensations: "une impression d'énergie et de passion" (2: 23). The intensity of Barrès's emotions was heightened by the form of religiosity he found in their churches, "neo-Catholicism: a way to combine sensuality and religion" (2: 90). Seeking starkly contrasted images that would stir the soul more than the mind, Barrès found in these cities the "atmosphere of death and fleeting bliss" (2: 96) that stimulated his ongoing "Culte du Moi." As previously noted, Spain is generally feminized—that is, reduced to a principle of boundless sensuality—in Barrès's work: "This race is worn down by pleasure. Whatever the hour may be, they have just left their bed" (*Mes Cahiers*, 13: 290).

Barrès's pilgrimages to the southern sources of instinctive vitality also provided inspiration for his more political writings: "So many higher interests compel the union [of France and Spain]" (*Mes Cahiers*, 20: 56).[33] The inherent vigor he detected in Spanish culture would provide a much-needed counterweight to the excessively intellectual tradition of Kantian German philosophy (20: 54). Meanwhile, an alliance between Latin, southern countries would strengthen France in its struggles against its adversaries to the north (20: 57). The professed admiration Barrès felt for Spain and its culture was not without its limitations, and certainly not without a note of condescension. The effusive literary impressions he recorded during his travels were colored by his obviously limited perceptions of what he felt to be the Spanish national character, or "l'hispanisme," a term as essentializing, if not as negative, as "le germanisme." Not above resorting to traditional climate-based stereotypes about excessive Spanish passion or indolence—such as those found, for instance, in Prosper Mérimée's *Carmen* (1845)—he tended to project a concomitant lack of intellectual depth onto the Spaniards he observed: "Under a violently-colored sky, they follow the dictates of their feelings" (*Du Sang*, 2: 33). As if to confirm the connection with Mérimée, Barrès visited "la manufacture des tabacs de Séville," admiring the beauty of its female workers and declaring it a microcosm of the region as a whole (2: 102).

Most of what has been said about how Barrès viewed Spain applies to Italy, the other southern, Catholic country where he found the contrasting sensations that stimulated his esthetic outlook: "Death and bliss, pain and love are linked in our imagination" (*Amori et dolori sacrum*, 7: 8). By spiritualizing extreme emotional states and estheticizing religious faith, Barrès found lyrical inspiration in the multifaceted architecture and art of Italian cities. As Yves-Alain Favre noted (241), these were not minor issues for Barrès, who often referred to the influence of Italian cities and art in his work. This influence appears in his more political texts as well. In this excerpt from Barrès's second trilogy, the violence of the terms used to describe the regions of Italy reflects the emotional state of "l'homme du Nord": "Under such a powerful sky, contrasting landscapes each had something to say to him . . . Nature, art, and history assaulted his soul" (*L'Appel au soldat*, 3: 382).

Seldom straying from his political aims, Barrès also kept abreast of Italian influence in European affairs, bemoaning France's weak postwar ties with its erstwhile World War I ally (*Mes Cahiers*, 20: 43). During one of his visits, ever conscious of national as well as literary symbolism, he visited Guiseppe Garibaldi's home. His last visit to Italy took place in 1916, in the middle of the war, when he was invited by its government to tour the front lines, something he was already in the habit of doing in France (and which furnished the basis for many of his thunderous prowar newspaper articles).[34] As always, he linked the alliance with Italy to its cultural and racial underpinnings: "Today we all want an extension of French-Italian friendship at all levels: intellectual, economic, financial, and military. Artists have always worked for a greater dissemination of Latin thought among the two peoples" (*Dix jours en Italie*, 9: 61–2). However, in an indication that Italy was for him more a source of esthetic inspiration than an important European state, he seems to have paid little attention to the significance of Benito Mussolini's rise to power in 1922.

In spite of his obvious affinity for Italian culture, Barrès was just as capable of rejecting Italian influence, of relegating it to a radically alien, foreign status similar to that of Germany's, political alliances or cultural interconnections notwithstanding. In an echo of the Dreyfus Affair, Barrès campaigned against the triumphal reinterment in the Panthéon of the remains of a novelist who had been his most effective adversary, Emile Zola. In a 1908 article, Barrès sought to explain Zola's pro-Dreyfus activism by the Italian ancestry of the author of

J'accuse: "Zola is violently struck, surprised, often shocked by what we do and how we behave, as a visiting foreigner would be" (4: 607). Barrès had already attacked Zola during *l'Affaire*, using similar tautological arguments based on geographic determinism: "What is Mr. Emile Zola? I look at his roots: this man is not French . . . between you and me, there is a border. Which border? The Alps . . . Emile Zola quite naturally thinks as would an uprooted Venitian" (*Scènes*, 5: 52–53). For Barrès, the parallel between the Italian intellectual and the Jewish traitor he was defending was obvious. The rigidly deterministic Barrésian logic inevitably led to a familiar and consistent conclusion; as a rootless foreigner, Zola could not immediately sense the instinctive rejection of Dreyfus by the French nation; he could only abstractly speculate about universalistic illusions such as truth and justice.

Orientalizing Greece

Barrès's trip to Greece in 1900 produced no paean to the "cradle of Western civilization." In a sharp contrast with the "feverish" dimension of his visits to Spain and Italy, Barrès describes a merely intellectual "voyage d'étude" (*Le Voyage de Sparte*, 7: 300), which in retrospect reinforced his sense of rootedness. Greece remained associated with Barrès's former teacher, Auguste Burdeau, whom he mercilessly depicted as the increasingly corrupt parliamentarian Bouteiller in his second trilogy. Barrès reproached Burdeau for his attempts at instilling a love for the "haute poésie essentielle" of classic Greek literature in his students: "A teacher should have taught us Lorrain discipline and explained to us the particular destiny of those who are born between France and Germany" (7: 162). With the code words "Lorrain" and "particular," Barrès immediately signals that Greece, especially Athens, is yet another incarnation of the abstract universalism he finds so pernicious. Although an elitist French scholar such as Burdeau, under the influence of Kant, Nietzsche, or other German philosophers, might claim an intimate link with Hellenistic thought, Barrès finds no prefigurement of any commonality among European cultures amid the ruins of Athens. While he admires the literature and architecture produced by the ancients Greeks, he feels no common bond with their civilization: "We are two different races" (7: 190). In his rejection of Greece as the starting point of a continuous series of connective links between European cultures, in his characterization of Hellenism as the spurious, relatively recent grouping of a dispersed and heterogeneous set of discursive formations, Barrès seems to prefigure Martin Bernal's critique of the notion of ancient Greece as the autonomous fountainhead for an interconnected framework of European cultural entities.

For Barrès, Hellenism is not just largely foreign to Greece and permeated with Oriental influences, but it is mainly alien to his roots in Lorraine, and therefore incompatible with his sensibility. In an interesting version of cultural relativism, Barrès does not seek to transcend his origins, feeling obligated to interpret Greek history and literature in strict accordance with his own roots. Just as he remains unmoved when standing in front of the remnants of the purportedly timeless and universal Parthenon, he declares himself incapable of appreciating or understanding Greek thought, using the lack of blood ties as a rationale: "Having no Hellenic blood, I can generate no Athenian thought" (7: 197). Such statements may seem merely ridiculous, because of their implication that presumed racial differences preclude the comprehension of philosophical texts: "With no Greek blood in my veins, I can little understand Socrates or Plato" (7: 300). They are, however, consistent with the exclusionary logic of Barrès's theory of rootedness. He cannot establish a link, intellectual or otherwise, with the land he visits, since he experiences no instinctive emotional attachment to it.

Greek civilization and philosophy remain intrinsically foreign at both the political and the personal level. Barrès's rejection of abstract universalism and his embrace of Herderian particularism are paralleled by his rejection of formalistic reason in favor of instinctual emotion. The two dichotomies are of course linked: intellect is rootless, while instinct is native. Barrès has amply demonstrated that which he believes to be more authentic, hence his dismissal of Greece, the traditional embodiment of universal reason. Of all the Barrésian paradoxes, his preference for feeling over thinking, painstakingly reiterated and elaborately justified in numerous erudite texts, is the most striking. It is also telling that the learned "intellectual" (how else could he today be described?) never seemed conscious of the paradox of trying to logically explain the ultimate lack of value of logic.

Where Does Europe End and the Orient Start?

Barrès sometimes indulged in the picturesque type of Orientalist descriptions that depend on a luxuriant, dreamy exoticism. *Un Jardin sur l'Oronte*, with its harem scenes, is typical of the sort of lush, languid atmosphere popularized by Pierre Loti. Another example is provided by the character of Astiné Aravian in *Les Déracinés*: "She comes from Asia and from regions shrouded in mystery and perfumed like beautiful veiled slaves . . . among the treasures of the Orient . . . as ingenious as Scheherazade with her sultan" (3: 82–83). Sturel, who considers himself "responsible for Europe in front of Asia," manfully tries to resist the hypnotic allure of Astiné's feminized Orient: "I would not like to slumber all day like women in the seraglio" (3: 91). It is not just that prolonged contact with Astiné would weaken his virility. Sturel's roots in Lorraine, "a military and disciplined province," render him constitutionally unsuited for the languorous pleasures Astiné embodies: "The dream of the Orient, the ashes of Asian centuries, can suffocate him" (3: 94). In the way Astiné Aravian describes her family to Sturel, her immutable status as a foreigner derives as much from her uprootedness as from her cultural and geographical origins: "You can see what kind of family we are, Turkish and Russian, in fact Armenian, which means not at all from Europe" (3: 84). As the embodiment of the prestigious but decadent civilizations of Asia, she also represents, through her rootlessness, the *apatride* cosmopolitanism that risks loosening Sturel's emotional ties to his homeland. In a particularly sordid episode (3: 298–305), she is murdered by two of Sturel's friends from Lorraine, both of whom are of lower-class origins. As is mentioned in the previous chapter, Sturel will eventually decide, due to the land-based solidarity he more acutely feels during the ceremonies linked to Hugo's funeral (3: 325–45), to refrain from informing the police as to the identities of the murderers of his former lover. The assassination scene of the character of Astiné Aravian provides one of the clearest examples of Barrès's misogyny. Her death represents the evacuation of a presence at once foreign and feminine: "It is natural that someone like Astiné Aravian should die assassinated" (3: 304).

Barrès, whom Huré calls "the last of the Orientalist writers" (223), produced several characters and texts that would fit into Edward Said's definitions of "Orientalism:" Marina in *L'Ennemi des lois*, Astiné Aravian in *Les Déracinés*, *Un Jardin sur l'Oronte*, and *Une Enquête au pays du Levant*.[35] The broad scope Barrès attributes to the Orient is one way to trace the limits he assigns to Europe.[36] As previously mentioned, Barrès tended to feminize and Orientalize countries, such as Spain and Greece, that are well within the traditional geographical and cultural confines of Europe as a continent. He also came to deny any "European" status to most of Germany. His treatment of the associated European and Oriental topoi provides an illustrative counterexample to what constitutes one of the major flaws of Said's book: the representation of "the West" as a monolithic presence.[37] Far from contrasting a culturally homogeneous Europe with the image of a similarly uniform Orient as a menacing or subaltern other, Barrès systematically positioned his own national culture at a remote, unbridgeable distance from such traditionally important European cultural forces as Greece and Germany. In effect, he "Orientalized" much of Europe, thus blurring the east-west opposition so thoroughly examined by Said. By symbolically relegating a country such as Germany to Asia (*Une Enquête*, 11: 463), Barrès tended to make the borders of Europe coincide with those of France.

Although he generally approved of France's efforts at extending its colonial empire—as long as they did not distract the country from its main objective along the Rhine[38]—Barrès did not posit an unchanging subject-object relationship between Europe and the Orient, neither of which is represented as a unified entity in most of his texts. His support of the French presence in the Ottoman Empire before the First World War, for instance, was to a great extent motivated by his desire to counter long-standing German influence. The superiority he ascribed to French culture, and the condescension or outright racism he often showed in his "Oriental" texts, did not derive from an underlying sense of belonging to a common, homogeneous European cultural field. The civilizational fault line Barrès perceived within the European continent was for him far more fundamental than what separated Europe from Asia. The same can be said for his version of the Orient, where he saw natural allies as well as enemies of France. In an aside on the forced Islamization of Persia, for instance, Barrès decries the loss of what he sees as its true nature: "What a disaster for the Persian race, which belongs, like the Indians, the Greeks, the Latins, and ourselves, to the great Aryan family, to be forced to adapt to Semitic thought, which is contrary to its nature!" (*Une Enquête*, 11: 234). Given his constant railing against "Germanism," one wonders why he dissociated "ourselves" from "the Latins." What is clear is that Barrès did not merely fabricate an immutable and unitary Oriental essence as a means of antithetically establishing a similarly reified European identity.

Conclusion

Barrès is not as easy to classify as such protofascists as Georges Sorel and Charles Maurras or such racist ideologues as Edouard Drumont and Arthur de Gobineau. The settled parliamentary career of his later years belied the revolutionary rhetoric and activities of his youth. Like many a young firebrand, he gradually evolved into a staid conservative, becoming in many ways a pillar of the very regime he had seemed bent on destroying. In his intellectual eclecticism, Barrès was capable of praising Michelet, Hugo, and even Rousseau, who incarnated the rationalist, universalistic tradition of the Enlightenment that he otherwise rejected. He could also show grudging respect for a contemporary political adversary such as Jean Jaurès. His reconciliation with his former enemies within France during the First World War seems genuine and stands in contrast with the frequently violent tone of his previous texts. The fact that critics remain bitterly divided over such a basic question as whether he was a prefascist or a pre-Gaullist is an indication of the lingering ambiguities of his literary and political heritage.[39]

There is little doubt, however, that Barrès was a major participant in the rise of a reductive, tribalist version of French patriotism at the turn of the century. The jingoistic fervor he exalted bore little resemblance to Hugo's version of French nationalism, which allowed for a vision of eventual European reconciliation and cooperation. Unlike Hugo, Barrès precluded any possibility of transcending nationalism or limiting its magnitude, perceiving only an uninterrupted series of conflicts—or at best an uneasy balance of power—between France and most of its neighbors. While he tended to relativize and particularize "abstract" concepts such as reason, truth, and justice, Barrès expressed his ethnocentric ethic of the Land and the Dead in absolute, all-encompassing terms, thus obviating any possible coexistence of national identity with a wider sense of European citizenship.

A nuanced and complex writer who initially showed signs of a genuine European sensitivity, Barrès evolved into a systematic nationalist with a comprehensive theory that made many of his political attitudes predictable and that seems to have limited his literary outlook. By assigning essentialized national characters to the countries he wrote about, and exalting or denigrating aspects of their culture according to his own estheticized nationalistic framework, he tended to reduce other European cultures to the status of alluringly (or threateningly) exoticized postcard images. His Europe soon became a blank screen onto which he could project mental pictures of contiguous foreign cultures that were either radically inimical to his native land or in a situation of reciprocal influence with it. Just as he dreamed of a Europe shaped according to the needs of France, his literary forays into other cultures always brought him back to his own: "In my youth, I thought beauty to be spread out across the world, and especially in its most mysterious regions, but today I find most of it on the unadorned face of my native land" (*Amori et dolori sacrum*, 7: 10).

Many of the themes so thoroughly developed by Barrès (national cohesion, Latin affinities, and the ongoing adversarial relationship with Germany) will reappear, albeit in far different form, in the next chapter. Jean Renoir produced his best films during the 1930s, in a European context largely shaped by World War I and its aftermath. As is reflected in some of those films, the *Entre-Deux-Guerres* was marked by a resurgence of pro-European sentiment and activism. However, it would take another world war for some countries to take the first tentative steps toward transcending the nationalistic divisions and hatreds that Barrès had sought to exacerbate.

CHAPTER 5

Europe Onscreen

Jean Renoir

Europe, the homeland of my heart's choice, is lost to me, since it has torn itself apart suicidally a second time in a war of brother against brother.
Stefan Zweig, *The World of Yesterday*

Jean Renoir (1894–1979) is widely regarded as one of the world's greatest film directors. Born the year of Dreyfus's trial, he had a privileged upbringing—materially, artistically, and by all accounts, emotionally—within the uncommonly stimulating environment of the studios in Paris and southern France of his father, the painter Auguste Renoir.[1] After his *Baccalauréat*, Jean Renoir enlisted in the French cavalry corps, seeking a military career. During World War I, he was wounded, which left him with a persistent limp. Nevertheless, he returned to active duty, serving in another elite unit, the air corps. Much of his wartime experience would later be depicted in his films—and it would be represented in a far different way from the Barrésian panegyric of enthusiastic martyrdom.

Renoir left France for the United States in 1940. In choosing exile during the German Occupation, he was part of a prestigious roster of French artists. Unlike most of them, Renoir did not return after the Liberation. Settling in Hollywood, he became an American citizen, and he did not visit his former homeland for ten years, which changed both his career and the reception of his films in postwar France (most of them were banned during the Occupation). Critics generally distinguish his pre-World War II films, which are arguably his best, from the rest of his cinematic production.[2] Renoir's American films were a mixed lot that included wartime propaganda efforts and a 1946 adaptation of Octave Mirbeau's novel, *Le Journal d'une femme de chambre* (1900). After the war, his career became international, with films shot in India (*Le Fleuve*, 1951), Italy (*Le Carrosse d'or*, 1953), and Austria (*Le Caporal épinglé*, 1962) as well as in France (from *French Cancan*, 1955, to *Le Petit Théâtre de Jean Renoir*, 1970).[3]

As Pascal Dethurens has amply documented, the interwar years constituted an exceptionally rich period for the literary treatment of Europe. It is therefore useful in this chapter to consider the issue from a cinematic perspective. While Renoir was never an obvious proponent of a unified Europe, several of his films are marked by an awareness of what Staël had called the "European spirit." They reflect the promise and the contradictions of what would become a trend toward integration among several countries of Western Europe. Renoir was also one of the first major filmmakers to lead a successful multinational career. As a quintessentially French director who chose to settle in the United States, who often depicted in his films encounters that spanned linguistic and national boundaries, and who would come to describe himself in universalistic and apolitical terms as "a citizen of the cinema" (*Ma Vie et mes films*, 259), Renoir provides an early example of cross-cultural cinematic production and representations. Some of his films embody a European sensibility, or an awareness of common patterns of thought and behavior, in a historical period when transnational interactions between the inhabitants of Europe had begun to multiply, no longer simply among the established economic and cultural elites, but across broader societal segments. Ironically, most of the films relevant to this chapter were produced during the 1930s, when the idea of a Europe potentially at peace and united was at a low ebb. Renoir's work is especially significant, not only in terms of its own merit and influence, but also because it spanned a crucial historical period, from the eve of the worst war on the continent to the first concrete steps toward European integration.

A Unified Corpus?

Few directors have been as wide-ranging in their filmmaking—in terms of the subject matter, technique, locales, and conditions of production—as Renoir. His career spanned the transition from the silent to the sound era as well as the subsequent transition from black-and-white to color films. Like most filmmakers of his generation, Renoir had no formal training in the field, and he learned the technical aspects of his craft through practical experience. During the apprenticeship period of his silent films, he developed a visual esthetic or style that came to define, following the auteurist tradition, "un film de Renoir," much as his father's paintings had come to be seen in terms of a generally recognizable style. Renoir's films have generally been characterized by long *plans-séquences*, with depth of field shooting that allows for a clear view of both foreground and background. The view of the characters in the background can thus provide an illustrative or contrapuntal complement to the action seen in the foreground, as in *La Règle du jeu*, when Octave and Robert appear ill at ease, standing behind Christine while she is speaking to her guests at la Colinière of her "friendship" for André. The style that Renoir gradually adopted is different from the *découpage classique* inspired by American cinema, which stresses narrative continuity through, paradoxically, a highly fragmented succession of takes, often involving a series of shots/reverse shots. As André Bazin noted (*Jean Renoir*, 77–84), in contrast with the meticulous *montage*, or editing, required by Hollywood standards, Renoir favored fixed or panning shots that privileged the time and space of each dramatic moment.

In spite of the disparities among his films, many critics have emphasized Renoir's status as a film "auteur," who attempted to control all the important aspects of his films, so as to produce an individual—and relatively constant—vision, to the extent possible in such a collective medium. Bazin and Alexander Sesonske have documented the recurrence in Renoir's work of thematic motifs (poaching, class distinctions, theatricalization, or murders accompanied by diegetic songs) and techniques (long takes, panoramic shots, and especially depth of field). In particular, Bazin describes Renoir as consistently a realist, in the nineteenth-century novelistic sense: "one of the masters of cinematic realism, a follower of the traditions of naturalistic novels and impressionistic painting" (*Jean Renoir*, 29). Several other critics of the influential review, *Les Cahiers du cinéma*, many of whom would go on to filmmaking careers—and who would be lumped together under the appellation of "la nouvelle vague"—championed Renoir's directorial style after the war.[4] The *Cahiers* did much to revive interest in a French director who had been living abroad for over a decade and whose films were not initially well received in his home country after the war. By stressing technical and thematic continuity within a highly differentiated body of work, by isolating the filmmaker from his social and cultural environment, auteurism, despite the often brilliant insights of its practitioners, tended to elevate Renoir to the lofty but somewhat inaccessible status of "genius" or "great artist," thereby minimizing the social and historical determinants of his cinematic production. More recent studies have provided a corrective to the auteurist tradition by inscribing Renoir as an important cultural actor within a complex set of social determinants, which include such factors as audience expectations, the influence of other forms of popular entertainment, the economic constraints of filmmaking, the evolving notions of class, sexual and national identities as well as overtly political activity and conflict.

Renoir was never an active politician seeking elective office. Unlike Hugo and Barrès, his political activity, which was considerable until 1939, remained that of an artist clearly identified with the major left-wing political movement of his time. Renoir's support for the Popular Front is well-known. Aside from *La Vie est à nous* (1936) and *La Marseillaise* (1938), he worked with Jacques Prévert and the *Groupe Octobre* on *Le Crime de M. Lange* (1935), participated in the creation of an independent association of filmmakers, *Ciné-Liberté*,[5] and contributed several articles to the communist newspaper *Ce Soir*, which were collected in his *Ecrits 1926–1971*. This period roughly coincided with the rise and fall of the Popular Front. After the infamous riot of February 6, 1934, the French Communist Party (PCF), following the lead of the Komintern, called for an alliance of the Left in order to counter the rising tide of fascism in Europe. No longer emphasizing class struggle or denouncing the socialists, the PCF, in one of its ideological U-turns, called for cooperation between the French working and middle classes, which were both being hard hit by the global economic crisis of the 1930s. For the PCF, emphasizing national unity, rather than class-based internationalism, meant promoting previously disparaged nationalistic symbols, such as the tricolor flag and the anthem of the French Revolution, projects in which Renoir participated through his filmmaking. As a "fellow traveler" (but not a member of the PCF), Renoir participated in the struggle for better living standards for French workers and against the spread of fascism in Europe.[6]

A Persistent Theme

Unlike Hugo, Renoir was never a prophet or theoretician of a united Europe, nor did he show great interest in, or openly advocate the gradual process of European integration after the war. In fact, as a film director, he was insistent, before the Second World War, on the necessity of independent national cinemas—if not exclusively national filmmakers. However, several of his pre- and postwar films show an obvious affinity, in terms of content as well as conditions of production, for the sort of transnational cooperation that the building of Europe continues to require. Similarly, some of Renoir's films, while they can include instances of negative stereotyping, also depict transnational minorities with a significant degree of both empathy and complexity, a rare achievement for their time. A discussion of the European thematics found in some of his films is inseparable from the dialectic of nationalism and internationalism that characterizes a great deal of his visual and textual output. Just as Renoir tended to disengage himself from left-wing political involvement after the Second World War, he also distanced himself from the version of French nationalism he had previously advocated in his writings and his filmmaking—a version that bore little resemblance to that of Barrès.

Renoir's own intellectual evolution is visible in his writings. In particular, his generally negative attitude toward transnational coproductions seems to have changed after the Second World War. Initially, while he in no way disparaged foreign films, he privileged the specificity of cinema as the reflection of an individual national culture. In a 1938 article, he saw film as, first and foremost, a national medium (*Ecrits*, 45). To his credit, Renoir showed no signs of chauvinism in his championing the necessity for authenticity in French cinema, nor did he advocate protectionism in terms of film production, although at that time he pronounced himself unwilling to direct anything but French films (46). In 1936, he opposed attempts to limit the number of foreign workers in the French cinema industry, many of whom were at that time refugees from Nazi Germany (85). However, in the same article, Renoir also called for levying special taxes on foreign films distributed in France, partly as a means of raising capital for the national film industry, which had remained financially weak since the First World War (83). The notion of a "French national cinema" (which Susan Hayward has studied at length), of which directors such as Renoir and Marcel Carné constitute prime examples, was partly formulated against the dominant American model of filmmaking. It is all the more ironic that Renoir, the French film director who never became fully fluent in English,[7] would find not just a safe haven, but a permanent home in Hollywood. Renoir's American film career was brief, and he began a new international phase with *The River* (1951), shot on location in India. He then went to Italy to shoot *Le Carrosse d'or* (1953). In 1958, he celebrated the multinational nature of its production process, while still referring to himself as a French filmmaker: "*La Carroza d'Oro*, shot in English, in Italy, by a French director" (*Ecrits*, 275). Nearly all his subsequent films, however, were shot in France.

Renoir described himself as being more concerned with "horizontal" than with "vertical" divisions—that is, class versus national boundaries (*Ma Vie*, 146). He came to believe that people from different countries who shared a similar educational and cultural background would more easily find common ground. Class distinctions, meanwhile, would more surely divide people living within the borders of a country. This form of internationalism, which was diametrically opposed to Barrès's wartime call for national unity, irrespective of class or religion, discounted ethnic conflicts and assumed the stability of class distinctions around the world. Renoir, after the war, was no doubt less of a militant but not necessarily more of a dreamer. One of his lighter post-World War II films, *Le Déjeuner sur l'herbe*, pointedly satirized the technocratic orientation of the European Economic Community, which had been created in 1957 by the Treaty of Rome. In this 1959 production, a brilliant scientist, played by Paul Meurisse, is a candidate for the office of "President of the United States of Europe." An aloof and somewhat pompous bureaucrat, he advocates a brave new world of societal betterment through generalized artificial insemination. He will be lured away from his somewhat sinister projects of methodical eugenics and from his intended bride (an equally rigid, uniformed German scout leader with whom he seems to enjoy communicating by television), by a French peasant girl played by Catherine Rouvel. This comic fable of science versus nature, or abstract rationalism versus sensual materialism, ends with a reconciliation, as Rouvel's pregnant character humanizes what Raymond Durgnat calls "an amiably glaciated biologist," leading him toward "a new, scientifically less fanatical policy" (349). The hypostatized representatives of the technocratic and pastoral domains, without abandoning either of their specificities, have thus managed to find what Renoir called "affinités spirituelles" (*Ma Vie*, 196). The new European entity, with its quest for standardization and efficiency, can coexist with the less structured *mores* of the traditional French countryside, and the two can learn from each other. The thrust of this dionysian morality tale is similar to *La Grande Illusion*'s prewar appeal for common understanding between ordinary Frenchmen and Germans; one difference being the far more favorable postwar historical context.

Renoir's gradual acceptance of "international" cinema has yet to find much concrete expression within Europe. The notion of "European cinema" is at least as problematic as that of "European literature." Although cinema is often considered a more easily accessible medium, most European films are still rarely screened outside of their home markets. Indeed, while the economic and even political integration of a large part of the continent has reached an advanced stage, cultural production remains highly fragmented, with negative consequences for films produced and distributed within Europe. Despite a tradition of coproductions, the film industries of each country of Europe remain largely provincial, producing films principally aimed at their individual home audience. Most trans-European films are thus, paradoxically, American. This asymmetrical situation of American global dominance and European fragmentation can be seen in a positive light, as the innovative resistance of local cultures against the homogenizing influence of entertainment conglomerates that tend to reduce cinematic cultural production to the lowest common denominator ("le degré zéro du cinéma," to paraphrase Roland Barthes). However, limited distribution within each country not only entails the competitive disadvantage of smaller markets and budgets, but it also carries the potential of perpetuating chauvinistic or provincial representations, encouraging the continued reification of local cultural patterns into mutually exclusive essences.[8] Within the European context of separate national film industries and audiences, what makes some of Renoir's films of the 1930s especially interesting is precisely the degree and complexity of the cross-cultural interactions they depict.

Latin Connections: *Toni* (1935)

A team of workers is in the middle of a routine maintenance job on the railroad tracks as a train carrying new immigrants arrives at a small town in southern France. While the train is slowly passing by, one of the railroad workers laments that these new arrivals will compete for scarce jobs in the area: "Foreigners coming to take the bread from our mouths." Echoing this protectionist cliché, his colleague concurs. Curiously, both of these presumably French xenophobes speak heavily accented French. Their short conversation soon reveals that one of them is from Turin, and the other from Barcelona. This opening scene from *Toni* appears strikingly contemporary, reminiscent of more recent popular jokes by Fernand Raynaud or Coluche about xenophobic attitudes within France. In the next scene, as the title character gets off the train and heads for the town in search of lodging, a pair of gendarmes stop him for a random, if fairly polite, "contrôle d'identité"—another everyday occurrence in contemporary France.

However, once the point is made that many of the characters are of foreign origins, *Toni* shows few instances of us-against-them adversarial relationships between French nationals and the diverse groups of immigrant workers. Few ethnic or racial epithets are heard, and the interactions between the different national and regional groups seem relatively frictionless. The multicultural, multilingual setting is introduced by the film's epigram: "The events occur in the south of France, in Latin country, where nature, by destroying the spirit of Babel, can so well merge races." The opening scene situates the practical motivation of the immigrants and the relative irrelevance of nationalistic sentiments within the narrative, as one of the workers admits, in spite of having complained about the new arrivals: "My country is the place that feeds me." The film's depiction of a functioning multiethnic society, as well as its downplaying of nationalism, constituted politically charged statements in the European context of the 1930s, which was marked by the spread of fascism and the overt institutionalization of racism.[9] *Toni* represents one extreme of Renoir's work in terms of the extent of multinationalism it depicts, with national institutions almost absent (the only representatives of the French Republic are a few gendarmes, who are briefly seen at the opening and closing of the narrative). He would move toward a clearer affirmation of French nationalism in subsequent films, particularly in *La Vie est à nous* and *La Marseillaise*.

Toni is one of the few films situated in the south of France that presents the languages of national and regional minorities (in this case, Italian, Spanish, and Corsican). Renoir thus initiated the undubbed intermingling of multiple languages and accents as an integral component of one of his films, a technique he would use so brilliantly in *La Grande Illusion*. The character of Toni is an Italian immigrant, while Josépha, the object of his unrequited love, is Spanish. Nearly all the characters speak French with an accent, including most of the French citizens in the area (some of whom are Corsican). The only major character who speaks standard, or "Parisian," French—Toni's rival, Albert, who will become Josépha's husband—is also the only unredeemably negative individual in the film. Albert, who rapes Josépha and marries her for her uncle's money (which he proceeds to squander), announces the character of Batala in *Le Crime de M. Lange*. He illustrates Renoir's theory of horizontal, or class-based, divisions; as the generally disliked manager of the quarry where many of the immigrants work, Albert is the only real outsider within the area's transnational community.

Renoir recounted real events that had occurred ten years earlier, filmed on location, hired several local inhabitants as part-time actors, and avoided exoticizing the characters or excessively dramatizing the plot.[10] Renoir's refusal to idealize or sentimentalize his "Latin" community is visible in such scenes as the negotiations between Josépha's uncle and Albert (prior to the latter's wedding to Josépha), which situate the bride as one of the economic assets to be haggled over, along with the house, the land, and the farm animals. This scene is not presented as some sort of exotic ritual, far removed from French societal practices. As Dudley Andrew (208) noted, a parallel could be drawn with the financial negotiations between Robert and André over Christine in the upper-class milieu of *La Règle du jeu*. In his analysis of *Toni*, Sesonske (164–65) emphasized the historical context of the 1920s, which saw a huge influx of immigrants (nearly three million) into France, many from Spain and Italy, after the First World War. These immigrants replaced, within the French economy, the generation that had been decimated during the war. In a parallel with the waves of immigration that followed the Second World War, French nativist fervor and protectionist rhetoric remained relatively muted—as long as the expanding economy continued to provide jobs. During the period between the two world wars, *Toni* was one of the few films that not only acknowledged the presence of large numbers of immigrants but also generally portrayed them in much the same way as their French counterparts, with neither excessive sentimentality nor demonization. Renoir's film is also a reminder that the cycle of high levels of immigration, later followed by anti-immigrant rhetoric, and ultimately by the permanent integration of most immigrants, does not constitute a new or isolated phenomenon in recent French history.

Some of the immigrants depicted in *Toni* have been settled in France long enough to acquire property; some have just arrived in search of employment. During the narrative, there is a constant weaving in and out of French, Spanish, and Italian, with diegetic songs accompanying the dialogue or providing transitions. Characters sometimes switch languages as they move from one conversational context to another. The south of France is thus presented as a somewhat unstable but functional Latin melting pot, or, as the film's epigrammatic introduction calls it, "pays latin." This fantasy of a specifically southern European, or Latin, commonwealth was already present in Barrès's work, albeit not at the level of peasants and proletarians. The spatial or geographic division suggested in *Toni* does not follow national borders. When speaking with his friend Fernand, Toni dreams of fleeing Europe altogether, of escaping to South America with Josépha: "We'll have another sky over our heads . . . it will be a new life, under other stars." European countries thus appear undifferentiated, with the notion of foreignness or alterity transposed to another continent.

Other ethnic and national groups are represented or mentioned in *Toni*, but they are not always seen. As will be the case in *La Grande Illusion*, a lone black character, whose origin is never elucidated, has a minor role.[11] Josépha's uncle, who is a fairly prosperous farmer, warns her against all the recently arrived foreigners in the area, especially the "Sidis" (Arabs). Josépha tells him not to worry, the irony being that she answers this xenophobic tirade in Spanish. The film's depiction of a harmonious "fusion des races" is obviously less than perfect, remaining limited in practice to southern European countries. In this sense, *Toni* is again contemporary (by present-day standards), presenting a relatively smooth process of integration within France for most Europeans and reflecting instances of xenophobic or racist reactions against immigrants from France's former colonial empire.

Somewhere between Paris and Moscow: *Les Bas-Fonds* (1936)

Renoir transposed the plot of Maxim Gorky's play from Czarist Russia to an unnamed location, apparently set in the present, at the time of the film's release. Renoir completely recreated *Les Bas-Fonds*, adding scenes, transforming characters, and changing the ending, producing a film that is much less somber in tone than Gorky's 1902 play. While the characters keep their Russian names and make frequent references to Rubles (usually their lack thereof), nothing else situates them in national terms. By contrast, Akira Kurosawa's 1957 film adaptation also transposed Gorky's play, this time to Japan, but remained much closer to the original in terms of plot and characterization. In 1968, Renoir sought to portray the lack of spatial and temporal specificity in *Les Bas-Fonds* in universalistic terms: "I did not attempt to make a 'Russian' film, my goal was human drama" (*Ecrits*, 239).

In Renoir's version, most of the narrative seems to occur in a sort of generic Europe in the throes of the Great Depression, rather than in the squalor of prerevolutionary Russia. However, the scene in which Pepel drags a sullen, inebriated Natacha away from her would-be suitor, a pompous *fonctionnaire*, takes place in the middle of a fashionable, and mostly open-air, café-restaurant. The luxurious decor of the spacious locale and the ridiculously genteel mannerisms of the clients and staff (which Pepel disrupts and deflates) are evocative of the Belle Epoque, thereby adding to the general impression of unreality. With the music and the elegant costumes of most of the clients, that scene could just as easily be set in Vienna as in Paris. Practical considerations, such as the difficulty of trying to pass off famous actors such as Jean Gabin and Louis Jouvet as Russians, apparently led to situating the plot somewhere between Paris and Moscow, but obviously closer to the former.

Renoir made a reference to the last scene of Charles Chaplin's *Modern Times* (and possibly to René Clair's 1931 film, *A nous la liberté*) by showing Pepel and Natacha walking down the road together.[12] The relatively optimistic ending of *Les Bas-Fonds* is more consonant with the initially heady atmosphere of the Popular Front—as exemplified by the communal solidarity of *Le Crime de M. Lange*—than with the despair of Gorky's play.[13] Both of these films portray an initially fragile community's symbolic exclusion, by murder, of an oppressive figure. Both end with the departure of the couple that was central to the community's development. However, *Les Bas-Fonds* ends with the couple, formerly a thief and a victimized household servant, escaping a static, hopeless community and thereby losing nothing. Meanwhile, *Le Crime*'s Valentine and Lange, respectively a small business owner and a popular artist, are forced to abandon a now-thriving community and to flee across the border. The departure from the sordid communal environment is a voluntary and comparatively hopeful event for Pepel and Natacha in *Les Bas-Fonds*. In *Le Crime*, however, the context in which the two main characters leave their community is one of fear and possible capture. Having killed the corrupt Batala, Lange, aided and accompanied by

Valentine, must seek refuge abroad, after being symbolically "judged" during an impromptu meeting in a café, by a de facto jury of his working-class peers. As in *Les Bas-Fonds*, the conclusion of *Le Crime* is indecisive, with the fugitive couple heading across the Belgian border and the future of the collective they leave behind uncertain. There is no particular significance to the choice of Belgium as the direction in which to flee; it is simply the closest border, and one that is fairly easy to cross clandestinely. Similarly, Pepel and Natacha do not seem to have any specific destination in mind. The couples in both films are fleeing in the hope of finding sanctuary or a new beginning. In 1936, areas of relative safe haven were already shrinking in Europe, and the idea of a better *ailleurs* was becoming increasingly phantasmic. *Toni* projected it toward South America, *Le Crime* featured Lange's imaginative recreation of an open Wild West in the United States, and *Les Bas-Fonds* presented a utopia (i.e., no-place) in the literal sense.

From Class to Nation: *La Vie est à nous* (1936) and *La Marseillaise* (1938)

The discontinuities within the Renoir film corpus are often glaring. His early body of work includes a (silent) musical comedy set in a futuristic, barbaric Europe (*Sur un air de Charleston*, 1926), and an embarrassing paean to French colonialism in Algeria (*Le Bled*, 1929). Among his postwar credits can be found an adaptation of Robert Louis Stevenson's 1886 novel, *The Strange Case of Dr. Jekyll and Mr. Hyde*, which makes use of the techniques of television (*Le Testament du Docteur Cordelier*, 1959). Within the overall "humanism" or "universalism" of his work that several critics have commented on, the two overtly political films he made in support of the Communist Party and/or the Popular Front stand out as celebrations of French nationalism, even more than as calls for class struggle. Made respectively for the PCF and the CGT labor union, *La Vie est à nous* and *La Marseillaise*, which were intended as propaganda films, correspond roughly to the beginning and the end of the Popular Front as a governmental alliance.

The extent of Renoir's participation in *La Vie est à nous*, a film with several directors, remains unclear. Georges Sadoul (75) emphasized Renoir's role, while Alan Williams (225) insisted on the collective nature of the making of this film. Alexander Sesonske (232) saw Renoir's work on this atypical film as an illustration of his lack of aesthetic or conceptual rigidity. Jonathan Buchsbaum (93) highlighted the links between the film's structure and the electoral objectives of the PCF. Within France, the use of the cinema as an instrument of what would today be called the communications strategy of a political party constituted an innovation. However, while political propaganda films were fairly new in France, they were a staple of Soviet film production. In Germany, Leni Riefenstahl's *Triumph of the Will* (1935) celebrated the rise of Nazism. As part of the PCF's campaign for the 1936 legislative elections, *La Vie* positions the party as the main line of defense against the enemies of France, both external (Hitler and Mussolini) and internal (the myth of "les deux cents familles"). It begins, didactically enough, with a teacher lecturing schoolchildren, and it ends with a series of speeches by PCF leaders. In between, three sequences illustrate the PCF's role in defending the rights of workers, farmers, and the middle class. *La Vie* often accurately depicts the effects of the Great Depression—high unemployment, harsh working conditions, bankruptcies—on individuals, something not often seen in commercial cinema. In customary propagandistic fashion, it interweaves accounts of real poverty and suffering with messages about the PCF's platform and activities. Not surprisingly, the Soviet Union is held up in *La Vie* as the alternative model to class-based exploitation in capitalist Europe. It is also presented by association as a natural ally against the increasingly menacing fascist countries that bordered France.

Renoir also participated, this time as the only director, in the other major film that sought to embody and project the ideology of the Popular Front. Ostensibly a filmic commemoration of the French Revolution, *La Marseillaise* remained a project structured around the already fading Frontist hopes and promises.[14] As Norman King (70) noted, in addition to the broader historical context, *La Marseillaise* was partly a reply to the authoritarian subtext of Abel Gance's film *Napoléon* (a new sound version had been released in 1935). Two interpretations of French history, each with its political aftereffects, were thus presented to French audiences, during a period of increasing polarization along class and party lines. In typically Barrésian fashion, Gance's film portrayed Napoleon as a Promethean conqueror, spreading the spirit of the French Revolution across Europe. Renoir's film, meanwhile, centered on the early part of the Revolution leading up to the battle of Valmy, stressing the isolation of France against external, particularly Prussian, enemies. Aside from their obvious differences, both films assert the primacy of French nationalism, and therefore national unity, rather than any universalistic ideals associated with the Revolution.

The French Revolution, especially in its initial stages, included a strong ideational element of internationalism that was expressed, for instance, by electing foreigners such as Thomas Paine to the National Assembly. The ideology of universalism that was an early component of the revolutionary process is not reflected in Renoir's film. The representation of the Revolution is clearly overdetermined by the political struggles of the period in which the film was shot, hence the emphasis on the menace coming from the German border, a danger enhanced by the complicity of some sections of the French upper classes. Against the backdrop of the disintegration of the Frontist coalition at home, and of the continuing spread of fascism abroad (the *Anschluss* and the Spanish Civil War), *La Marseillaise* stressed the need to counter the threats from foreign aggressors and their French supporters. Overall, *La Vie est à nous* and *La Marseillaise*, the films that most closely followed the PCF line, or that reflected the dangerous international context of the short-lived Popular Front, are the most overtly nationalistic of Renoir's films, and the least European.

Europe in a Camp: *La Grande Illusion* (1937)

Just as Renoir attempted to represent the French Revolution from the point of view of its average participants in *La Marseillaise*, he sought in *La Grande Illusion* to represent the First World War as it had been experienced by its ordinary combatants. And just as *La Marseillaise* reflected the struggles linked to the Popular Front within France, *La Grande Illusion* reflected the rising tensions linked to the spread of fascism across much of the European continent, one year after the beginning of the Spanish Civil War and one year before Munich. The filmic representation of the Great War, nearly twenty years after the Armistice, was not an isolated instance. Films set during the First World War were fairly common at the time, in France as elsewhere in Europe.[15] What distinguished *La Grande Illusion* from other war films of the period was not any "realistic" reconstruction of scenes from famous battles, but the complexity and richness of its depiction of the (enforced) interactions among different European national groups. In this sense, Renoir's film adumbrates the postwar situation in Europe (or rather western Europe), with an initially uneasy truce and the belated recognition of the need for dialogue and accommodation across national borders.

Renoir's 1937 film was, among other things, a retrospective look at the state of Europe during the First World War—just as the clouds of World War II were gathering. With two German prisoner-of-war camps serving as microcosms and metaphors, Renoir represented several European nationalities in his film, along with gender, class, and religious rivalries. Although the narrative of *La Grande Illusion* takes place during what was still called "la Grande Guerre" when the film was released, the war itself constitutes a mostly invisible presence. There is no infantry assault, pitched battle, or artillery barrage anywhere in the film. Indeed, there are few examples of any form of physical struggle between uniformed soldiers; few shots are fired; few corpses are shown. Even the aerial battle that turns the characters of Maréchal and de Boeldieu into prisoners of war remains unseen. The news from the front, which seems quite distant, arrives at the camp late, filtered through posters or newspapers. Despite the well-known brutality of the Great War, an aura of antiquated gentility envelops the camps in which German soldiers guard French, British, and Russian prisoners.

True to Renoir's theatrical tradition, the war itself is represented indirectly, on the makeshift stage of the Hallbach camp,[16] with the British and French actors/prisoners defiantly singing *La Marseillaise*, thereby provoking a walkout by the German guards/spectators. This lone scene of patriotic fervor is captured through a panoramic shot, when Maréchal's announcement of a French victory at Douaumont, in the middle of the stage show put on by the prisoners, is followed by a full clockwise movement, starting with a British officer removing his wig and asking the pianist to play *La Marseillaise*, moving to the other British and French officers onstage, highlighting Maréchal in a low angle shot as he ostensibly turns the lyrics "ces féroces soldats" into a show of defiance toward the German officers situated offstage, then moving to the spectators/prisoners, and finally back to the initial British officer. This long shot then continues in a counterclockwise direction back to the assembled prisoners, who are no longer passive spectators of a play but are active participants in a long struggle, standing together and singing proudly. The sweeping camera movement magnifies the collective enthusiasm of all the prisoners, on and off the stage.[17] However, the battlefield victory that leads to the singing of the French national anthem turns out to be only temporary. The recapture by the French army of the Fort of Douaumont was simply one of the back-and-forth swings in the battle of Verdun, the longest and bloodiest of the war. A poster later informs the prisoners and the viewers that the German army had in turn retaken the disputed fort. The impression that results is not one of military enthusiasm or disappointment but one of the absurdity of war itself. Renoir was clear about his intentions when making this film: "Because I am a pacifist, I directed *La Grande Illusion*" (*Ecrits*, 240). The bitter irony is that the film's pacifist subtext was doomed to be misunderstood or ignored, due to the rise of Nazism.

The failure of pacifism as a practical possibility, in the European context of the late 1930s, did not transform Renoir into a xenophobic nationalist. In 1957, he seemed to have abandoned none of his hopes for reconciliation across national borders. He bemoaned the aggressiveness promoted by modern nationalism and longed for a new flowering of internationalism, which he felt could be facilitated by the film medium (*Ecrits*, 65–66). Ironically, *La Grande Illusion* records, in a retrospective way, the Europe-wide triumph of modern nationalism, of the sort of nationalism that seeks to transcend class antagonisms. The First World War represented for Barrès the apotheosis of his patriotic movement, the triumphant culmination of his revanchist dreams. With few exceptions, the French nation temporarily set aside all forms of internal class and religious divisions, forming the sort of *union sacrée* he had long been calling for. United against a common, foreign foe, the French were able to recover the regions of Alsace and Lorraine that had been forcibly annexed by Germany in 1870. Despite the war's horrendous cost in human lives, France recovered, through its defeat of the German military machine, both its former military glory and its sense of common purpose, if only for a brief period. In *La Grande Illusion*, there is a similar sense of national unity, but it is far from unequivocal, nor is it imbued with the sort of religious fervor in battle that Barrès celebrated. Class and religious divisions are openly examined in Renoir's film, not swept under the rug. What is also missing is a clearly defined eternal enemy, at least in the way that Barrès had designated Germans as a monolithic horde of aggressive invaders.

It might be excessive to consider *La Grande Illusion* as a prefiguration of the sort of transnational exchanges and interactions that have become institutionalized in the European Union, with its perennial rivalries and endless negotiations. However, the film is full of references to diverse European countries, cultures, languages, and food. For instance, a Russian officer gives a language lesson to a French counterpart at the Hallbach camp, patiently pointing out morphological similarities and differences. In the Wintersborn camp, the French character Demolder is busy translating Pindar, declaring, to everyone else's bewilderment: "He's the greatest Greek poet." During a search of the prisoners' quarters, von Rauffenstein, amused by Demolder's obsession, inspects the French prisoner's face in profile, no doubt comparing it to classical Greek esthetic standards. In Hallbach, the French prisoners are digging a tunnel, seeking to escape to Holland, which was neutral during the First World War. The engineer, played by Gaston Modot, tells his fellow prisoners: "Rendez-vous à Amsterdam." In Wintersborn, the goal of Maréchal and Rosenthal, played by Jean Gabin and Marcel Dalio, is to escape to Switzerland. Also in Wintersborn, the excited Russian prisoners invite their French counterparts to witness the opening of a highly anticipated crate they have just received, a "gift from the Empress"— which turns out to contain only surplus books instead of the hoped-for vodka and canned food. In an echo of prerevolutionary tensions, they angrily set fire to the crate and its contents, preventing the horrified Demolder from saving any of the books.

All the characters use their native language, one of the major innovations of the film.[18] The simultaneous use of different languages plays both a technical and a thematic function, alternately separating or uniting characters of different national origins. Language is one of the major factors, along with class, religion, and gender, which determine relationships and alliances among the characters. Some of them seem to break the language barriers with relative ease: the de Boeldieu/von Rauffenstein couple, Rosenthal, some of the German guards, some of the Russian prisoners, and the Maréchal/Elsa couple. Others remain confined to their own national group, even if there are characters from other countries who speak their language; aside from the theatrical representation, the British prisoners are never seen amicably interacting with representatives of other countries. In a 1938 speech in London, Renoir pointed out the importance of hearing all of the different languages in the films, without the filter of dubbing: "The authenticity of accents, terms, and languages is crucial" (*Ecrits*, 48).

One of the other distinguishing attributes of European nationalities in this film is food, which is consistent with Renoir's aim of presenting *la Grande Guerre* from the point of view of its average participants. According to the level of its abundance or quality, food serves to divide the characters, or bring them together, across class or national lines. Shared meals can provide the setting for pacific encounters, where all forms of societal divisions are momentarily set aside. De Boeldieu and Maréchal politely have lunch with the German air corps unit responsible for shooting down their plane; all social classes at Hallbach, from the aristocrat to the proletarian, commune at what can only be called Rosenthal's table; and Elsa, unafraid despite the wretched appearance of the escaped prisoners whom she finds in her barn, instantly shares her food with them. Alternately, in a scene that tests and ultimately cements their friendship, Maréchal and Rosenthal, before they reach the warmth and safety of Elsa's house, are reduced to blaming each other when their meager provisions run out. Within the camps, access to food, as well as its quality, depends on one's nationality. The relative position of each group is neatly summarized in the mess hall of the Hallbach camp, with a portrait of the Kaiser on the wall, when three German soldiers sardonically complain about their rations:

>   —This tastes like an old sock.
>   —What do they feed the French?
>   —Cabbage, but they have their parcels.
>   —And the Russians?
>   —Cabbage roots, but no parcels.
>   —And the English?
>   —Plum pudding! [laughter]

Representing Germany

This film's universalism, much discussed by critics, is in practice circumscribed to Europe. The narrative of *La Grande Illusion* takes place in 1916, before the United States entered the war, and there is almost no trace of the soldiers drawn from the British and French colonial empires who were sent to the front.[19] The European theme of Renoir's film was not an isolated one, whether in the artistic or political domains. During the interwar period, there were several organizations and projects, such as Richard Coudenhove-Kalergi's *Paneuropa* and Aristide Briand's 1930 memorandum on an "union fédérale européenne" (written by his assistant, Alexis Léger, better known as Saint-John Perse), that called for European unity. In the literary field, Romain Rolland was instrumental in creating the review *Europe*, which attempted to extend his wartime calls for peaceful coexistence within the European continent.[20] Of course, these projects or movements, which were designed to bring peace and prosperity to Europe, all remained dead letters. A central feature of most of them was a call for reconciliation between France and Germany. The Schuman Declaration of 1950 would also stress the Franco-German relationship as the building block of a united Europe, with somewhat more success, since it led to the first of the postwar institutions that later developed into the European Union. The main focus of *La Grande Illusion*'s European theme is also the interactions between the French and German characters. While these interactions are not devoid of conflict—the context is, after all, a prisoner-of-war camp where German soldiers are guarding French prisoners—they are characterized by a degree of common understanding and the possibility of reconciliation. As Andrew (298) noted, the depiction of coexistence, effective if not frictionless, across religious, class, or national divides, provides one of the common threads of many of Renoir's films.

The generally positive representation of Germans—especially Germans in uniform—accounts for much of the negative reaction in France to *La Grande Illusion* when it was rereleased in 1946.[21] Overall, German soldiers are depicted as fundamentally decent individuals who perform their military duties without sadism or bloodthirstiness. As he stated in 1938, Renoir sought to portray Germans as individuals the French could empathize with and see as similar to them (*Ecrits*, 240–42). There is none of the systematic demonizing of "Prussians" in the Barrésian vein. The message is one of common humanity, with reminders that soldiers of other countries would behave in a similar fashion, a point reinforced by von Rauffenstein when he informs Maréchal and de Boeldieu that he has decided to apply French military regulations at the Wintersborn camp. Correspondingly, after being shot during the diversion he organizes to assist the escape of Maréchal and Rosenthal, de Boeldieu responds to von Rauffenstein's obviously sincere apology with a laconic: "I would have done the same." At the film's end, a German border patrol spots the two escaped prisoners trudging through the snow toward the sanctuary of Swiss territory. As some of them start firing, one of the soldiers yells: "Don't shoot! They're in Switzerland." Another responds with apparent envy: "All the better for them." One of the most moving moments, as silently witnessed by Maréchal and Rosenthal, occurs when Elsa comments on the pictures of her husband and brothers, all killed at once famous, now meaningless battles—"our greatest victories," she states in a flat tone, at once bitter and empty—reinforcing her sense of loss by showing her long dining table, at which only she and her daughter now sit. In France, with its 1.4 million death toll, almost every family could identify with Elsa's litany of relatives swallowed up by a seemingly endless war.

The most favorable portrayal of a German soldier occurs when Maréchal, desperate after languishing in solitary confinement at Hallbach, is comforted by an older guard who, out of concern over the French prisoner's distress, offers him a cigarette and a harmonica. Almost absentmindedly, Maréchal starts playing "Frou-frou," the recorded song he was singing along with at the film's opening scene. Although he is reassured by Maréchal's reaction to his kindness, the weary German guard observes, "the war is lasting too long"—an understated comment that could have been echoed by soldiers and civilians of any other nation. The question often asked by critics is whether such a generous depiction was naive or worse in the historical context of the film's release. Of course, as an artist, Renoir cannot be held accountable for, or somehow represented as complicit with, the new form of inhumanity developed by the Nazi regime. In 1946, obviously aware of the criticisms directed against the positive representation of Germans in uniform in *La Grande Illusion*, Renoir stressed that his film depicted Germany before the rise of Hitler (*Ecrits*, 243).

Renoir had a long and productive association with Germany and German filmmakers during the first part of his career. In his autobiography (146), Renoir warmly remembered Carl Koch, who had served in a German antiaircraft unit during the First World War. Koch became a close friend of Renoir and worked with him as a screenwriter on several films. *Nana*, Renoir's first important film, was also the first French film shot in Berlin after the First World War.[22] The practice of producing French films abroad, particularly in Germany, rapidly became widespread. Since France's cinematic industry had lost its prewar supremacy, many French films had German producers and were shot in German studios during the interwar years, sometimes in separate bilingual versions. Hitler's rise to power slowed, but did not stop, German participation at all levels of French filmmaking.[23] As Rémy Pithon detailed, many French actors, screenwriters, and directors continued to travel to Germany for coproductions until 1939. During the Occupation, meanwhile, German authorities tended to encourage the production of French films, albeit heavily censored.[24]

Sadoul (74) characterized Renoir's film as a last-ditch appeal to ordinary Germans, a desperate plea to avert another generalized conflagration. This call for transnational fraternization is sometimes expressed comically. Within the temporary sanctuary of Elsa's farm, Maréchal jovially addresses the cow he is feeding: "You were born in Württemberg, and me in Paris. Doesn't keep us from being buddies." Renoir's openness to German culture and his generally positive characterization of Germans in *La Grande Illusion* illustrates the difficulty inherent in any pro-European position in the context of German Nazism. In 1937, he insisted on the need to resist conflating Germans and Nazis (*Ecrits*, 125). However, in a 1938 article written after the already infamous Munich accords, Renoir showed that he was also conscious of Nazi brutalities (178).

Britain versus Europe

At his arrival in Hallbach, a British soldier stubbornly resists being searched, apparently believing he will only be robbed: "Keep your hands away! Don't touch me! What do you want, my watch?" Incensed at the insistence of the German guard standing in front of him, the Briton ends up throwing down his watch and crushing it under his boot, contemptuously telling the unfazed guard: "Pick it up now!" As if to present a contrasting attitude, a French soldier also exhibits resistance as he is being searched, but with far less aggressiveness directed at the German guard: "Leave that alone, buddy! That's my stuff!" These parallel presentations of anonymous soldiers are typical of the generally negative depictions of Britons in *La Grande Illusion*, all the more negative by comparison with the film's more generous representations of Germans. This scene shows British characters for the first time, and it situates them as marginalized, relative to representatives of other countries. If Renoir's film consigns a national group to a position of alterity, it is not France's enemy during the war but, paradoxically, its main ally.

There are two other unflattering portraits of British prisoners in the Hallbach camp (significantly, none are seen helping in the escape attempt at Wintersborn). The first features the dancing line of British officers when they are rehearsing for the show. Their comically (and stereotypically) light-hearted song, "Tipperary," complete with a ridiculous chorus line, stands in contrast to the rousing French anthem of war and victory that will symbolically unite all the prisoners. The participants in the chorus line will later be seen fully costumed in drag on stage, thus connoting the stereotypes of British effeminacy and homosexuality; while the French prisoners might fondle the recently arrived women's garments with fetishistic longing, it is mostly the British who actually wear them. The group of Britons will only attain dignity, virility, and solidarity with the other prisoners when one of them removes his wig and asks the musicians to play *La Marseillaise*, in celebration of the French victory at Douaumont. Gender distinctions are thus straightforwardly established along national lines.

Another, more ridiculous, scene, this time centering on frivolity, occurs when a new group of British prisoners arrives in the Hallbach camp just as its current occupants are being transferred. The British officers are seen carrying tennis racquets—as they arrive in a prisoner-of-war camp. The lack of comprehension with their French counterparts is highlighted when Maréchal vainly attempts to inform one of the incoming British officers about the tunnel originating in the barracks that the French officers are vacating. The Briton, as annoyed as any nonchalant tourist would be at having to repack the contents of his suitcase, makes no effort to understand Maréchal's obvious sense of urgency, politely but dismissively answering that he does not speak French. Most of the French officers themselves do not seem to be sure if they should inform the newly arrived British—who are, after all, their allies in the war—about the tunnel, implying a relative lack of trust. By contrast, the departing French prisoners are fairly warm when saying goodbye to the German guard they call "Arthur."

The French Jew

As a rich Jew whose family has not long been settled in France, the character of Rosenthal represents the ultimate outsider (or the untrustworthy *cosmopolite*) in the Europe of the 1930s. In *La Grande Illusion*, that perceived stateless or *apatride* status does not prevent his forming a close friendship with the working-class Maréchal—who has the sort of fixed national roots that Barrès would have approved of. By making his Jewish character part of a rich banking family, Renoir links him to the popular image of the Rothschilds, thus directly confronting the issue of anti-Semitism, which was all the more virulent since the Popular Front was led by the first Jewish prime minister of France, Léon

Blum.²⁵ While highlighting Rosenthal's status as a wealthy landowner, Renoir also portrays him as brave, generous, and eager to fit in with his fellow French prisoners, as opposed to the aloof, aristocratic de Boeldieu. Not surprisingly, Renoir was attacked in some right-wing circles for this generally positive representation of an important Jewish character. In 1938, he angrily responded to Céline's *Bagatelles pour un massacre*, which accused *La Grande Illusion* of being "Jewish propaganda" (*Ecrits*, 148). This depiction of a Jewish character as a regular, albeit rich, fellow, as patriotic as any other Frenchman, did not have any German counterpart in the film, even though German Jews had fought and died for the Reich during the First World War. Perhaps current events at the time of the film's making—German eliminationist policies directed against Jews—were inescapable.

Responding to the actor's barbed comment ("He was born in Jerusalem"), Rosenthal provocatively highlights his *cosmopolitisme*: "Excuse me! In Vienna, capital of Austria, of a Danish mother and a Polish father, now French citizens." In an ambiguous statement that reflects the complex, unresolved dialectics between class, religion, and nation in the film, Maréchal jokingly responds: "Old Breton nobility." As a descendant of immigrants, Rosenthal is always in an intermediary position: between de Boeldieu and Maréchal in terms of class and between Elsa and Maréchal in terms of national origin and language. On Christmas Eve, it is Rosenthal who carves for Elsa's daughter Lotte the characters of the nativity scene (including Jesus, "my racial brother") out of potatoes.²⁶ He is thus the only character who always transcends borders, saying at the end of the film: "You can't see borders. They're a human invention. Nature doesn't give a damn about them." During the disastrous first part of their escape, before they stumble onto Elsa's secluded house, Maréchal's anti-Semitic outburst against the limping Rosenthal—"I never could stand Jews"—has a cathartic function, bringing into the open hatreds that were shared by workers as well as aristocrats. The fact that Maréchal can overcome his latent prejudice illustrates *La Grande Illusion*'s constant portrayal of all characters (with the exception of the aristocrats) as ordinary people, with whom it is possible to reach an understanding. By the end of their escape to Switzerland, what would once have been a vicious insult—"Goodbye, dirty Jew"—is transformed into something approaching a reconciliatory joke between Maréchal (who now knows better) and Rosenthal. During the Occupation, the hope expressed by the film's representation of solidarity across religious divides would prove to be just as illusory as that of the decency of German soldiers. Renoir's film came too early or too late.

An Aristocratic Couple

The twilight of one idea of Europe is embodied by the doomed friendship—or courtship—between the French and German aristocrats (de Boeldieu and von Rauffenstein, played by Pierre Fresnay and Erich von Stroheim), whose narrow class-based solidarity cannot withstand the generalized assault of modern nationalism. By contrast, the central figure, the working-class Maréchal, does manage, in spite of initial misgivings and prejudices, to establish relationships based on friendship (with Rosenthal) and love (with Elsa). While Rosenthal uses his multilingualism to bring characters together, de Boeldieu and von Rauffenstein use theirs as a means of exclusion. As career officers and representatives of a fading aristocratic class, they have common tastes and activities, which they nostalgically reminisce about (often in English, another "snobbish" trait they share): social contacts, horse racing, restaurants, and women. After Maréchal jokes about Maxim's in the context of camp food, von Rauffenstein addresses de Boeldieu in English, thus excluding the French commoner: "Maxim's . . . That reminds me: I used to know a girl there in 1913. Her name was Fifi." De Boeldieu responds laconically: "So did I." Interestingly, de Boeldieu, a fluent English speaker, never attempts to communicate with the British prisoners, while Maréchal does, to no avail. Whereas Maréchal can manage, despite his monolingualism, to communicate with a German guard and with Elsa, he is unable to tell a British officer about the tunnel in one of the barracks. This is in keeping with the rather negative portrayal of the British in most of *La Grande Illusion*.

The civility—indeed, the chivalry—that von Rauffenstein shows to his French counterparts in the mess hall early in the film is strictly based on their status as officers. Von Rauffenstein is following a rigorous code of conduct that today seems particularly outdated: "If they are officers, invite them over for lunch." He immediately finds a common bond with his French counterpart de Boeldieu, having met his cousin, a military attaché, in Berlin before the war. Despite the fact that it is von Rauffenstein who has shot down his plane, de Boeldieu is instantly more comfortable with him than with the working-class Maréchal, who in turn is happy to meet a French-speaking German mechanic. At Wintersborn, the sole flower serves as the symbol of the singular friendship between the two aristocrats. Von Rauffenstein reacts very much like a jilted lover when de Boeldieu risks his life, not in a bid for his own freedom, but to ensure the escape of his lower-class compatriots. There is also something of a lovers' triangle in the relationship between Maréchal, Rosenthal, and de Boeldieu. Maréchal is the center of attention throughout, with de Boeldieu apparently having renounced any attempt at forming a bond with Rosenthal, despite their common upper-class backgrounds. The tension will ultimately be resolved by the self-sacrifice of de Boeldieu, which will allow Maréchal and Rosenthal to escape.

Europe on the Brink: *La Règle du jeu* (1939)

La Règle du jeu is one of the most famous examples of a commercially unsuccessful "film maudit" that belatedly received vindication from critics and audiences. It was very badly received at its opening, in the volatile European context of

1939. In a frantic effort to improve its popular reception and to forestall a commercial disaster, it was significantly cut, to no avail. Renoir's last prewar French film was banned as demoralizing by the French government at the beginning of the war, and then during the German Occupation. Its shortened version did not fare any better after the Liberation. After a painstaking restoration in 1959, it finally became accessible in its near-original form to audiences and critics. It took decades for *La Règle du jeu* to be widely recognized as a masterpiece.[27] Based on classical eighteenth- and nineteenth-century French comedy,[28] the film's funereal mixture of unheroic tragedy and dark comedy was apparently too unsettling immediately before and after the war.

La Règle du jeu inserts several disruptive characters into an otherwise smugly closed upper-class milieu: the ne'er-do-well Octave, the hero/misfit André Jurieux, the poacher Marceau, the Alsatian gamekeeper Schumacher, and the foreigner Christine de La Chesnaye. Although it is less obvious than in *La Grande Illusion*, Renoir also mixes representatives of several European nations. While the national conflicts suggested in the narrative are mostly limited to France and Germany, class and sexual distinctions are more consistently highlighted. As in many of Renoir's films, a diverse assortment of characters is assembled in a collective, albeit luxurious, environment. One of the guests at the rural mansion called la Colinière has a very noticeable Spanish accent, while one of the servants is identified as British. Lisette nonchalantly tells him: "if you please." In a scene that recalls *Toni*, and suggests an uncomplimentary parallel—across perceived differences between social classes, in terms of character, education, and behavior—Robert dejectedly comments to his rival André, after their ungentlemanly fistfight over Christine: "I sometimes read in the newspapers that in some remote neighborhood, an Italian construction worker wanted to steal the wife of a Polish laborer, and that it led to a knifefight!"

Although Renoir does not make full use of multiple languages, as he had in *La Grande Illusion*, the national identities or origins of several characters are clearly designated, along with conflicts and alliances that follow national lines. André Jurieux is thus identified as "le héros national," or as the embodiment of France, while Christine is repeatedly situated as a foreigner. The upper-class Robert/Christine/André triangle has its corollary among the servants with the Schumacher/Lisette/Marceau triangle, one of whose members has a German-sounding name—which is reinforced when Christine pronounces Schumacher's name in German. As played by Nora Gregor (who, with her husband, was forced into exile after the *Anschluss*), Christine de La Chesnaye's status as an expatriate, specifically a German-speaking Austrian, is mentioned several times by Octave, Geneviève, André, Robert, and Saint-Aubin. She also alludes to it herself, dressing for the costume party as "une Tyrolienne," and mockingly replying to Octave that if she refuses to invite André to la Colinière, "people will talk about foreign influence." Geneviève, Robert's mistress, pointedly plays up her rival's foreignness and lack of Parisian sophistication when he ineffectually tries to end their long-standing affair: "A Parisian would understand, not her." As an ironic visual counterpoint to this declaration of Frenchness, Geneviève is wearing a Chinese robe, and she and Robert are standing next to impassive, almost smirking Chinese statues. Octave, the character in an intermediate social position, is alone in giving a positive account of Christine's foreign background, stressing his emotional and artistic links to her father, a famous orchestra conductor from Salzburg.

Christine is somewhat indifferently married to Robert de La Chesnaye, a rich, idle French aristocrat who is identified as the descendant of "un métèque" (in this context, a Jew, preferably of foreign origin). As in *La Grande Illusion*, Renoir inserts a character of Jewish descent into a micro-society that is quite capable of activating exclusionary mechanisms. In *La Règle du jeu*, however, the character is not in an intermediate position, but at the top of the social scale by both his title and his wealth. As if to reinforce the intertextual relationship, Marcel Dalio plays both Rosenthal in *La Grande Illusion* and La Chesnaye in *La Règle du jeu*, and the latter is mentioned as related to the former. Although the character's Jewishness is less emphasized in the 1939 film, it is pointed out, interestingly, by one of the servants: "La Chesnaye's mother had a father named Rosenthal who came straight from Frankfurt." This is one of the instances in which the servants who toil at la Colinière exhibit as much class consciousness and snobbery as their masters.[29] As opposed to the micro-society depicted in *Le Crime de M. Lange*, there is no progressive or nurturing community in *La Règle du jeu*, nor is it the corrupt and oppressive character who is physically eliminated.

When faced with conflict, disagreement, or the necessity of making a painful choice, Robert constantly utters lenitive replies designed to temporize and to assuage his interlocutors: "Lisette, don't exaggerate." When he wants to leave Geneviève, his attempt to mollify her makes him sound as weak as Louis XVI in *La Marseillaise*:[30] "I'm sorry, my dear. I had no intention of distressing you; only put yourself in my shoes." He ineffectually seeks to appease his mistress in much the same way as his wife: "Lying! You're exaggerating . . . " As he pathetically tells Marceau, "I wouldn't like to hurt anyone, especially not women." Of course, through his indecisiveness and lack of resolve, he ends up hurting everyone. Robert's constant and useless appeasement, at a farcical level, recalls a more tragic pattern of appeasement on the part of French and British politicians.[31] In 1939, with Europe on the brink of another war, Renoir did not reiterate his previous calls for common understanding across national lines. La Chesnaye's unrealistic internationalism stands as a pale reflection of Rosenthal's in *La Grande Illusion*: "I'm opposed to borders or walls." He tells Octave this is why he'll invite his rival to la Colinière, despite André's obvious attraction to Christine: "They might as well see each other and reach an understanding." All conflicts, no matter what the context, can apparently be resolved through discussions or, in fact, through acquiescence—a widely shared and easily recognizable attitude, after Munich. Robert's love of openness can also reach a ridiculous level, as when he forbids his gamekeeper Schumacher from fencing off the rabbits that are damaging the grounds. This reduced form of internationalism, which refuses to recognize often conflicting practical realities, stands in somewhat pathetic contrast to Rosenthal's recognition of the artificiality of borders.

Many of Renoir's films offer their characters a means of escape, however imaginary or fantastic, from the harsh realities of contradictory social and political forces. As previously mentioned, in *Le Crime de M. Lange*, the two lovers seek a new beginning in a neighboring country (one of the few that has not succumbed to fascism). In *Les Bas-Fonds*, there is at least some hope on the open road. In *Boudu sauvé des eaux*, the title character similarly finds symbolic refuge from confining societal strictures in the openness of a pastoral, if unromanticized, setting. At a somewhat more shallow and superficial level, art transcends jealousy and ambition in *French Cancan*, just as love provides an apparent antidote to greed and the lust for power in *Eléna et les hommes*.[32] While the representatives of an outdated aristocratic social order come to accept the inevitability of their demise in *La Grande Illusion*, their downfall allows the reconciliation and escape to freedom of the men who exemplify the dynamism of the working and bourgeois classes. The world of *La Règle du jeu*, however, is totally closed, with a determinism seemingly as inescapable as that of Gabin's doomed character in *La Bête humaine*. Those who do not conform to its norms have no means of escape. They are either reduced to conformity (Christine) or shot and killed (André). The film's mixture of tragedy, farce, and dark foreboding does not allow for the deliverance of any of the characters. Despite numerous instances of slapstick comedy, this is Renoir's bleakest film.

A Shooting War

The lengthy hunting—or, more accurately, shooting—scene, one of the most famous in *La Règle du jeu*, imparts a lingering sense of foreboding, given the film's historical context (by 1939, France was largely surrounded by fascist regimes in Italy, Germany, and Spain).[33] Whether or not Renoir intended it, the scene of the massacre of the small animals, who are inexorably led to the waiting, immobile shooters by a group of servants commanded by the gamekeeper, Schumacher, constitutes a troubling premonition.[34] While Marceau was content with small-scale poaching, Schumacher supervises industrial-scale slaughter. When he is shot by Schumacher, André Jurieux will crumple into the same position as a twitching, dying rabbit. It should be noted that even in this film made just before the war, distinctions are drawn between characters identified as Germanic; unlike most of the participants, Christine does not seem to enjoy the hunt. The uselessness, in practical terms, of the hunt is highlighted by the fact that the game was not shot for food; even the servants are uninterested in eating rabbit. La Chesnaye and his privileged guests are merely indulging in hunting as a fashionable aristocratic pastime—one which turns into illegal poaching when practiced by the impoverished Marceau. While all people on earth may "have their reasons," as Octave puts it, the reasons of this shooting party are particularly paltry.

Schumacher, the meticulous, orderly, and ultimately murderous gamekeeper, is from the eastern region of Alsace, where a German dialect is widely used and which was, along with part of the region of Lorraine, the motive for *la revanche* championed by Barrès. Schumacher's animus toward Marceau (who "poaches" on both his hunting and conjugal territory), quickly takes on national and warlike overtones. Abruptly announcing to his wife, "I'm taking you to Alsace," Schumacher tells her that "over there," shiftless troublemakers like Marceau are ruthlessly dealt with: "Poachers, scum, you know, guys like Marceau: we know how to take care of them. Just shoot them! At night, in the forest: that way, no more problems." Meanwhile, in a contrapuntal use of depth of field, Marceau is grotesquely quivering with fear in the background. Also, when he first catches Marceau poaching, Schumacher tells a bemused La Chesnaye that "during the war, I shot guys who weren't even as big troublemakers as him." Although it is not specified, the reference to "la guerre" can only be to the First World War. On which side would Schumacher, the Alsatian, have been fighting? In the context of 1939, the implication of a booted, rifle-bearing character, who has a German-sounding name, ruthlessly pursuing a hapless Frenchman (Marceau), is inescapable. Of course, the gamekeeper Schumacher will end up killing "le héros national," André Jurieux, while believing he is shooting at Octave.

Marceau and Schumacher each exhibit stereotypical traits of the country they respectively incarnate. With his facial tics and quaint slang, Marceau incarnates a comically theatrical form of Frenchness: charming and imaginative, but unreliable. He can ingratiate himself to La Chesnaye and Lisette, but he always attempts to disappear if there are complications. By contrast, Schumacher generally remains severe in tone and stiff in body language. Unlike the amusingly unpredictable Marceau, the stolid, disciplined Schumacher often arouses reactions of hostility. As Jean-Pierre Boon (343) pointed out, it is no doubt easier for spectators to identify with Marceau, the prey, than with Schumacher, the hunter (the parallel with the hunting scene is obvious). When Schumacher has resolved to shoot Octave, who is apparently courting his wife Lisette, he peremptorily tells a hesitant and frightened Marceau: "Now, we're in this together." The doubly mistaken Schumacher's target will in fact be André, as he runs toward Christine.[35] The embodiments of France and Germany, both upper- and lower-class, are thus locked together when the real shooting begins.

Andrew compared *La Règle du jeu* to Renoir's adaptation of Flaubert's *Madame Bovary*, describing André Jurieux as a romantic figure, as doomed and out of place as Emma Bovary: "In both films, spontaneity being impossible, the romantic is doomed to die, leaving the suffocating structure intact" (281). This portrait of André derives from his repeatedly mentioned status, by Octave and other characters, as a gallant if somewhat befuddled hero, a technologically updated embodiment of the tradition of chivalry. However, this modern-day knight turns out to be almost as useless and egotistical as his rival, La Chesnaye, who spends his time collecting mechanical toys. André's much-hailed exploit, his transatlantic flight in a retrospectively more sinister mechanical toy, achieved nothing of practical value. As André himself points out, his sole motivation was to impress Christine. Once the flight is over, he seems to have no more interest in aviation. At la Colinière, André, the *chevalier du ciel*, joins other self-styled, and similarly self-absorbed, modern-day knights: the General and the knights of industry (the La Bruyères).

In the opening scene of *La Règle du jeu*, the arriving solo aviator is compared by the radio reporter to Charles Lindbergh, whose 1927 solo flight across the Atlantic created the sort of enthusiastic pandemonium depicted in the film, upon his arrival at Le Bourget Airport. By 1939, however, Lindbergh was no longer simply an intrepid and somewhat innocent aviator. He had visited Nazi Germany, had praised the technical sophistication of the Luftwaffe, had received a medal from Hermann Goering, and was advocating American isolationism as a response to the threat of a new war in Europe. In retrospect, given the deadly role of aviation during the war, the character of André adds another element of foreboding to Renoir's film. The enthusiasm of the crowd that greets André at Le Bourget also recalls the arrival at the same airport, on September 30, 1938, of Prime Minister Edouard Daladier, who along with his British counterpart, Neville Chamberlain, had just capitulated to Hitler's ultimatum by signing the Munich accords. Desperately wanting to believe that the risk of another war had been averted, half a million people turned out to cheer Daladier, caught up in what Léon Blum had previously called "cowardly relief."[36] With the search for peace in Europe having been reduced to the appeasement of dictators, the term "grande illusion" had thus acquired a new meaning, one that Renoir was aware of when he wrote that he was "less proud of being French" (*Ecrits*, 178) after the abandonment of Czechoslovakia.

Conclusion

The thematic diversity of the Renoir corpus includes not just an isolated satire of technocratic European institutions (*Le Déjeuner sur l'herbe*) but also several films containing a favorable perception of cross-cultural points of contact that transcend, but do not negate, nation-based identity and solidarity. Renoir, it should be noted, never became a propagandist for a united Europe. However, many of his most important films are marked by an awareness of the inextricability of European interrelationships, not just at the traditional level of elites, but inclusive of a wide spectrum of citizens. The widespread prewar illusion of national self-sufficiency (often associated with a colonial empire) was thereby implicitly undermined. While Barrès could make Europe end at France's eastern border, Renoir, with some exceptions, does not present in his films a splendidly isolated French nation, inherently at odds with its permanently hostile neighbors. Although they may not always be free of tensions and conflicts, exchanges between Europeans, across national borders, are generally depicted as both inevitable and potentially beneficial. This relatively favorable European topos is all the more remarkable in the increasingly disastrous historical context of the 1930s, when Nazi Germany was preparing to carve out its own version of a "New Europe."

In spite of this context, *La Grande Illusion*, perhaps Renoir's best-known film, emphasizes the Franco-German relationship, generally portraying Germans in a sympathetic light, more as potential partners than as immutable adversaries. Through frequent references to other European countries, it outlines a limited form of transnationalism, one that takes into account nationalism as an established force but also gives a broader content to human self-definition. It is generally inclusive of minority groups such as Jews, who have often been excluded by more traditional forms of nationalism in Europe. However, it represents Great Britain as somehow more distant and separate than other European countries. A Europe that is mainly structured around the reconciliation of France and Germany and that allows a more limited form of participation for some of its members: it is difficult not to detect a parallel with the postwar process that led to the creation of the European Union.

The extremes in French attitudes toward Germany might be represented by Germaine de Staël's laudatory reevaluation of German literature on the one hand and Maurice Barrès's denunciation of inherent German barbarism on the other. Such attitudes partly reflect the level of nationalistic ideology as well as the shifting balance of power between the two countries during the nineteenth century. Renoir, while no theoretician of literary influence or nationalism,[37] generally portrayed Germans as he did other Europeans, with neither excessive sentimentality nor demonization. His films acknowledge the inescapably central place of Germany among France's potential European partners. In this sense, both Barrès and Renoir were right too early; just as Barrès's worst predictions about German behavior became all too true during the Nazi regime, Renoir's depictions of transnational interaction and exchanges at all social levels, with Germans as privileged interlocutors for the French, would become self-evident during the postwar years.

Renoir's work provides an important transition from the age of nationalism to a growing realization of interdependency and the need for practical cooperation between countries—a realization that would only yield results after the Second World War. By stressing the need for dialogue, without occluding real conflicts, some of his films (particularly *Toni* and *La Grande Illusion*) present a less romanticized view of Europe, with its promise as well as its contradictions, that is distinct from both Barrès's negation of the very idea of European commonality of interests and Hugo's utopian prophecy of European unity as the foundation for everlasting peace and progress. Through Renoir's work, the idea of Europe can be seen as becoming a less fanciful and more of a practical—and therefore less exalting—issue. After the slaughter and devastation of the Second World War, the obvious urgency of such a nonutopian, practical political project for Europe finally led to a partial degree of fruition. The work of Denis de Rougemont, one of the literary advocates and participants in this project, will be discussed in the next chapter.

CHAPTER 6

Institutionalizing the Dream

Denis de Rougemont

The truth is that the spirit of conflict and conquest is at the origin and in the center of Western nationalism; its basis is not social cooperation.

Rabindranath Tagore, *Nationalism*

Even though he wrote thirty-eight books and countless articles,[1] Denis de Rougemont (1906–1985) is remembered almost exclusively as the author of *L'Amour et l'Occident* (Love in the Western World), which, although initially published in 1939, did not receive its "definitive" edition until 1972. The lasting success and influence of that book has tended to obscure the rest of Rougemont's work as a literary critic, as well as his role in the Personalist movement, in the creation of the journal *Esprit*, and, in particular, as a cultural activist and literary proponent of European federalism based on a continuous dialectic of cultural unity and diversity. A Swiss Protestant Francophone writer, Rougemont left Switzerland and moved to Paris in 1930, where he quickly became associated with the Personalist movement, whose members were trying, during a period of extreme political polarization, to find a middle ground between what they saw as the twin perils of aimless bourgeois culture and rigid Marxist ideology, between capitalistic self-centeredness and Soviet collectivism, as expressed in the movement's credo: "Neither individualists, nor collectivists, we are personalists." Rougemont's lifelong insistence on the value and the importance of "la personne humaine" was forged during a period that saw the triumph of mass societies in which the impending dissolution of personality or individualism was announced, if not heralded, by intellectuals from both the left and the right.

From Personalism to European Federalism

As a non-Marxist intellectual confronted with rising ideological extremism, Rougemont found in the largely unstructured Personalist movement an appropriate combination of the values of personal freedom and responsibility to one's community. As Bruno Ackermann (499) noted in his biography, Rougemont's 1936 book, paradoxically—and typically—entitled *Penser avec les mains* (Thinking with One's Hands), reads as a sharp rejoinder to Julien Benda's advocacy of disinterested contemplation and analysis in his famous polemical work, *La Trahison des clercs* (The Treason of the Intellectuals, 1927).[2] Rougemont opposes *la personne* (free, responsible, and fully engaged) and *l'individu* (isolated, atomistic, and passive). Skirting the dual risk of being co-opted by communism or fascism, Rougemont's reiterated metaphor of "manual thought" was a means for this very pragmatic intellectual to go beyond abstract principles and categories, to stake a claim for the practical value of intellectual work: "The only real form of action involves *thinking*, and my turn of phrase implies the primacy of thought in all action, no less than the necessity of that action through thought" (154).[3] Rougemont used his metaphor as a reminder that issues of freedom and responsibility are played out through concrete actions that call for authentic *engagement*, a term that Jean-Paul Sartre would later quietly appropriate and loudly overuse.[4] An echo of "thinking with one's hands" is found in a later historical text on European cultural unity: "We will only find Europe by making it . . . The real way to define it is to build it" (*Vingt-huit siècles d'Europe*, *EE*, 1: 487–88).

Rougemont was in 1932 one of the founders of the journal *Esprit*, bringing his Protestant outlook to the Personalist movement, in which participated several Catholic intellectuals, most notably Emmanuel Mounier. Rougemont remained deeply concerned with religious issues throughout his life: "Christian, or rather Protestant, morality is thus central to Rougemont's concerns" (Ackermann 186). Many of the articles Rougemont published in *Esprit*, as well as in another Personalist journal, *L'Ordre Nouveau*, were collected in one of his first major works, *Politique de la Personne* (1934). The author's call for "active pessimism," for ethical activism during—and in spite of—desperate times, reflects his growing concern over the rise of totalitarianism during the 1930s. A Swiss national, Rougemont was not forced into exile, like many French intellectuals, during the Occupation. It was his own government that sent him to the United States, ostensibly to give a series of lectures, after one of his articles had been judged too critical of Hitler and therefore incompatible with Swiss neutrality. During his lengthy stay in America, he established links with several exiled French writers, such as Antoine de Saint-Exupéry, Alexis Léger, and André Breton.[5] Among other activities, Rougemont wrote some of the texts read by Breton for "La Voix de l'Amérique parle aux Français," an Office of War Information radio series that was broadcast to occupied France.[6] He also wrote one of his best—but least-known—books, *La Part du Diable* (The Devil's Share, which will be discussed later), while he was living in the United States. He would later claim that his undifferentiated status as an exiled "European" intellectual helped to crystallize his thinking about the reality of a European identity, and therefore of the need for European federalism: "It is in the United States that I discovered the European continent. Since I was repeatedly considered as a European by people who had no more concern for my country than for the *canton* where I was born, in the eyes of Americans I saw Europe as a real unit,[7] and I intuited that upon this unit could be founded a union" (*La Suisse ou l'histoire d'un peuple heureux*, 9).

In 1946, Rougemont returned to Europe, after six years of what he considered forced exile, spent mainly in the United States. Ever conscious of symbolism, he chose to live in the French town (near the Swiss border) where Voltaire had spent his later years, now renamed Ferney-Voltaire. Like many intellectuals returning from abroad after the end of the war, he was appalled by the devastation he saw, and he sought to participate in the reconstruction and reorganization of what had become a diminished Europe, divided between the two superpowers. During the postwar period, Rougemont became one of the best-known and most active advocates of European federalism. His evolution from Personalism to European federalism was the topic of a colloquium organized in Geneva three years after his death.[8] For his part, Rougemont consistently sought to portray that evolution in terms of continuity, even as the focus of his work shifted from literary and philosophical concerns to the political and administrative spheres: "There is, to use philosophical terminology, an essential homology between Personalist philosophy and federalist politics" (*Inédits*, 114).

Personalism and *Esprit* have received much belated critical attention, some of it revisionist in nature. The best-known studies of the movement and the journal, respectively by Jean-Louis Loubet del Bayle and by Michel Winock, provide a very different picture than do the books by John Hellman, Bernard-Henri Lévy, and Zeev Sternhell (*Ni droite ni gauche*).[9] While the broader controversy over whether at least some members of the Personalist movement were tempted by, or somehow associated with, fascism during the 1930s is not the main focus of this chapter, given that Rougemont's European federalism can be directly linked to his longstanding affiliation with Personalism, his attitude toward "la tentation fasciste" before the Second World War needs to be briefly addressed here. Rougemont, who was fluent in German, described his impressions after his yearlong stay in Nazi Germany in his 1938 *Journal d'Allemagne*.[10] In this as in all of Rougemont's texts, it is impossible for any honest reader to find anything remotely similar to the customary components of fascist discourse. In particular, the anti-intellectualism, the willing surrender of individual thought and behavior to mass sentiment fueled by a charismatic leader, is simply antithetical to anything found throughout Rougemont's writings, both literary and political—which, as Pierre Verdaguer (263) and Fabrizio Frigerio (121) both point out, are remarkably consistent in this regard. The best illustration of why it is inherently nonsensical to attempt to link Rougemont to fascism is found in Eugène Ionesco's preface to his 1959 play, *Rhinocéros*. Ionesco refers specifically to Rougemont's description of a Nazi party gathering in 1936, citing the case in point of his decisive rejection of the collective fascination and delirium that surrounded him as what inspired the similar reaction of the character Bérenger in the play.

After his return from the United States, Rougemont became one of the leading activists in the European federalist movement that emerged, or rather reemerged, after the Second World War. Painstakingly conceived during the interwar years (notably in Richard Coudenhove-Kalergi's work), the practical project of European federalism was rearticulated and promoted by intellectuals from several countries, some of whom had met during the years of Occupation, while in exile in Great Britain or the United States. Rougemont participated in several postwar conferences on European unification: *le Congrès de l'Union Européenne des Fédéralistes* (Montreux, 1947) and *la Conférence Européenne de la Culture* (Lausanne, 1949).[11] In particular, he was deeply involved in the organization of the Congress of the European Unity Movement, which was held in The Hague in May 1948 and provided part of the impetus for the establishment of the Council of Europe the following year.[12] While this institution (which is still in existence and is based in Strasbourg) largely failed to fulfill its promise, the very fact of its creation, so soon after the war, did in turn help to set the stage for the 1950 Schuman Declaration, which constitutes the starting point of the current European institutional framework. Since outright federalists such as Rougemont have been few in number and relatively little known, the extent of their influence remains unclear. Tony Judt dismissed idealists of his ilk as having had "no discernible real-world impact" (*A Grand Illusion*, 4). Eric Roussel (706) mentioned close links between Rougemont and Jean Monnet, but the limited institutions that evolved under Monnet's aegis fell far short of federalist goals.

Rougemont was also a participant in the creation of several European cultural and scientific organizations: *l'Association Européenne des Festivals de Musique* in 1951, *l'Agence de Presses Européennes Associées* in 1952, and *le Conseil Européen pour la Recherche Nucléaire*, or CERN, in 1954. Most notably, there was *le Centre Européen de la Culture*, based in Geneva, which he directed from its founding in 1950 until his death and where he attracted over time a small cult following, not unlike Sartre's role in Paris.[13] Obviously, the recurring terms in the names of these conferences and organizations—Europe, Federalism, and Culture—bear the stamp of Rougemont's concerns and influence. As he put it in an article entitled, appropriately enough, "Fédéralisme culturel": "It seems to me that in Europe, the federalist cause is linked to the cause of culture" (*EE*, 2: 152).[14] One of the ways in which Rougemont's thought and activities evolved is reflected by his growing commitment to environmentalism,[15] which eventually put him in the ironic position of expressing concern regarding the work of an institution that he had once championed and that provided an example of a joint European research project. Although he had participated in the creation of the CERN, which he felt would allow for European cooperation over the peaceful use of atomic energy, he came to fear the environmental impact of a technology that, even in its least warlike form, still constituted a potential menace.[16]

In addition to, or rather in association with his activism, most of Rougemont's written output after the war revolves around the idea, and therefore the goal, of Europe. There are enough articles, speeches, and interviews on this topic to fill up two thick volumes (*Ecrits sur l'Europe*). Some of these texts are closer to programmatic political science treatises that lay out the foundations of European federalism and that often depict the Swiss federation as a model. Many are hortatory speeches, calling for citizens of established nation-states to participate in the process of elaboration of a European federation.[17] Others are more literary in nature, with the multilingual Rougemont displaying his impressive grasp of European literary history. In this category, most notably, Rougemont was one of the first writers to attempt a comprehensive literary history of the idea of Europe. In *Vingt-huit siècles d'Europe* (*EE*, 1: 485–777), which was published in 1961, he discusses, for instance, Madame de Staël and her cosmopolitan "esprit européen;"[18] Victor Hugo and his much-derided call for "les Etats-Unis d'Europe;" Alexis Léger, better known as Saint-John Perse, who wrote Aristide Briand's 1930 memorandum on an "union fédérale européenne;" and Paul Valéry, who in "La Crise de l'esprit" famously referred to Europe as "a sort of promontory of the old continent, a western appendage of Asia."[19] In general, Rougemont tended to inscribe the authors and texts he investigated within a teleological framework, in an attempt to ascertain to what extent each one had announced or refuted the idea (or his idea) of European unification. Literary history thus became a window and a mirror for this erudite activist, who sought to construct Europe, or to reveal its underlying existence, in large part by establishing European studies as a valid literary field. Unlike previous authors (Voltaire and Staël) who had presented and embellished foreign cultures as an indirect means of criticizing their own society, Rougemont used an inexistent social and cultural model whose future outline he perceived within the diversity of the Europe of his time.

Geopolitical Imperatives

It is of course no coincidence that the first practical steps toward a European union began with the stark geopolitical decline that followed the end of the Second World War, a decline marked by the east-west division of Europe, the dismantling of its colonial empires, and the loss of political and economic centrality. Long before Dipesh Chakrabarty sought to relativize or "provincialize" European cultural norms, it was clear that the "Age of Europe" had come to an end. As Raymond Aron would sum it up: "The period of European domination is over" (189). With the exception of Great Britain, postwar intellectuals throughout the continent were faced with the lingering evidence of defeat, occupation, and decline. Modern ideologies born in several countries of Europe—nationalism, fascism, Nazism, and communism—had to varying degrees contributed to the worst period of slaughter in history, far surpassing the death toll of the First World War. After Auschwitz, there could also be no doubt that Europe had sunk to a new moral nadir. Like James Joyce's character Stephen Dedalus, an entire continent was trying to awaken from the nightmare of its recent history, from what Enzo Traverso appropriately analyzed as a European civil war.[20] For federalist intellectuals like Rougemont, it was clear that the system of nation-states, inherently unstable and conflict-ridden, had contributed to the nightmare. A new Europe had to be built, one that could transcend nationalistic hatreds and avoid reproducing the inherently bellicose centralized state apparatus. With unchecked European states always ready to resort to war, lasting peace, as Rougemont would stress for the rest of his life, could not be produced through merely a new continental balance of power. It could only result from the establishment of a European federation. In almost every postwar European country, it had thus become possible to paraphrase José Ortega y Gasset's famous pronouncement that Spain was the problem and Europe the solution.[21]

During the cold war, many western Europeans thought of their smaller countries as precariously situated between the two rival superpowers, threatened by military domination on one side and by cultural asphyxiation on the other. The challenge for the would-be European pawns was to chart an independent course between this modern form of Charybdis and Scylla, by preserving an autonomous political and cultural sphere in Western Europe. Throughout his post-World War II texts, Rougemont projected the recurring image of a weakened Europe caught between two larger powers, the United States and the Soviet Union: "physically squeezed between two great empires whose immense shadows struggle above [Europe], reduced and ruined at its borders, morally closed within itself" (*L'Europe en jeu, EE*, 1: 19). European disunity and weakness left a vacuum that would inevitably be filled by one of the superpowers: "The lack of European unity leaves the Atlantic alliance unbalanced and carries the risk of relegating half the world to American hegemony" (*L'Aventure occidentale de l'homme*, 116). Rougemont was keenly aware of the fact that whatever actual progress was made toward European unity had in large part resulted from the weakened postwar state of a previously dominant continent that, as he put it, "felt menaced" (244).

Rougemont was not alone in stressing this image of a divided Europe surrounded by vast empires, an image designed to increase support for an independent European federation. Régis Debray, for instance, would later take up that image in *Les Empires contre l'Europe* (1985), coincidentally published the year of Rougemont's death: "For European societies, American power is *internally* pervasive; while Soviet power, even though it is based in our continent, is *externally* pervasive, including in the part of Europe that it has subjugated" (113). Charles de Gaulle's famous invocation of an autonomous Europe "de l'Atlantique à l'Oural"—at a time when the continent was in fact sharply divided—also reflected this fear of effective elimination through absorption, gradual or otherwise, into one or the other of the global spheres of influence. Interestingly, the image of Europe caught between external powers was not a uniquely postwar phenomenon. As was discussed in Chapter 3, one of the authors—and prophets of a united Europe—examined by Rougemont in *Vingt-huit siècles d'Europe*, Victor Hugo, also presented the European cultural sphere in the seventeenth and nineteenth centuries as besieged from the east and the west by what he considered to be two great external empires.

Rougemont, for his part, instead of portraying the empires of his day, the United States and the Soviet Union, as military or political threats, tended to situate them as extremes on a cultural continuum, neither of which provided a model for a future federated Europe. Using terminology that carried Orwellian overtones, he described them as constituting only partial, imperfect outgrowths of Europe itself: "The rhythms of history are today set by two antagonistic powers that nevertheless already resemble each other: Euramerica and Eurasia" (*L'Aventure occidentale de l'homme*, 254). As early as *La Part du Diable* (187), Rougemont made reference to federalism as the only means of avoiding what he saw as the unacceptable alternatives of American-style isolation and Soviet-style mass societies. Coming from an intellectual with a liberal and religious background, a strong critique of Marxism and especially of postwar Stalinism is not surprising. What is surprising—and amusing—is the way in which Rougemont criticizes the materialism he found in the United States, thereby sounding more like a traditional French Catholic than like a Swiss Protestant: "The morality of success, which has been the true American morality for a century, has always seemed diabolical to me. Its superficial manifestations are deceptively attractive: optimism and cordiality, self-confidence, a firm handshake, and a big, friendly smile that reveals shining teeth!" (*La Part du Diable*, 126).[22]

Through his postwar characterization of the United States as one of the great empires that was external to Europe, Rougemont was not indulging in gratuitous anti-Americanism. Like most discerning intellectuals of his time (the most notable of whom was Raymond Aron), Rougemont was fully aware that the United States had indirectly facilitated the emergence of European institutions, both economically (the Marshall plan) and militarily (the NATO alliance). And he certainly envisioned a united Europe that would share common values and would be an equal partner with its American cousin. But it was clear to Rougemont, who was naturally drawn to the values of liberal democracy represented by the United States (and who was denounced on the left as an apologist for American capitalism and imperialism), that Europe would in many ways remain different from the American societal model. Just as the United States had initially developed a sense of national identity by distinguishing itself from Europe, a European federation would necessarily define itself by its level of divergence, no matter how small, from the established American standard.

Europe as a Practical Project

In addition to his critiques of hegemonic superpowers, Rougemont insisted on the positive aspects of his European federal model. One of the most appealing features of European federalism has always been the promise of taming the exclusionary tendencies that lead to racism and warfare. Comprising several ethnic, religious and cultural groups, a federated Europe should thus be, if not immune to the temptations of internecine rivalries, at least more capable of managing or resolving them through peaceful means. Similarly, a culturally diverse Europe should be less inclined than a more homogeneous nation-state to resort to oppressing or excluding minority groups in order to establish an "identity" for its majority, an issue that has become all the more crucial since the level of ethnic and religious diversity within the European Union was increased by the arrival of immigrants from Turkey, North Africa, and sub-Saharan Africa. While Europe has amply displayed its capacity for intolerance and racism, it also has a tradition of cultural syncretism. In an insightful analysis, Rémi Brague finds cultural "secondarité" to be one of Europe's defining features, with Rome and Christianity each acknowledging their respective debt to Greece and Judaism, and thereby establishing a historical pattern of cultural borrowing and reformulating for Europe as a whole.

To his own question, "So who is European?" (1007), Valéry replied with one of the many definitions that have so far been offered, his own being based on the Roman Empire, Christianity, and, perhaps less predictably, Greek geometry. Needless to say, this particular definition has yet to gain wider acceptance than any other. While Rougemont did often link his vision of Europe to the classic sources of Greece and Rome, his attempts at a definition of a European identity—"A cultural creation if there ever was one" ("L'Europe comme invention de la culture," *EE*, 2: 699)—were usually so broad that they would be useless to any form of exclusionary nationalism: "Valéry considered as European every population that in the course of its history was decisively influenced by the Roman Empire, Greek philosophy, and Christianity. A famous definition, which leaves out the Celtic, Germanic, Arabic, Slavic, and Oriental contributions, but which would especially lead us to forget that Athens, Rome, and Jerusalem left us at least as many elements of discordance as of harmony" (*Lettre ouverte aux Européens*, *EE*, 2: 269). Neither was he particularly preoccupied with the issue of geographical limits or borders. Rougemont's Europe would be a federation of regions, with nation-states remaining, but not dominating, within what he called a "plurality of allegiances" for Europeans. An updated form of eighteenth-century cosmopolitanism, Rougemont's plurality of allegiances is best expressed in the description he gives of himself in his 1970 book, *Lettre ouverte aux Européens*:

In terms of birth, tradition, and accent, I am from Neuchâtel. It is therefore toward this canton (which was for centuries a sovereign principality) that I feel a patriotic allegiance. Neuchâtel is a part of the Swiss federation: my passport and my sense of national allegiance are thus Swiss. I am also a French writer: Francophone Europe, which means three-fourths of France, as well as parts of Belgium, Italy, and Switzerland, provides my sense of cultural allegiance. But I am also Protestant, which represents a worldwide sense of allegiance (it would obviously be the same if I were Communist or Catholic). And I belong to several social networks—family, professional, intellectual, spiritual, or emotional—*which share no common borders*, and generally have no borders whatsoever. (*EE*, 2: 340)

Rougemont advocated a bottom-up approach to European federalism, from the person to the region to the federation, with cities and regions freely establishing cross-border ties: "The regions will gradually set up a diversified network of exchanges" ("L'Europe des régions," *EE*, 2: 187). In one of his first programmatic texts of the postwar period, he insisted on this process of elaboration for his vision of a European federation: "A federation is created by neighbors, through people and organizations, and not starting from a center or through governments" (*L'Europe en jeu*, *EE*, 1: 37). In this perspective, a united Europe would not be a superstate, or a larger version of existing nation-states, but a new form of association and government: "We must transcend the nation-state, by establishing the Regions below and the Federation above it" (*L'Un et le divers*, *EE*, 2: 249). Rougemont was, however, increasingly disappointed with the top-down methodology that has been used since 1950 by nation-states in order to forge largely unelected supranational institutions. In his often repeated view, instead of a European federation evolving as a natural outgrowth of a multiplicity of cultural links, the existing European institutions merely came to constitute a new level of statist bureaucracies, reproducing the centralized pattern of laws and directives flowing from the government to the masses. Rougemont often expressed his dismay at the slow pace of progress toward his vision of European federalism, largely faulting established nation-states for having systematically resisted attempts at creating a true European federation: "I think this is a sufficient explanation for the fact that we have not moved an inch toward a political union" (*Inédits*, 101).[23] There is no doubt that his version of federalism, which was inspired by the Swiss model, derived from a "sustained intellectual critique of the concept of the nation-state" (Loyer 413).

Although he lived through a period that saw the triumph of ultranationalism, Rougemont adopted a daring rhetorical strategy, counterintuitively opposing what he called *l'Europe des réalités*, built around regions and a European federation, to what he saw as increasingly outdated national myths. Even though Europe was bitterly divided, following the worst war in history, Rougemont calmly presented the paradox that European culture (what he referred to as "a non-unitary unity") was the actual, underlying reality, while established individual national cultures ("the so-called national cultures") constituted so many myths: "There is no French painting or German chemistry, just as there is no Soviet mathematics" (*Lettre ouverte aux Européens*, 1970). Similarly, intra-European warfare was less the result of rivalries between differentiated nation-states and more of a civil war. Whether his Europe could itself in turn constitute a supranational myth was an issue he did not directly address. While Rougemont often seems to adumbrate the now-familiar postmodern critique of nationalist "Grand Narratives," his European federation, built successively around groups of persons and regions, is an even more elaborate discursive construct.

During his stay in the United States, Rougemont presented a similar form of logic in *La Part du Diable*, a curious and fascinating book based on the paradox that the author calls the reality of the myth: "The devil is a myth; therefore he exists and is ceaselessly active" (27). This book begins with a quote from Baudelaire's *Petits Poèmes en prose*: "The Devil is so cunning that he has convinced us he doesn't exist" (21). Rougemont's penchant for paradox is reflected at a stylistic level, through his repeated references to an unresolved "dialectic with two factors" (*L'Aventure occidentale de l'homme*, 84), to oppositions that are productive when maintained, not combined into a integrated whole: "They cannot be transcended by reducing one of their factors, and they are immune to theoretical mediation; it is precisely through their tension that they must be experienced" (231). Instead of a fully resolved Hegelian dialectic (concluding in synthesis), Rougemont tended to find durable sets of Kantian oppositions fruitful (such as unity versus diversity), often pointing out that his vision of a European federation would not seek to reduce the level of cultural diversity within the continent. Based on religious inspiration ("*real man* and *real God*," 85), Rougemont exhibited a penchant for turning the logic of contradictory terms ("*la liberté* et *l'engagement*," 86) into complementary terms: "Federalist theory has developed as a response to the dual challenge of individualistic (or nationalistic) anarchy and of totalitarian reaction: the goal being to seek an *optimum* between two contradictory maxima" (90). Just as he found that in the Swiss constitution, "the union is real and so is [local] autonomy" (*La Suisse ou l'histoire d'un peuple heureux*, 97), he discerned preestablished complementarities between national particularisms and federalist interconnections. Instead of some supranational melting pot, a European federation would be the means by which to preserve and enhance "Europe as the homeland of diversity" (*Inédits*, 60). Not only was Europe, therefore, greater than the sum of its parts, it was also more real than the apparently random conglomeration of nation-states that had never ceased feuding:

> The idea that there would somehow be within Europe a certain number of national cultures, quite distinct and autonomous, whose sum would make up European culture, is simply a grade-school-level optical illusion. It disappears, as sunshine dissipates mist, in the light of historical study. European culture is not

and has never been the sum of national cultures. It is the achievement of all the Europeans who thought and created over three thousand years, independently from the nation-states that today divide up Europe. Most of these nation-states (including some of the most important) have existed for only a century: it must at least be conceded that culture had developed before them! (*La Suisse*, 196)

With this insistence on a less visible but more harmonious form of reality, we are not far from Rougemont's religious frame of reference, discreetly but repeatedly stated, and particularly to his ecumenical version of Protestantism as an inspiration.[24] Just as he had presented European authors and texts within a teleological framework, the European federation he advocated, although it was never presented in naïvely utopian terms, was part of a broader teleology, one that in many ways echoed Hugo's vision of *les Etats-Unis d'Europe*: "A European federation can only be a steppingstone for a worldwide federation. There can only be peace, and therefore a livable future, through the task of establishing a truly worldwide government" (*L'Europe en jeu*, *EE*, 1: 28). While never pompous or boring, some of his texts took on the tonality of prophecy (ironically reminiscent of the Marxist prediction that the state would wither away), and some of his analyses included performative statements, becoming rhetorical acts of creation or foundation: "The nation-state will thus disappear of its own accord, at the end of the regionalization process. It will have become obsolete" ("L'Europe des régions," *EE*, 2: 187). Rougemont's repeated references to Europe as a common culture and civilization could often be somewhat tautological; Europe should be a united, or rather federated, civilization because it has a common form of civilization, which is, in turn, based on the diversity of its cultures. In an article entitled "Vingt Langues, une littérature," he returns to his concept of unity within diversity: "Europe is a union of cultures, which was constituted through the combined influences of several civilizations (the Middle East, Greece, Christianity, the Celts, the Germans, the Arabs and the Slavs), and which, in the course of history, became at once integrated and diversified" (*EE*, 2: 174).

Persistent Challenges

Having presented Rougemont's paradoxical strategy of the "reality of the myth," it might now be useful to insert a little cynicism and to point out the disquieting or unpleasant fact that, outside of literature, Europe has never existed. As the 2005 popular votes in France and the Netherlands (as well as in Ireland in 2008) against the proposed European Constitution remind us, the slow process of elaboration of supranational institutions remains widely perceived as an artificial construct, superimposed on existing national traditions. The Europe that Rougemont so ardently advocated has so far only achieved partial reality, certainly not to the extent of the federation he envisioned. As Ferdinand Kinsky put it, in a laconic and sobering assessment shortly after Rougemont's death: "The federalist utopia has not come into being" (66). But then, Rougemont's literary construction of Europe is as much a creative projection into the future as it is a retrospective examination of perceived cultural commonalities. Benedict Anderson's analytical framework, with its emphasis on the cultural dimension of nationalistic development, is consistent with Rougemont's version of the ascent of modern nationalism, which he presents as an artificial and largely malevolent invention: "The division of culture was the result of compulsory schooling and of newspapers. Nationalism was manufactured during the nineteenth century" (*Le Cheminement des esprits*, 75).[25] The question is whether a European identity and a European federation can be built through a process of creative imagination, rather than by selective remembering.

It is difficult to discuss the concept of Europe without stumbling into the collective myth that many authors articulated even as Europeans conquered and colonized much of the world, a myth that can roughly be summarized as follows: based on an ancient spiritual heritage composed of Judeo-Christian values and Greco-Roman culture, Europeans gradually achieved a scientifically advanced, morally superior form of civilization, characterized by humanistic, rational thought and by liberal, democratic political systems. As in the case of most myths, that of the inherent superiority of Europe (or of *l'Occident*, when necessary, with the United States cast as a super-Europe) started from established facts at a certain historical period—the military conquest, by European countries, of much of the rest of the world—and proceeded toward a retroactive series of justifications in the form of rationally based explanations, whether they be sociocultural, racial, or religious, of why these conquests were both unavoidable and historically legitimate. As V.Y. Mudimbe put it: "It is, in any case, troubling to note that since the fifteenth century the will to truth in Europe seems to espouse perfectly a will to power" (212). Well-known critiques or deconstructions of various versions of the Eurocentric myth have since been developed by numerous authors. Rougemont's European activism, meanwhile, roughly coincided with the period of decolonization and loss of geopolitical supremacy for European powers. His responses to the aftermath of the colonial period remain ambiguous, and they include some disturbing references to the lands that Europe "discovered" and to the colonized peoples that it "civilized." By seeking the underlying reality of a common European culture that transcends national divisions, Rougemont sometimes succumbed to the temptation of defining a European essence. While never crudely reverting to Kipling's dichotomy, Rougemont does tend to essentialize his oppositions between East and West.[26]

Rougemont's vision of federalism had its blind spots. In "L'Attitude fédéraliste," a speech given at the 1947 Montreux conference, he seemed to posit that the issue of ethnic, linguistic, or religious difference would somehow be settled simply through the transition from the nation-state to the federalist paradigm:

"Federalism knows no minority problems" (*L'Europe en jeu*, *EE*, 1: 36). He added that neither did totalitarianism, but that was because it simply suppressed or eliminated minorities.[27] For him, the very concept of minorities was linked to the centralized system of power established within the nation-state, a system that would not apply to a decentralized European federation, where difference, having become the norm, would presumably be reconciled with unity. However, large and small federal constitutional systems already exist in various forms throughout the world. Countries as diverse as Canada, Germany, and Switzerland share common constitutional principles but also diverge widely in terms of their forms of organization. Belgium, a very small country, has adopted a uniquely complex federal system. None has truly reached the point where the issues of minority rights have simply ceased to be a public policy consideration. All continue to grapple with the question of difference that minorities still represent. Even within small, decentralized, largely self-governing political entities, the fear of the "Other" still materializes, and the risk of tribalism does not disappear within a broad federation.

Conclusion

Once he had become an activist for European federalism, Rougemont remained consistent until the end of his life. He relentlessly attacked the prevailing system of competing nation-states, with its legacy of increasingly chauvinistic ideologies and wars. He criticized many of the European institutions that were eventually created, not only because he found them too limited in scope or based on narrow considerations of economic efficiency, but especially because they were unelected, technocratic structures that lacked democratic legitimacy and that had been superimposed on existing nation-states through largely secret negotiations. He often pointed out that the multilingual Swiss Federation, which he tended to present as a blueprint for the rest of Europe, had been created within a matter of months, not years or decades, and that its eventual emergence had met with a similar level of skepticism: "More of an idea than a reality, Switzerland was then [before the 1848 Constitution] fairly comparable to our Europe of the twentieth century" (*La Suisse*, 89). Most saliently, he constantly insisted that a European federation was not an artificial concept, but a natural outgrowth of cultural and especially literary commonalities (see for instance "De l'unité de culture à l'union politique," *EE*, 1: 285–89). The Europe he projected into the future was largely based on his perception of a shared and lengthy literary history.

Perhaps not surprisingly, there is a self-fulfilling characteristic to Rougemont's literary construction of Europe. It has many of the attributes of traditional forms of fiction: internal coherence, founding and/or heroic characters, conflict, tribulation, and eventual resolution. And since Europe has been elaborated through literary means, through texts and the links they establish and are based upon, the authors of the texts are in turn retrospectively identified as Europeans, a designation that is for Rougemont, once again, more real than their national affiliation. Trying to define Europe thus became an illustration of the hermeneutic circle. The analysis of textual Europe in turn became a foundational act in Rougemont's extended body of work, which in this sense makes him the closest successor to Hugo's European vision. Whether they are naïve or a tribute to the power of literature, the conceptions of Europe presented by Rougemont are still both influential and controversial. In an involuntary tribute to his contribution to the creation of Europe as a literary artifact, the postwar institutions that evolved through a gradualist—and pointedly nonfederalist—approach have been named through a consistent use of euphemisms (community, union) in order to avoid such terms as "Federation" or "United States." For Rougemont, a literary critic, Europe became his only fictional creation, which was (in keeping with the pattern he established in *La Part du diable*) therefore all the more real and effective.

Afterword

Let us imagine an American Union (AU) encompassing nearly every country of North and South America, a Union whose underlying goal, unlike the current Organization of American States, would be the establishment of a supranational federation. The nominal capital of the AU might be Panama City, but its institutions would be decentralized. For instance, its parliament might meet in Brasilia, while its central bank would be headquartered in New York. The multilingual AU would seek to promote cross-cultural competency as a means of forging an ever closer political union. New transnational regional entities would evolve (Baja and Southern California, for example, or British Columbia and Washington state) and seek influence and representation directly at the AU level. Meanwhile, elected officials at the national level would find the scope of their authority progressively reduced as a result of the development of both supranational and regional institutions. Periodic bouts of resistance from movements defending traditional forms of national sovereignty might impede the process of transnational integration and lead to temporary agreements that would paper over unresolved issues. Higher levels of opposition to the ever increasing scope of AU activities would likely come from prosperous countries with a long established sense of national identity (in particular, from the United States, whose inhabitants might have mixed feelings as to the new content of their status as "Americans"). However, the trend toward closer union would gradually acquire a dynamic of its own, backed by growing institutions and by support from a wide range of artists and intellectuals. And of course, books similar to this one would be written, with the aim of exploring the literary origins of the invention of America.

From Fiction to a Degree of Reality

The purpose of this book has been to argue that Europe is best understood as a literary invention and that the ongoing movement toward European unity, which has come to be institutionalized in the European Union (EU), cannot be understood without reference to the literary works that helped bring it about. There is no doubt that Europe continues to inspire novels (Alain Lacroix's

Constellation) as well as films (Cédric Klapisch's *L'Auberge espagnole*, 2002). Meanwhile, Michel Blain has attempted to systematize twelve "foundation myths" that are apparently shared across the continent. More broadly, however, the creation and development of durable European institutions after the Second World War, at first limited to a small group of countries, has changed the terms of the European literary topos and has led to a flurry of publications—almost a separate genre—that seek to explain the conditions in which these institutions were created, how they are likely to evolve, what their impact will be in social and cultural terms, and to what extent their development has been accompanied by the emergence of a shared European identity.[1] European unity having been partly accomplished, its concept is no longer perpetually beyond the historical horizon. The partial reality has eliminated some of the more fanciful predictions, positive or negative, about what would result from the creation of multinational institutions in Europe. Unlike the numerous grand schemes for a *République européenne* that periodically surfaced and failed in the course of previous centuries, the current process of European integration has progressed slowly and fitfully through a series of limited but cumulative stages. Through this process, European unification or federalism has ceased to be an often derisive synonym for some kind of new Golden Age. It has moved from the comprehensive, if often unrealistic, visions of individual writers to the practical and circumscribed domain of public opinion. This move from dream to partial reality has been reflected in the type of literature that deals with Europe, a literature that for the most part no longer bears the imprint of utopianism.

As outlined in Chapter 6, the first effective steps toward some form of political union coincided with the stark geopolitical decline of the once dominant European centers of power. If there is such a thing as "Western Civilization," Europe is no longer its political, economic, or even cultural center. The current drive toward a European union is notable for its limited ambitions—indeed, that is part of its appeal. The twentieth century has amply demonstrated that utopian dreams of transforming the world can lead to historical nightmares. With the collapse of communism, the last major secularized chiliastic ideology, the utopian goal of an ideal society, which for so long had been one of the characteristic elements of European politics and literature, has dissipated, having largely been inverted into dystopia. These are dreams now shared only by religious fundamentalists. Instead of the "last utopia" (as Dominique Wolton put it), Europe thus represents the first postutopian project, most of whose advocates carefully eschew soaring Hugolian rhetoric. As opposed to the strong emotional mystique of traditional patriotism, no one is willing to die for Europe, nor is there any European equivalent to such a transformational concept as the creation of a "new Soviet man." In its postwar institutional application, the concept of a united Europe has not—to put it mildly—given rise to a widespread new form of idealism. It remains a painstakingly lengthy and arduous process that has not been accompanied by movements of mass enthusiasm. The day-to-day process of European integration over the past half-century, even though it has achieved positive, tangible results, has been less than awe-inspiring; usually far removed from participation by ordinary citizens, it has mostly involved haggling between bureaucrats of several countries over such mundane matters as sugar quotas, competition in the telecommunications industry, and the pricing of dairy products. Yet, through this protracted and arguably mediocre process has been elaborated the most successful attempt, so far, at multinational cooperation and integration, while any foreseeable threat of war among the member states of the EU has been banished.

At its narrowest, the goal of the European process of unification is simply to avoid a reoccurrence of the increasingly destructive wars that have periodically ravaged the continent. To (perversely) paraphrase Napoleon III, Victor Hugo's nemesis, *l'Europe, c'est la paix*—a sufficient rationale in itself, one that has inspired a number of authors. In its most extensive form, proponents of stronger European unity point to an established pattern of intercultural commonality within the current ethnic, religious, and linguistic diversity of the continent, a commonality that in turn calls for a greater degree of political integration. It is therefore increasingly artificial national borders, and not fundamental cultural distinctions, that divide Europeans. While the idea of a united Europe is several centuries old, the driving force for its actual, and modest, beginnings derived in large part from the carnage and rubble of World War II—as well as that of World War I and the Franco-Prussian War. Despite its initial focus on economic development and trade between its members, what is now called the EU started out with a clearly political objective: to achieve lasting peace between France and Germany, by rendering the two countries so economically interdependent as to make another war seem unthinkable. In practical terms, the French-German partnership has remained the basic building block of European integration since the Treaty of Paris was signed in 1951. To a surprising extent, the step-by-step approach initially advocated by Jean Monnet has proven to be remarkably successful. Indeed, within a half-century after the end of World War II, the EU has gone from the sort of concrete, specific areas of economic cooperation outlined by the French Planning Commissioner (1945–52) to a novel form of political integration.

The difficulty of reconciling future aspirations toward a united Europe with its warfare-ridden past is evident when one considers the symbolism of May 9, the date chosen for the commemoration of the official "Europe Day" (albeit with much less fanfare than for most national holidays). On that day in 1950, the French foreign minister, Robert Schuman, in agreement with Monnet, proposed in a speech to act swiftly on "a limited but decisive issue," the creation of a common Franco-German organization, which was also open to other European countries, to oversee the production of coal and steel.[2] While this focus on two industrial raw materials today seems incongruous, coal and steel, which were at the time the essential elements of the armament industry, carried an important practical and symbolic weight after the Second World War. By pooling their resources on these items, France and Germany sought to prevent the reemergence of rival arms industries, while laying the foundations of future European institutions. A period of lasting peace in Europe was thus initiated, in part, by merging and consolidating the basic industrial components of modern warfare. Declared Europe Day in 1985, May 9 falls, fittingly or ironically, the day after most of Europe commemorates the surrender of Nazi Germany in 1945. The celebration of European unity thus follows closely the remembrance of what is arguably the worst and the most divisive period in the history of the continent.

The evolution of the EU constitutes a unique social, political, and constitutional experiment; never before have established, developed nation-states, with separate languages (although, arguably, with interlinked literatures and cultures), attempted to achieve political integration or unity through peaceful means. The supranational institutions that have evolved in the course of this attempt, such as the European Parliament, the European High Court, and the European Central Bank, are also unique, both in their current roles and in their potential development. The successive treaties signed by the member states of what is now the EU compose a legal and political corpus that increasingly resembles a constitution. What is less clear is whether the passage of time, along with each institution created by the treaties, strengthens any emerging sense of permanence of a shared European identity. The progressive process of integration through limited, practical steps seems to have developed a dynamic of its own, but it has yet to elicit any form of widespread public allegiance, as was abruptly demonstrated in 2005 when French and Dutch voters rejected the proposed Constitutional Treaty, and again in 2008 when the revised treaty was rejected by Irish voters. Since Europe lacks the customary components of national identity (common ethnicity and language, recognized territoriality), whether its institutions can represent the emergence of a postnational form of collective identity remains the object of sharp debates. For the foreseeable future, Europe will continue to mean different things, to evoke different emotional connotations, within the different member states. Nationalistic sentiment, meanwhile, does not appear likely to wither away anytime soon. Ernest Renan, one of the nineteenth-century authors who predicted such an outcome—"Nations are not eternal. They began, they will end. The European confederation will probably take their place" (*Qu'est-ce qu'une nation?* 242)—added the caveat that his was a prediction for the very long term, as is borne out by the historical resilience of the nation-state.

Us and Them

The breakup of the Soviet Union (preceded or accompanied by the demise of communism as a credible internationalist ideology) put an end to a decades-long military threat and removed one obstacle toward broader European integration. With the end of the cold war and of the East-West division of Europe, the EU has expanded in the direction of its previously closed eastern border, an unfinished process that represents a peaceful triumph but also raises new questions and challenges. The current lack of an obvious adversary, or Other, has renewed the debate over the European identity (or identities) and over the limits of Europe, by removing a fixed point of reference, however negative. The development of the EU has encountered significant popular opposition within the past few years, even as it has begun to assume a more substantial and visible role in the daily life of its "citizens."[3] The main motive for opposition—and the political left and right wings converge on this point—is that Europe risks losing the diversity of its cultural heritage, becoming one vast, soulless marketplace where what Paul Valéry called *l'esprit* has been eliminated, albeit peacefully. The negative model usually invoked in this regard is the United States, whose status has been inverted; it is no longer a federal model for Europeans to emulate, but a pervasive economic and cultural menace that tends toward a reductive homogenization of smaller cultural groups.

It seems unlikely that a united Europe will totally avoid what René Girard calls the *mimésis de l'antagoniste*, whereby a formerly disunited group coalesces around the opposition to a common adversary. To a large extent, the role of *l'antagoniste* has been transferred from the defunct Soviet Union to the United States—where, as the reasoning goes, anonymous, atomistic individuals, devoid of cultural links, have been reduced to their purely economic dimensions. Within the current opposition to Europe as a clone of some vague American dysfunctional model, we could be witnessing the partial displacement of traditional nationalism onto a Greater Europe, leading to new and perhaps less warlike rivalries between larger multinational blocks. Of course, the simplistic and somewhat self-serving dichotomy between the soulless American marketplace and the European gathering of cultures tends to obscure the numerous instances of barbarity that contributed to much of the original driving force for European integration. However, such a dichotomy—and with it, the establishment of a negative model against which unity can be fostered—may well be an unavoidable stage of the process. While largely unsuccessful, the attempt by Jürgen Habermas and Jacques Derrida to turn widespread European opposition against the 2003 invasion of Iraq into the beginning of a specifically European shared identity—"a sign of the birth of a European public sphere" (4)—constituted a symptomatic episode, reminiscent of the ways in which was developed, over the past two centuries, a national consciousness among the elites of many countries seeking unity and/or independence.

With some exceptions, EU member states do share certain societal traits that stand in contrast to those of the United States. Most Europeans remain attached to the comprehensive social welfare systems that have long been crucially important and largely uncontroversial institutions (with a history that stretches back to the days of German Chancellor Bismarck). As a reaction against the continent's record of jingoistic hatred and warfare, its inhabitants tend to be less inclined toward both aggressive displays of patriotism and the unilateral use of military force. Due to similar causes, they are generally suspicious of the conflation of religious dogma and political rhetoric. Opposition to the death penalty has also become one of the defining characteristics of EU membership. As Tony Judt detailed (*Postwar*, 803–31), nearly all of contemporary Europe has come to be shaped by the recovered memory (which had long been partly suppressed) of the Shoah or Holocaust, a self-critical process of acknowledgement and historical investigation that has lent new urgency and weight to the debates over the moral limits of political activity. Whether such societal commonalities, some of which appear unrelated, can provide the basis for a sense of collective identity across national borders remains to be seen.

The degree of success of the European experiment can be measured by freely crossing national borders that were once tightly controlled and that are now open. For those who live in the countries that have adopted the common currency, the Euro represents the most tangible symbol of European institutions. Yet the simple fact that some member states still have border crossings or continue to use their own national currency is a reminder that the EU encounters resistance at each attempt to develop beyond the level of a free-trade zone.[4] While Europe's successes remain limited in scope, its failures are usually glaring; during the 1990s, the EU demonstrated its inability to halt the slaughter in the former Yugoslavia, which finally required decisive American intervention.[5] European economic achievements are thus matched neither by the EU's geopolitical weight nor by the democratic exemplarity and inclusiveness of its institutions. Even its ranking in the global economy is less than secure. While T.R. Reid discerns the emergence of a European "superpower," Alberto Alesina and Francesco Giavazzi forecast that, absent vigorous reforms, "the twenty-first century will be the century of European decline" (14).

The fact that European institutions have come into existence does not guarantee their continued development, nor does it address the lingering issue of the lack of public participation. In a bout of Euroskepticism, Judt argued that the period between World War II and the end of the cold war was more of a historical interlude or anomaly. After its passing, Europe is unlikely to sustain the momentum toward union: "*This* is the foundation myth of modern Europe— that the European Community was and remains the kernel of a greater, pan-European prospect" (*A Grand Illusion*, 41). The EU thus remains in limbo, neither a simple free-trade zone nor a federal polity. In any case, nation-states have so far retained their primacy, with European institutions remaining too abstract and remote to elicit any form of citizens' allegiance. Various proposals have been put forward to generate or define what would be a new form of citizenship, from Habermas's "constitutional patriotism" (best articulated by Jan-Werner Müller) to the recent redefinition of a "cosmopolitan Europe" by Ulrich

Beck and Edgar Grande. While its specific applications have often shifted, the broad opposition, outlined in the introduction, between Kantian universalism and Herderian particularism still remains relevant. As a unique transnational entity, the EU thus continues to be the object of an extraordinary level of debate over its origins, its degree of democratic legitimacy, its long-term prospects, and, ultimately, its cultural relevance.

Notes

Introduction

1. For lack of a better term, I will refer to Europe as a continent, even though its geographical limits remain unclear (see Jacques Lévy, ch. 1). The dividing line between Europe and Asia, traditionally set along the Ural Mountains, is even more problematic than such outlying nations as Iceland, Malta, or Turkey or such leftovers of European colonial empires as the French *Départements d'outre-mer*. The difficulty of defining Europe in geographical terms leads to what Defay calls the "imaginary cartography of Europe."
2. Such symbols include Europe Day (May 9), a flag (12 gold stars on a blue background), a motto ("United in diversity"), a common passport (with the bearer's nationality in smaller print), and an anthem (Beethoven's *Ode to Joy*, customarily played after the national anthem).
3. See Heater for the main projects aimed at achieving peace and unification in Europe, from Sully's "Grand Design" to the more limited proposals of Monnet and Spaak.
4. The word "author" is used in a broad sense, thus including the filmmaker Jean Renoir.
5. See Sternhell (*Les anti-Lumières*, 98–117) for Herder as a pioneer of the "counter-Enlightenment."
6. Unlike the famous question from *Lettres persanes*, Valéry's "Mais qui donc est Européen?" has no satirical connotation.
7. Of course, the presentation of Europe as a product of the literary imagination could be inverted, thereby confirming Kundera's intuition (193–202), which links European diversity to the emergence of the modern novel.

Chapter 1

1. The War of Austrian Succession (1740–48) and the Seven Years War (1756–63) figure prominently in the Voltairean corpus.
2. Quotes from Voltaire's correspondence refer to Besterman's "Definitive" edition. Quotes from his other works refer to the 1885 Moland edition. It should be noted that Voltaire's travels were often the result of forced exile. He visited or lived in northern Europe: England, Germany, Holland, and Switzerland. He never saw Spain, Italy, or Greece, and he never crossed the ocean to visit the New World or

the Asian countries of which he wrote at length. After 1728, he never returned to the British model he had extolled. Perhaps because of the humiliating outcome of his stay at the Prussian court (1750–53), he never visited the Russia of Catherine II, whom he so admired.
3. See Schlereth (chapter 1) and Dziembowski (chapter 3). Besterman highlighted his multilingualism: "Voltaire had a far greater knowledge of modern languages than was general in France at that time, or since for that matter. He wrote a large number of letters in English and Italian, and a certain number wholly or partly in Latin, Spanish, and German" (263).
4. Voltaire did not long remain in favor with Louis XV. See Pomeau (2: 193–230) and Milza (*Voltaire*, chapter 9).
5. In particular, Voltaire struggled against a cruel and arbitrary judicial system, defending victims of religious persecution, such as the Calas and Sirven families, as well as the Chevalier de la Barre. See Pomeau (4: 131–59 and 4: 288–306).
6. See Maillard (chapters 6–8).
7. See Masseau (chapter 3) and Schlereth (11–17).
8. In a text written during the Napoleonic regime, Germaine de Staël noted that the French Revolution had put an end to unhampered transnational travel: "Twenty years ago, it was possible to freely travel from one end of Europe to the other" (*Dix Années d'exil*, 191).
9. A typically ironic critique of Bossuet's *Discours* is found in Voltaire's *Lettres d'Amabed*: "We read a strange book from his country, a universal history of the whole world, in which there is no mention of our ancient empire, nothing about the immense lands beyond the Ganges, nothing about China, nothing about the vast Tatar territories. The authors of this part of Europe must be quite ignorant" (21: 438). As Bessire noted (206), Voltaire also sought to rebut Bossuet for having given Jews a central historical role.
10. As will be argued in Chapter 3, Victor Hugo's concept of history came to resemble Voltaire's. For a study of Voltaire as a historian, see Leigh.
11. See Badir (167–76).
12. For lists of the works in which Voltaire mentions China, see Guy (440–41) and Song (235–42). See Song (153–74) regarding Voltaire's understanding of Confucian thought and its status as a philosophical model in his writings.
13. Voltaire did not consider all Asian cultures as worthy of praise. He was particularly categorical about Mongols and Turks: "The vast Tatar lands, far larger than Europe, have only been inhabited by barbarians" (*Essai sur les mœurs*, 11: 435).
14. For his part, Rousseau was less sanguine about the "purported wisdom of the laws" (*Discours sur les sciences et les arts*, 3: 11) in Voltaire's China. See Guy (227–31, 338–40) concerning the quarrel between Voltaire and Rousseau over the representation of China. Rousseau was not the only philosophe to differ from Voltaire on this issue. In his *Commentaire sur l'esprit des lois* (1777), Voltaire tried to refute Montesquieu's description of China (30: 430–31) and India (30: 443–44) as despotic states.
15. See Meyer (167–90). As Habermas suggested, Kant's conceptual framework now seems, paradoxically, more relevant.
16. For a comparison of the positions of Voltaire and Saint-Pierre, see Perkins.

17. See Mason.
18. Another Voltairean survey of the varying levels of progress in Europe is found in the allegorical *Eloge historique de la raison* (21: 513–22).
19. See Vercruysse (26–66).
20. The other small European republic that Voltaire praised in terms similar to Holland was Switzerland, where was found "that form of equality through which citizens are subject only to the law, and which upholds the freedom of the weak against the ambition of the strong" (*Essai sur les mœurs*, 11: 528).
21. Voltaire, who was imprisoned for nearly a year in the Bastille, who was banished for much of his life, whose works were often condemned and burned, had concrete reasons to feel persecuted in general and to fear censorship in particular (see Gay 66–87).
22. See Vercruysse (11–23) and Van Strien-Chardonneau (chapter 6).
23. See Pomeau (1: 203–11).
24. See Dédéyan (*Le Retour de Salente*, 103–14).
25. Concerning Locke, see Hutchison (202–22).
26. Concerning Voltaire's love-hate relationship with Shakespearean drama, see Gunny (26–48), André-Michel Rousseau (447–95), and Dédéyan (*Le Retour de Salente*, 37–59).
27. The stylistic aspects of the forty-year correspondence between Voltaire and the openly gay Frederick have been studied by Mervaud, who characterizes their reciprocal flattery as a prolonged instance of "narcissisme de couple" (*Voltaire et Frédéric II*, 46). Voltaire certainly sounds like a jilted lover in his letters to Mme Denis, when reacting to Frederick's infamous comment: "I will need him for at most another year; once the orange has been squeezed, the peel can be discarded" (D4564 and D4597). As Magnan showed (1–72), Voltaire later rewrote the letters he had sent to his niece from Prussia in an effort at exacting revenge against the erstwhile "Salomon du nord."
28. For a chronology of Voltaire's stay in Prussia, see Magnan (399–421).
29. See Pomeau (2: 176–92).
30. See Meyer (30–38) and Lavicka.
31. See Pomeau (4: 116–18) and Milza (*Voltaire*, 592–95).
32. See Wilberger ("Peter the Great," 19–62, and *Voltaire's Russia*, 199–233).
33. See Pomeau (5: 47–63) for Voltaire's approval of Russia's armed expansionism directed against Turkey and Poland.
34. While he often praised the Arabs for their relative tolerance and their contributions to the arts and sciences, Voltaire consistently depicted the Ottoman Empire as the archenemy of Christian Europe. His idea of the essential otherness of the Turks is found in the *Essai sur les mœurs* (13: 178).
35. See Fiszer concerning Voltaire's negative view on Catholic Poland, which was a natural target for his anticlericalism and which he felt would be better off ruled by an enlightened monarch.
36. For Voltaire's possible personal motivations, see David Lévy (227–34). While the term is an anachronism—"antisémite" was coined in the nineteenth century—it is unavoidable in the context of Voltaire's writings.

37. For a reevaluation of Poliakov's analysis of Labroue's book, see Pellerin. Voltaire's writings on Jews have generated some of the most acerbic critical literature devoted to his work. Both Schechter and Schwarzbach, for instance, defend the philosophe against accusations of having fostered racialist anti-Semitism. See also Chisick's distinction between Voltaire's history and ethics. The paradoxes of Voltaire's obsessive animus against Jews, within the context of his struggle against intolerance, are aptly detailed by Sutcliffe (chapter 9).
38. The Voltairean dictum on the necessity of God's existence—"Si Dieu n'existait pas, il faudrait l'inventer"—is found in the *"Epître à l'auteur des Trois Imposteurs"* (10: 402–05), which predicts the triumph of philosophical tolerance and the end of Jewish particularism.
39. Similar passages are found in other texts, situating the Jews as immutably barbaric and degenerate, based on their innate and unvarying ethnic character, rather than on traditional religious bigotry. It is not difficult to see the propaganda uses someone like Labroue, during the Occupation, could make of such statements as "ennemis du genre humain" (*Essai sur les mœurs*, 11: 209).
40. A similar theme of Judaism and Christianity as perversions of a deistic, or natural, religion is found in the *Examen important de Milord Bolingbroke* (26: 298).
41. See Gay (chapter 5), Milza (*Voltaire*, chapter 20), and Pomeau (4: 230–60).
42. Ironically, Voltaire also produced a text on albinos that satirized racial prejudice: "if we imagine ourselves superior to them, we are gravely mistaken" ("Relation touchant un maure blanc amené d'Afrique à Paris en 1744," 23: 191).
43. The *Essai sur les mœurs* (12: 417) includes a strong condemnation of slavery that recalls the well-known encounter with a mutilated slave in *Candide* (chapter 19).
44. See Abanime. For the representation of slavery in Voltaire's 1736 play, *Alzire*, see Miller (71-80).
45. See Montaigne's *Essais*, "Des cannibales" (1, 31) and "Des coches" (3, 6).
46. Voltaire also used Aztec sacrifices to highlight the Inquisition as an example of European barbarity: "Montezuma was condemned for sacrificing prisoners to his gods. What would he have said if he had witnessed an *autodafé*?" (*Essai sur les mœurs*, 12: 351).

Chapter 2

1. I will generally drop the *particule*. For Staël's family background, see Fairweather (chapters 1–3) and Balayé (*Madame de Staël. Lumières et liberté*, chapter 1).
2. The issue of French citizenship was not fully formulated until the Revolution. Necker was not the only eighteenth-century French government minister of foreign extraction. During the Regency (1715–1723), John Law unsuccessfully attempted to modernize the country's monetary system. Although born and raised in Paris, Staël, who could claim French, Swiss (strictly speaking, Genevan), and Swedish citizenship, was suspected as a foreigner during the later phases of the Revolution. Ironically, in its early phase, the Revolution would grant citizenship (and even elective office) to foreigners such as Thomas Paine and Jeremy Bentham. Benjamin Constant, for his part, gained access to a French legislative body, the *Tribunat*, after Napoleon's 1799 coup d'état.

3. For Staël's political activities during the Revolutionary period, see Gwynne (13–48).
4. For instance, see Kramer (143–54) regarding the friendship between Staël and Lafayette. For Staël's friendship with Byron, see Forsberg (47–55) and Goodden (chapters 8-9).
5. See Balayé, "Le Système critique de Madame de Staël: théorie et sensibilité" (*Madame de Staël: écrire, lutter, vivre*, 307–20).
6. See Lotterie (158–79) and Rosset (chapter 2).
7. See Mortier (125–33).
8. Critics have emphasized Staël's complementary juxtaposition of the rationalism of the Enlightenment and the emotion of Romanticism. In "A propos du 'Préromantisme:' continuité ou rupture chez Madame de Staël" (*Madame de Staël: écrire, lutter, vivre*, 291–306), Balayé situates Staël as a continuator of the eighteenth-century literary tradition. Meanwhile, Staël's central role within the development of European Romanticism has been detailed by Isbell, who argues that she represents "a mythic parent to link all Europe's Romantic movements, and the vast spread of Romantic civilization" (9).
9. See Rosenblum (chapter 2).
10. See Szmurlo concerning Staël's depiction of individual languages as the discursive organizational framework for the "spirit" of their respective national groups.
11. As Isbell put it, "Staël has linked her fame to Napoleon: like Byron, she thus creates her own myth, both in her life and in her books" (105–6). For Staël's early encounters with Bonaparte, see Goodden (chapter 2).
12. For the various forms of French military occupation, see Laurent.
13. During the Revolution, the word "nation," which had in the eighteenth century simply designated the inhabitants of a country, came to refer to a collective political entity of citizens. The term "nationalism," which would dominate political thought in the nineteenth century, appeared shortly afterward.
14. For the various forms of resistance by European intellectuals to the cultural uniformity of the Empire, see Broers (105–25).
15. See Gwynne (254–61). While Staël analyzed the British system in terms of political liberalism, she largely ignored such issues as the industrial revolution.
16. See Forycki.
17. See Balayé, "Madame de Staël et l'Europe napoléonienne" (*Madame de Staël: écrire, lutter, vivre*, 155–71).
18. See Fairweather (chapter 23). Staël's account is found in *Dix années d'exil* (535–44).
19. Staël, who coined the term "vulgarité" (*De la littérature*, 1: 8), also displayed her class-based prejudice, commenting for instance on the "commissaires de la classe la plus subalterne" who wanted to search her house in August 1792 (*Considérations*, 281).
20. For a discussion of how the issue of abolitionism is reflected in Staël's fictional writing, see Miller (141-57).
21. "*Delphine* and *Corinne* had a success and a popularity that were, simply, immense. *Corinne* alone was published in more than forty editions between 1807 and 1872"

(Gutwirth 285). As Vallois noted (110), the novel's success was not limited to France, nor was it apolitical.
22. Quotes from *Corinne* are by book and chapter.
23. See Gutwirth (295–301).
24. See Vallois regarding the identification established between the main character and her native land ("une Femme-Pays," 113).
25. See Corinne's letter to Oswald (6, 3), responding to his characterization of Italians as lacking in virility. See Vallois (133–50) and Gutwirth (209–15) for the feminized representation of Italy in *Corinne*. Staël was not alone in her characterization of Italy as essentially feminized. As is discussed in Chapter 4 of this book, Barrès developed a discourse of feminization in his writings on Italy, albeit for different esthetic and political purposes.
26. See Balayé, "*Corinne et la ville italienne*" (*Madame de Staël: écrire, lutter, vivre*, 91–109).
27. See Polowetzky (131–38).
28. See Soloviéff (chapter 1) for the main German authors discussed by Staël. See Isbell (70–90) for Staël's presentation of Goethe's *Faust*.
29. Staël's "portrait d'Attila" (1: 373) is often described as an unflattering allegorical reference to Napoleon. See Balayé, "Pour une lecture politique de *De l'Allemagne*" (*Madame de Staël: écrire, lutter, vivre*, 213–29), and Isbell (90–107).
30. See Gsteiger.
31. See Isbell (chapter 1) and Soloviéff (chapter 5).
32. Staël's presentation of the Schlegel brothers' work is found in *De l'Allemagne* (part 2, chapter 31). See Soloviéff (chapter 6) regarding the intellectual and personal links between Staël and Schlegel. For Staël's 1803–4 stay in Germany, see Fairweather (chapter 18) and Goodden (chapter 4).
33. See Balayé (*Madame de Staël. Lumières et liberté*, 177–81) and Isbell (131–41).
34. Projecting her north/south dichotomy within Germany, Staël saw the northern part of the country as more developed and more inclined toward thoughtful deliberation, due to the influence of the colder climate. Meanwhile, the more temperate southern part had a lesser degree of the sort of climatic stimulus that would encourage intellectual activity (1: 76).
35. See Louis Réau (388–90) for a depiction of Staël as an irresponsible literary Germanophile, applauding the defeat of Napoleon and France. It should be noted that Staël met and wrote about Fichte (*De l'Allemagne*, 2: 141–54) before he became an ultranationalist.
36. Savary's letter is also found in Staël's *Dix Années d'exil* (200–201).
37. See Pellegrini. One of the great ironies of French literary history, in light of the officially sanctioned neoclassicism of the Empire, is the transformation of the historical figure of Napoleon Bonaparte into a tragic icon of Romanticism after his loss of power and death in forced exile, a literary and political process in which Stendhal (along with Victor Hugo and other writers) was a major participant. The Romantic generation that owed so much to Staël created a cult around the image of the Emperor against whom she had so long struggled.
38. See Hofmann and Rosset.
39. See Rosset (chapter 3).

40. See Calame, Fink, and Tilkin.
41. See Dijn (chapters 3–4) and Manent (chapter 8) for Constant as a theoretician of liberalism. For a comparative presentation of Staël and Constant on this issue, see Jaume (25–117).

Chapter 3

1. Other revolutionary moments include the failed insurrection of 1832 (depicted in *Les Misérables*, parts 4–5).
2. See Winock, *Victor Hugo*.
3. As Nash put it: "Hugo, Lamartine, and Vigny were all dedicated to the belief in the redemptive power of language as a means of altering the course of history . . . For them politics was very much a part of the poet's domain" (17).
4. For the largely negative Hugolian references in Proust's work, see Leriche.
5. See Robb (273–78).
6. As Ward noted, Hugo's poetic notions of cosmic finality were interrelated with his political positions: "Hugo shared with others of his century the obsession with discovering the laws of historical development. But much of this interest in finding the end of history stemmed from personal convictions that the future must justify his own political choices" (85).
7. See Laforgue (25–48) for a comparison of the speeches of the conventionnel and Enjolras in *Les Misérables* as complementary expressions of revolutionary myths.
8. See Robb (chapters 2–3).
9. Like Voltaire, Hugo was a practitioner of almost every literary genre: "He is the only major French nineteenth-century writer to have felt equally at home in lyric and epic poetry, in the novel, and in the theater—and to have made a powerful impact in all these genres. No similar claims, whatever their genius, can be made for Stendhal, Balzac, Flaubert, Zola, Dickens, Dostoevsky, or Tolstoy" (Brombert 10).
10. See Dédéyan (1: 70–95).
11. See Aref (133–67) for Hugo's paternalistic representation of Africans in *Bug-Jargal*.
12. This fascination is visible in such poems as "A la colonne" (4: 691–98) and "Lui":

    > Napoleon, always dazzling and somber,
    > Is standing at the threshold of the century. (4: 535)

13. Barrès privileged the patriotic component of Hugo's work, which he integrated into his revanchist discourse. In chapter 18 of *Les Déracinés*, garishly entitled "La Vertu sociale d'un cadavre," Barrès organized his version of national unity around Hugo's funeral ceremony. As Ben-Amos noted (513), the Barrésian interpretation eliminated the liberal, cosmopolitan aspect of the Hugolian heritage and transformed the event into a reductively nationalistic celebration.
14. In Romains's *Les Hommes de bonne volonté*, Hugo's irenic expectations regarding the consequences of scientific progress are ridiculed by a character who, ironically, represents the Hugolian ideal of a peaceful Europe: "[Hugo] thought it obvious that air travel would lead to the elimination of borders and to universal brotherhood.

He would be happy to learn that during the next war, if it breaks out, airplanes will destroy more than half of Europe" (*Comparutions*, 24: 158).

15. For Hugo's representation of Voltaire as a "héros mythologique," see Trousson (chapter 5).
16. In *Choses vues*, Hugo cites the atrocities committed by French troops during the "pacification" of Algeria, concluding with, "L'armée—faite féroce par l'Algérie" (11: 1256)—thereby attributing the colonizers' actions to the influence of the colonized.
17. Occupied Poland is represented as a suffering "sister" of France in an 1835 poem (*Les Chants du crépuscule*, 4: 718). In 1853, Hugo would return to the issue of oppression in Poland, this time committed by Russian troops. By then, he envisioned that nineteenth-century nationalistic struggles would be transcended by future European federalism: "Let us greet, beyond all these convulsions and all these wars, the blessed dawn of the United States of Europe!" (10: 445). By contrast, Voltaire, it will be recalled, acquiesced in the 1772 partition of Poland by Austria, Prussia, and Russia.
18. See Pena-Ruiz and Scot (chapter 7).
19. However, in his 1868 letters of support for the establishment of a republic in Spain (10: 610–14), Hugo included the country in his future Europe.
20. Hugo did, however, often make use of English words in his writings (see Barrère). See Leuillot for an account of the translation of Shakespeare's works by Hugo's son, a project with polemical ramifications that was undertaken during the period of exile.
21. For the impact of Hugo's work in Russia, see Sokologorsky. For an analysis of Hugo's influence on Dostoevsky, see Babel Brown.
22. See the Hugo-Schœlcher correspondence.
23. See Dédéyan (2: 425–35) regarding Hugo's trips to Germany and Switzerland in 1839 and 1840, which led to the publication of *Le Rhin* in 1842.
24. Hugo's poetic impressions of the Rhineland would become a major reference in Barrès's 1921 *Le Génie du Rhin*.
25. See Dédéyan (2: 404–24).
26. In a prescient pamphlet, "Après Sadowa" (159–83), published after the 1866 Prussian victory over Austrian troops at Sadowa, Quinet noted that German unity was being achieved not in the spirit of democratic self-determination but through despotic militarism that was reminiscent of *Ancien Régime* practices. The exiled Quinet warned that the process of German unification, long called for by artists and philosophers, would be completed against France.
27. In his presentation of the Rhine as the uniting line between France and Germany, Hugo pays little attention to Holland and Switzerland.
28. See Morrissey.
29. Since Paris was surrounded by Prussian troops, the Assembly met in Bordeaux. It would later meet in Versailles instead of Paris, a move laden with conservative symbolism. See Rosa for Hugo's political action during the Franco-Prussian War and the Commune.
30. Marx did share Hugo's contempt for the "single individual," Louis-Napoléon Bonaparte. It is at the beginning of this text that Marx made his famous pronouncement,

in comparing Napoleon I to his nephew, about the uneven recurrence of historical events: "Hegel remarks somewhere that all facts and personages of great importance in world history occur, as it were, twice. He forgot to add: the first time as tragedy, the second as farce" (15).
31. See Milza (*Napoléon III*, chapters 14–15) regarding the Second Empire's economic program.
32. For the role of railways in Hugo's vision of progress, see Charles (30–41).
33. See Petrovska (chapter 5).

Chapter 4

1. For an overview of French right-wing reactions to the 1870–71 war, see El Gammal. I will use the commonly accepted term "Alsace-Lorraine," even though only part of the Lorraine region was occupied by Germany ("Alsace-Moselle" is more historically accurate).
2. See Blum (543–45) for his disappointment when Barrès became an anti-Dreyfusard (see also Lacouture 37–39). See Miguet for Barrès's relationship with Proust. For appraisals of Barrès by Cocteau and Malraux, see Boisdeffre (184–86 and 197–98, respectively). See Montherlant's preface in *L'Œuvre* (11: ix–xviii).
3. See Bonnet. This rejection of a prewar literary giant can be compared to the symbolic expulsion of Anatole France by the Surrealists in their 1924 pamphlet, *Un Cadavre* (Nadeau 197–200).
4. Aragon's reexamination of Barrès, as well as his belittling of Gide, corresponded to the French Communist Party's repositioning as a nationalist movement since the Resistance, and it attacked the erstwhile fellow traveler who had become heretical by criticizing the Soviet Union in *Retour de l'U.R.S.S.* (1936).
5. Concerning the political aspects of Barrès's thought, critics are generally divided into two broad types of interpretation: those who, like Sternhell, see in him one of the precursors of fascism and those who maintain his links to a democratic, albeit authoritarian, tradition, not unlike Gaullism (in a division Barrès might have appreciated, most of the latter are French). The differing views are often sharply expressed. Denouncing any comparison between Barrès's "Land and Dead" and the German doctrine of *Blut und Bloden* that Nazism would later draw upon, Domenach rails against the "semi-ignorants who see in Barrès a prefascist" (142). Broche mentions Sternhell's first book in his bibliography, only to summarily dismiss it (536). Meanwhile, Kirscher does not deign to mention the names of Barrès's "censors," whose "unfounded prejudices pass for knowledge" (10). For overviews of the differing interpretations by historians of the emergence of fascism, see Burrin (606–32) and Soucy (*French Fascism: The Second Wave*, 1–11).
6. See aphorism 475 of *Human, All Too Human*.
7. To use Rémond's terms, Barrès and Maurras represent the "Bonapartist" and "Legitimist" branches, respectively, of the French Right. See the Barrès-Maurras correspondence, *La République ou le Roi*.
8. In *La Grande Pitié des églises de France* (1914), the quest for an unbroken chain of the Dead leads Barrès to attempt to link Christianity with the paganism that

preceded it within the same Land: "it is time to complete the reconciliation of the vanquished gods and the saints" (8: 172).
9. The ambiguities of Barrésian rootedness are highlighted by his first electoral campaign. As Serman pointed out (124), Barrès, who had been living in Paris, initially had few contacts in his district of Lorraine and knew little about it.
10. At the end of *Une Journée parlementaire* (1894), Madame Thuringe, whose husband, a crooked Député, has been forced to commit suicide—by other crooked members of the National Assembly—tells her young son: "Look, my child, look at these men and learn to hold them in contempt: they are all scum!" (4: 551).
11. Having already participated in Boulanger's attempt to create a new regime, Barrès supported Déroulède's coup attempt in 1899. Both of these episodes degenerated into farce. See Bécarud for Barrès's parliamentary career.
12. See Berstein (1: 344–52).
13. The founder of the first overtly fascist party in France, Georges Valois, proclaimed Barrès's work in *La Cocarde*, along with Georges Sorel's *Réflexions sur la violence* (1908), to be among the originating documents of fascism: "Barrès was the first to see the possibility of merging socialism and nationalism" (6). See Sternhell (*Ni droite ni gauche*, chapter 3) and Soucy (*French Fascism: The First Wave*, chapter 5) concerning Valois's paradoxical political evolution.
14. See Sabourin (49–73) for nationalistic counterarguments against European supranationality.
15. Germany was also, since Immanuel Kant, the national embodiment of the universalistic model of logic that Barrès rejected. A major theme of Barrès's second trilogy is the perverting influence of Kant's philosophy, through his disciple Bouteiller, on a group of young French men who are briefly his students at a lycée in Nancy. A rootless intellectual, Bouteiller vainly attempts to raise his pupils "above the passions of their race, up to reason, up to humanity" (*Les Déracinés*, 3: 19).
16. Barrès typically—and absurdly—presented one of his literary models as exclusively rooted: "Hugo is the child of a military family from Lorraine" (*Les Maîtres*, 12: 142). Paul Verlaine was also posthumously enlisted into Barrès's *cocardier* form of patriotism, albeit with somewhat more reason ("Les Funérailles de Verlaine," 2: 406–09).
17. The issue of just how personal has been addressed at length by Tronquart.
18. "The nation, like the individual, is the end point of a long history of effort, sacrifice, and devotion. The cult of our ancestors is the most legitimate of all. Our ancestors have made us what we are" (Renan 240). See Todorov (*Nous et les autres*, 247–61) concerning the links between Renan's formulation of nationalism and Barrès's determinism. See Birnbaum (*La France aux Français*, chapter 4) for Renan's paradoxical status as an intellectual reference for both left-wing republicans and right-wing nationalists.
19. Taine had already elaborated the critique of Rousseau's "social contract" as a blindly abstract concept, applicable only to the purely fanciful notion of a society composed of atomistic individuals who lack historical links: "These are abstract persons, of no specific century or country, pure entities conjured up by a metaphysical wand" (183).

20. Through his denunciation of Zola and other Dreyfusards, Barrès contributed to the wide use of the term "les intellectuels," which he consistently used in a pejorative sense. They were the rootless propagators of Kantian abstraction: "Kantism cuts off one's roots: the land and the dead" (*Scènes*, 5: 66).
21. During the Dreyfus Affair, as Noiriel argued (259–63), Barrès used rhetorical devices that were similar to those of Drumont.
22. Ironically, Barrès did in fact have much in common with Dreyfus, a patriotic career officer who had been forced to leave his native Alsace after the Franco-Prussian War.
23. It was the integration of anti-Semitism within a systematic theory of nationalistic determinism that also set Barrès apart from the more instinctual (and less well-known) distaste for Jews of his ideological adversaries, Gide and Rolland (see Bourrelier, 960–62 and 750–53).
24. See Soucy (*Fascism in France*, chapter 7) and Sternhell (*Maurice Barrès*, chapter 5).
25. See Birnbaum (*Le Peuple et les Gros*, chapter 1) for the political variations of the "deux cents familles" metaphor.
26. Although he sharply criticized Staël for her "Germanophilia," Barrès largely adopted her conceptual model of opposition against enforced universalism through the revalorization of individual national cultures. However, he inverted the poles of that model; while Staël sought literary renewal outside of the dominant French tradition at the beginning of the nineteenth century, Barrès saw Germany as the domineering embodiment of abstract universalism at the century's close.
27. Hugo's *L'Année terrible* (6: 3–182) covers both the Franco-Prussian War and the Paris Commune.
28. Fustel de Coulanges's text is found in Hartog (376–82).
29. For the disputed status and representations of Alsace, see Mayeur.
30. As Birnbaum (*La France aux Français*, 306–08) and Sternhell (*Les anti-Lumières*, 418–23) noted, Barrès's version of nationalism also shares common traits with Herder's organic societal model. For the reception of Fichte's work in France, see Espagne (243–66).
31. Fichte took the nationalist concept of economic self-sufficiency to an absurd extreme, positing in *L'Etat commercial fermé* (1800) a system of totally autarchic nation-states, with sealed borders.
32. Ironically, while Barrès does not seem to have found much intellectual depth in Spain, his work was influential among Spanish writers, particularly among the "generation of 1898" (see Storm).
33. See *Chronique de la Grande Guerre* for examples of the cultural and political links between France and Spain that Barrès promoted: "Les Affinités franco-espagnoles" (2: 35–43) and "Les Voix françaises de l'Espagne" (2: 195–205).
34. Barrès's account of this wartime trip was published as "Le Voyage d'Italie" in *Chronique* (8: 120–202). It was reprinted as *Dix Jours en Italie* in *L'Œuvre* (9: 61–121). See also *Chronique* (4: 317–35) for Barrès's enthusiastic reaction to Italy's decision to enter the war in 1915.
35. Said devoted a few paragraphs to Barrès, defining the author of *Une Enquête aux Pays du Levant* as advocating "the cultivation of intellectual imperialism, as ineradicable as it is subtle" (245).

36. For instance, Russia is for Barrès clearly not a part of Europe. In *Scènes et doctrines du nationalisme*, he contrasts Anatole France, "ce véritable Français," with Leo Tolstoy, "ce véritable Asiatique" (5: 62).
37. See Ahmad (chapter 5), Clifford (chapter 11), and Irwin (chapter 9) for detailed critiques, from very different perspectives, of Said's construction of an essentialized European entity.
38. Barrès provides an example of the ambiguity that some revanchist right-wing elements exhibited toward the colonialist policies of the Third Republic (see Michel).
39. Doty argues that the Barrésian corpus was sufficiently protean to have inspired two opposing versions of French nationalism: "Malraux is a prime example of how one could move on to the Barrès of 'the novel of national energy' and 'bastions of the East' as preparation for Gaullism; one must remember that Charles de Gaulle, himself, was a student in those same prewar years. Read differently, that same Barrès could prepare fascists, Pétainists, and the backers of *Algérie française*" (246). However, the contrasts between the political legacies of Maurice Barrès and Charles de Gaulle remain glaring; de Gaulle never called for, or participated in, a coup d'état as a means of achieving his political goals. Instead, he scrupulously adhered to democratic principles and institutions while in office. He also advocated and practiced reconciliation with Germany. For the differences between the two forms of nationalism, see Charlot.

Chapter 5

1. See Bertin (chapter 2) and Bergan (chapters 3–5).
2. For the consequences of Renoir's prolonged absence from France on his postwar films, see Bergstrom.
3. For a complete listing of Renoir's visual and textual output, see Viry-Babel.
4. See Truffaut's (in)famous distinction between *les auteurs* and *la tradition de qualité*.
5. For the *Groupe Octobre*, see Buchsbaum (36–42) and Ory (350–53). For *Ciné-Liberté*, see Buchsbaum (185–234) and Ory (439–47).
6. Renoir devoted only three pages of his autobiography to the Popular Front (112–14), thereby diminishing the scope of his political engagement.
7. The Indian filmmaker Satyajit Ray, who met Renoir in India while he was working on *The River*, refers to his "charming broken English" (113). By then, Renoir had been living in the United States for nearly a decade. He was, at least, more willing to learn English than had been Hugo.
8. Of course, the mere capacity for global distribution of cultural products does not necessarily make them less chauvinistic or provincial, as is visible in many American films.
9. Paradoxically, by filming *Toni* on location in the south of France, Renoir remained temporarily absent from the Parisian political struggles and realignments that followed the riots of February 1934.
10. Bazin (*Jean Renoir*, 34) described *Toni* as a precursor to postwar Italian neo-realism. See Forlin (395–98).

11. Sesonske suggests that this was an early case of color-blind casting, making *Toni* "one of the very few 1930s films in which a black man is treated as simply another person" (167).
12. Renoir reviewed *Modern Times* (*Ecrits*, 79–81), which was released a few months before *Les Bas-Fonds*.
13. By the time Renoir made *La Règle du jeu*, the promise of the Popular Front had dissipated (although paid vacations for French workers remained as a lasting achievement of the short-lived movement).
14. See Ory (448–62) and Buchsbaum (250–70).
15. Sorlin estimated that "in the 1930s, Europe made more films on the years 1914–18 than Hollywood" (24).
16. Such a theatrical representation was at the time less unlikely than it would appear. As Rearick (13–14) noted, shows staged by soldiers were fairly common during the war.
17. In *Le Crime de M. Lange*, the famous circular shot of the courtyard has a similar effect, turning Lange's individual act of murder into a collective act of exclusion of the exploiter and thief, Batala. See Bazin (*Jean Renoir*, 41–42) and Sesonske (215–18).
18. In a linguistic sense, *La Grande Illusion*, with its use of English, German, and Russian, constitutes the northern European counterpart to *Toni*, albeit in a very different historical context. See Sesonske (319–22) and Triggs.
19. The only reminder of the French colonial empire is a minor character known as "le Sénégalais," who at Wintersborn, attempts to strike up a conversation with Maréchal about the drawing he has just finished: "la justice poursuivant le crime." Maréchal is as uninterested about this as he is about Pindar.
20. See Racine for the review's reactions to the rise of Nazism in Germany.
21. See Ferro (184–90).
22. See Bertin (85–87). Interestingly, in *Nana* as in *La Bête humaine*, both adaptations of novels by Emile Zola, Renoir eliminated the French Second Empire context of impending war against Prussia.
23. See *Ma Vie* (85–89) for Renoir's account of a trip to Germany that coincided with Hitler's coming to power.
24. For the paradoxical situation of French filmmaking during the Occupation, see Siclier (310–16). The Vichy regime also reorganized the French cinema industry, creating the national film school (Institut des Hautes Etudes Cinématographiques, or IDHEC) and the Comité d'Organisation de l'Industrie Cinématographique (COIC). Most of the structural changes implemented during the Occupation were retained after the Liberation, with the COIC becoming the Centre National de la Cinématographie, or CNC (see Williams 249–51 and 276–78). As for l'IDHEC, it became la Fémis in 1986.
25. See Samuels.
26. Céline's anti-Semitic tirade against *La Grande Illusion* (268–74) reached a particularly venomous level when quoting Rosenthal's jocularly ecumenical line in the film: "Jésus, mon frère de race."
27. For the film's tribulations, see Sesonske (438–40).
28. See Sesonske (386–95).

29. The supercilious butler, ironically named Corneille, expresses more contempt than La Chesnaye when he addresses Marceau and even the fearsome Schumacher as "mon ami."
30. The parallel between the two characters is reinforced by the often mentioned Austrian origin of La Chesnaye's wife Christine and by the couple's monarchical status at the center of a fractious, dying society.
31. See Tifft for an analysis of farce and the historical moment of *La Règle du jeu*.
32. A 1956 Franco-Italian coproduction, *Eléna et les hommes* depicts a Polish princess who attempts to influence the political career of Rollan, a French general (who is obviously modeled on Boulanger). As opposed to Barrès's grandiloquent treatment of the Boulanger episode, Renoir portrays it as comic opera, with the indecisive general ultimately renouncing power for love, while Eléna finds happiness with the unheroic but devoted Henri: "Eléna, c'est Vénus" (*Ecrits*, 281). Although Rollan exhibits a tendency toward fascist-style grandstanding in front of enthusiastic crowds, his saber-rattling against Germany turns to farce, as love conquers all and international tensions evaporate. Such a film, lightly depicting a Polish aristocrat, a French general, and the threat of a war with Germany, could probably not have been made in the 1930s.
33. Other instances of foreboding include the shadows on the wall of the closing scene and the skit that features skeletons dancing to the sounds of Saint-Saëns's *Danse macabre* (produced by a player piano).
34. This scene is one of the most vivid illustrations of the ominously closed environment of *La Règle du jeu*. The forest, normally an open space for the animals, gradually becomes a restricted and deadly enclosure as they are led toward the shooters.
35. This tragedy of errors concludes the numerous parallel constructions that Sesonske detailed (chapter 21). For instance, during the stage show, the shots of the spectators reveal two illicit couples (Christine and Saint-Aubin; Lisette and Marceau), with each one being spied upon (by André and Schumacher, respectively).
36. See Lacouture (334–40).
37. In the last chapter of his autobiography (259–62), Renoir somewhat hastily predicts the coming demise of national identities in favor of worldwide "horizontal" or class-based stratifications. Hugo, it will be recalled, had similarly announced that the twentieth century would see the end of national borders within Europe.

Chapter 6

1. For Rougemont's publications, see Ackermann (1152–1227). Many of the quotes refer to Rougemont's *Ecrits sur l'Europe* (hereinafter *EE*). As was the case in Chapter 2, I will generally drop the *particule* when naming the author.
2. See *Penser avec les mains* (115). On the issue of Europe, Rougemont would come to have more in common with Benda, the author of *Discours à la nation européenne*. See also *L'Esprit européen*.
3. An echo of the importance and the risks of writing is found in Rougemont's *La Part du Diable* (1944): "It is true that for certain authors, the act of writing is simply the result of an intellectual itch that can be soothed by scratching paper, with no

thought as to the consequences. But those who write in order to better understand always take on a certain level of risk" (16).
4. See Starobinski (163).
5. For accounts of this transitional but important period of Rougemont's life, see Ackermann (677–802) and Mehlman (chapter 4).
6. See Loyer (286–306).
7. "Unité" could be translated as unit or unity.
8. See Puymège.
9. See Verdaguer for an overview of this issue.
10. See also Ackermann (445–95). Rougemont's stay in Germany was unexceptional for French intellectuals during the 1930s. Others included Aron and Sartre (see Granjon).
11. See Deering (223–397), Ackermann (835–66), and Rougemont's own account ("Vingt ans après ou la campagne des congrès, 1947–1949," *EE*, 2: 193–209).
12. See Olivi and Giacone (13–18) and Elisabeth du Réau (165–88).
13. A sense of rivalry with Sartre, over issues as varied as the origins of Existentialism and the notion of *engagement*, often emerges from Rougemont's writings. His fiercest polemic was written after the publication of Sartre's virulently anti-European preface to Fanon's *Les Damnés de la Terre*. Rougemont's sardonic rejoinder is found in the appendix to *Les Chances de l'Europe* (*EE*, 2: 97–100). Overall, however, as the studies by Judt (*Past Imperfect*) and by Ory and Sirinelli confirm, Rougemont's was one of the relatively marginalized non-Marxist voices in the French postwar intellectual landscape.
14. Sidjanski (52–57) provides some examples of the activities of the *Centre Européen de la Culture* (see also Rougemont's own brief 1958 description, *EE*, 1: 324–28).
15. See, for instance, his "Manifeste écologique pour une Europe différente" (*EE*, 2: 586–95).
16. See Sidjanski (58).
17. The beginning of *Lettre ouverte aux Européens* (1970) provides a striking example, ostensibly addressing a list of citizens of nation-states in alphabetical order ("Albanaises, Albanais!" etc.), who are, finally, symbolically united into: "Européennes, Européens!" (*EE*, 2: 253–54).
18. Rougemont's background has some similarities with Staël's: a well-traveled Swiss Protestant multilingual writer, with family ties in several European countries. See his 1980 article, "Madame de Staël et 'l'Esprit européen'" (*EE*, 2: 740–44).
19. As Rougemont points out, Valéry did not invent the geographical concept of Europe as "un appendice occidental de l'Asie" (*Vingt-huit siècles d'Europe, EE*, 1: 506–07).
20. For an analysis of the war's aftermath, see Judt (*Postwar*, part 1).
21. For the historical context, see Jáuregui.
22. Rougemont was particularly scornful of Dale Carnegie's *How to Win Friends and Influence People* (first published in 1936): "Mr. Carnegie's ideal individual is chatty and always smiling, willing to flatter others in order to be flattered, accustomed to using false modesty as a self-serving stratagem, and tirelessly ready to exhibit methodical friendliness toward any neighbor who might one day prove to be useful" (*La Part du Diable*, 104).

23. Rougemont provides his own brief history of federalist efforts after World War II in *La Suisse ou l'histoire d'un peuple heureux* (284–85), ending the book on a proposal to turn Switzerland into a "district fédéral européen" that would reconcile traditional Swiss neutrality with a united Europe.
24. As his biographer put it: "It is thus upon these two principles, federalism and ecumenism, both essential according to him, that Rougemont undeniably establishes himself as a theologian of Europe, a theologian of European unity" (Ackermann 74).
25. Passion, Revolution, and Nation make up the "maladies spécifiques" of the Western world, according to Rougemont (*L'Aventure occidentale de l'homme*, 94). They constitute the sacred dimension of our modern societies.
26. "Due to the nature of Christianity and the nature of Hinduism or Buddhism, real life in the West conflicts with faith, while real life in Asia is symbiotic with its religions" (*Les Mythes de l'amour*, 259).
27. Rougemont probably had recent history in mind. In 1937, he had contributed an article to *Les Juifs* (Claudel, et al.), a collective work intended as a response to German anti-Semitism. Like many of the articles in this book, Rougemont's "Vocation et destin d'Israël" (143–61), in which he interprets the Jewish predicament within his religious and philosophical framework, in retrospect appears clumsy at best.

Afterword

1. Derrida's opposition between "an old Europe" and "a Europe that does not yet exist" (14), outlines the developing European identity by the very pursuit of it—an ongoing process rather than an established fact.
2. "Europe will not be built all at once, nor as part of a comprehensive plan. It will be built through concrete achievements that initially produce effective solidarity. In order to bring together the nations of Europe, the outdated antagonism between France and Germany must be eliminated: any practical project must therefore concern first and foremost these two countries" (Schuman Declaration). For overviews of the creation of the European Coal and Steel Community, see Judt (*Postwar*, 153–59), Sutton (chapter 2), and Wasserstein (451–61).
3. It should be recalled that the 1992 Maastricht Treaty created a "citizenship" of the EU.
4. On the other hand, even the fact is free trade is now widely considered the minimal or baseline level of European integration constitutes an improvement over the protectionist policies of the 1930s. See Wasserstein (165–73).
5. See Judt (*Postwar*, 665–85).

Works Cited

Abanime, Emeka. "Voltaire antiesclavagiste." *SVEC* 182. Oxford: Voltaire Foundation, 1979. 237–51.
Ackermann, Bruno. *Denis de Rougemont: une biographie intellectuelle*. 2 vols. Genève: Labor et Fides, 1996.
Agathon (Henri Massis et Alfred de Tarde). *Les Jeunes Gens d'aujourd'hui*. Paris: Imprimerie Nationale, 1995.
Ahmad, Aijaz. *In Theory: Classes, Nations, Literatures*. London: Verso, 1992.
Alesina, Alberto, and Francesco Giavazzi. *The Future of Europe: Reform or Decline*. Cambridge: MIT P, 2006.
Amin, Samir. *L'Eurocentrisme. Critique d'une idéologie*. Paris: Anthropos, 1988.
Anderson, Benedict. *Imagined Communities: Reflections on the Origin and Spread of Nationalism*. 3rd ed. London: Verso, 2006.
Andrew, Dudley. *Mists of Regret: Culture and Sensibility in Classic French Film*. Princeton: Princeton UP, 1995.
Aref, Mahmoud. *La Pensée sociale et humaine de Victor Hugo dans son œuvre romanesque*. Genève: Slatkine, 1979.
Aron, Raymond. *L'Opium des intellectuels*. Paris: Calmann-Lévy, 1955.
Babel Brown, Nathalie. *Hugo and Dostoevsky*. Ann Arbor, MI: Ardis, 1978.
Badir, Magdy. *Voltaire et l'islam*. *SVEC* 125. Oxford: Voltaire Foundation, 1974.
Balayé, Simone. *Madame de Staël: écrire, lutter, vivre*. Genève: Droz, 1994.
———. *Madame de Staël. Lumières et liberté*. Paris: Klincksieck, 1979.
Barrère, Jean-Bertrand. "Victor Hugo et le franglais." James 15–22.
Barrès, Maurice. *Chronique de la Grande Guerre*. 14 vols. Paris: Plon, 1931–39.
———. *L'Œuvre*. Ed. Philippe Barrès. 20 vols. Paris: Club de l'Honnête Homme, 1965–68.
Barrès, Maurice, and Charles Maurras. *La République ou le Roi*. Paris: Plon, 1970.
Bazin, André. *Jean Renoir*. Paris: Champ Libre, 1971.
———. *Qu'est-ce que le cinéma?* 4 vols. Paris: Cerf, 1958–62.
Bécarud, Jean. *Maurice Barrès et le Parlement de la Belle Epoque*. Paris: Plon, 1987.
Beck, Ulrich, and Edgar Grande. *Cosmopolitan Europe*. Trans. Ciaran Cronin. Cambridge: Polity, 2007.
Ben-Amos, Avner. "Les Funérailles de Victor Hugo. Apothéose de l'événement spectacle." Nora 1: 473–522.

Benda, Julien. *Discours à la nation européenne*. Paris: Gallimard, 1933.
Benda, Julien, et al. *L'Esprit européen. Rencontres internationales de Genève, 1946*. Neuchâtel: Baconnière, 1947.
Bergan, Ronald. *Jean Renoir. Projections of Paradise*. Woodstock, NY: Overlook, 1992.
Bergstrom, Janet. "Jean Renoir's Return to France." *Poetics Today* 17.3 (Fall 1996): 453–89.
Bernal, Martin. *Black Athena: The Afroasiatic Roots of Classical Civilization*. 3 vols. New Brunswick, NJ: Rutgers UP, 1987–2006.
Berstein, Serge. *Histoire du Parti Radical*. 2 vols. Paris: Sciences Politiques, 1982.
Bertin, Célia. *Jean Renoir*. Paris: Rocher, 1994.
Bessire, François. *La Bible dans la correspondance de Voltaire*. SVEC 367. Oxford: Voltaire Foundation, 1999.
Besterman, Theodore. *Voltaire*. New York: Harcourt, 1969.
Birnbaum, Pierre. *"La France aux Français." Histoire des haines nationalistes*. Paris: Seuil, 1993.
———. *Le Peuple et les Gros. Histoire d'un mythe*. Paris: Grasset, 1979.
Blain, Michel. *Douze Mythes qui ont fondé l'Europe. Une Table ronde de grands récits*. Paris: L'Harmattan, 2007.
Blum, Léon. *Souvenirs sur l'Affaire*. 1935. *L'Œuvre*. Vol. 4 (2). Paris: Albin Michel, 1965. 511–78.
Bock, Hans-Manfred, Reinhart Meyer-Kalkus, and Michel Trebitsch, eds. *Entre Locarno et Vichy. Les Relations culturelles franco-allemandes dans les années 1930*. 2 vols. Paris: CNRS, 1993.
Boisdeffre, Pierre de. *Barrès parmi nous*. Paris: Plon, 1969.
Bonnet, Marguerite, ed. *L'Affaire Barrès*. Paris: José Corti, 1987.
Bonstetten, Charles-Victor de. *L'Homme du midi et l'homme du nord, ou l'influence du climat*. Genève: Paschoud, 1824.
Boon, Jean-Pierre. "La Chasse, la règle et le mensonge: éléments structuraux dans *La Règle du jeu*." *French Review* 53.3 (Feb. 1980): 341–50.
Bossuet, Jacques-Bénigne. *Discours sur l'histoire universelle*. Paris: Firmin-Didot, 1892.
Bourrelier, Paul-Henri. *La Revue Blanche. Une Génération dans l'engagement, 1890–1905*. Paris: Fayard, 2007.
Brague, Rémi. *Europe, la voie romaine*. 2nd ed. Paris: Criterion, 1993.
Brewer, Daniel. *The Enlightenment Past: Reconstructing Eighteenth-Century French Thought*. Cambridge: Cambridge UP, 2008.
Broche, François. *Maurice Barrès*. Paris: Lattès, 1987.
Broers, Michael. *Europe under Napoleon 1799–1815*. London: Arnold, 1996.
Brombert, Victor. *Victor Hugo and the Visionary Novel*. Cambridge: Harvard UP, 1984.
Buchsbaum, Jonathan. *Cinéma engagé: Film in the Popular Front*. Urbana: Illinois UP, 1988.
Burrin, Philippe. "Le Fascisme." Sirinelli 1: 603–52.
Calame, Christophe. "Bonstetten et l'Europe." Kloocke 107–17.
Carroll, David. *French Literary Fascism. Nationalism, Anti-Semitism, and the Ideology of Culture*. Princeton: Princeton UP, 1995.

Céline, Louis-Ferdinand. *Bagatelles pour un massacre*. Paris: Denoël, 1937.
Césaire, Aimé. *Discours sur le colonialisme* suivi de *Discours sur la Négritude*. Paris: Présence africaine, 2004.
Chakrabarty, Dipesh. *Provincializing Europe: Postcolonial Thought and Historical Difference*. Princeton: Princeton UP, 2000.
Charles, David. *La Pensée technique dans l'œuvre de Victor Hugo*. Paris: PUF, 1997.
Charlot, Jean. "Le Gaullisme." Sirinelli 1: 653–89.
Chisick, Harvey. "Ethics and History in Voltaire's Attitudes toward the Jews." *Eighteenth-Century Studies* 35.4 (2002): 577–600.
Claudel, Paul, et al. *Les Juifs*. Paris: Plon, 1937.
Clifford, James. *The Predicament of Culture. Twentieth-Century Ethnography, Literature and Art*. Cambridge: Harvard UP, 1988.
Condorcet, Jean-Antoine-Nicolas de. *Esquisse d'un tableau historique des progrès de l'esprit humain*. Paris: Flammarion, 1988.
Coudenhove-Kalergi, Richard. *Paneurope*. Trans. Philippe Simon. Paris: Paneuropéennes, 1927.
Custine, Astolphe de. *La Russie en 1839*. Bruxelles: Wouters, 1843.
Debray, Régis. *Les Empires contre l'Europe*. Paris: Gallimard, 1985.
Dédéyan, Charles. *Victor Hugo et l'Allemagne*. 4 vols. Paris: Minard, 1965–77.
———. *Le Retour de Salente ou Voltaire et l'Angleterre*. Paris: Nizet, 1988.
Deering, Mary. *Combats acharnés: Denis de Rougemont et les fondements de l'unité européenne*. Lausanne: Fondation Jean Monnet, 1991.
Defay, Alexandre. "La Cartographie imaginaire de l'Europe." *Les Frontières de l'Europe*. Ed. Elie Barnavi and Paul Goossens. Bruxelles: De Boeck, 2001. 35–42.
Derrida, Jacques. *L'Autre Cap*. Paris: Minuit, 1991.
Dethurens, Pascal. *De l'Europe en littérature. Création littéraire et culture européenne au temps de la crise de l'esprit (1918–1939)*. Genève: Droz, 2002.
Dijn, Annelien de. *French Political Thought from Montesquieu to Tocqueville: Liberty in a Leveled Society?* Cambridge: Cambridge UP, 2008.
Domenach, Jean-Marie. "Barrésisme et révolution conservatrice." Guyaux 139–43.
Doty, Stewart. *From Cultural Rebellion to Counterrevolution: The Politics of Maurice Barrès*. Athens: Ohio UP, 1976.
Durgnat, Raymond. *Jean Renoir*. Berkeley: California UP, 1974.
Duroselle, Jean-Baptiste. *L'Idée d'Europe dans l'histoire*. Paris: Denoël, 1965.
Dziembowski, Edmond. *Un Nouveau Patriotisme français, 1750–1770*. SVEC 365. Oxford: Voltaire Foundation, 1998.
El Gammal, Jean. "La Guerre de 1870–1871 dans la mémoire des droites." Sirinelli 2: 471–504.
Espagne, Michel. *Les Transferts culturels franco-allemands*. Paris: PUF, 1999.
Fairweather, Maria. *Madame de Staël*. New York: Carroll & Graf, 2005.
Fanon, Frantz. *Les Damnés de la terre*. Paris: Maspéro, 1961.
Favre, Yves-Alain. "Barrès, l'Espagne et l'Italie." Guyaux 241–50.
Ferro, Marc. *Cinéma et histoire*. 2nd ed. Paris: Gallimard, 1993.

Fichte, Johann. *Addresses to the German Nation*. Trans. R. F. Jones and G. H. Turnbull. Westport, CT: Greenwood, 1979.

———. *L'Etat commercial fermé*. Trans. Daniel Schultess. Lausanne: L'Age d'Homme, 1980.

Fink, Béatrice. "L'Europe de Constant vue à travers *De l'esprit de conquête*." Kloocke 97–105.

Fiszer, Stanislaw. *L'Image de la Pologne dans l'œuvre de Voltaire*. SVEC 2001: 05. Oxford: Voltaire Foundation, 2001.

Forlin, Olivier. *Les Intellectuels français et l'Italie (1945–1955)*. Paris: L'Harmattan, 2006.

Forsberg, Roberta. *Madame de Staël and the English*. New York: Astra, 1967.

Forycki, Rémi. "Madame de Staël et la Russie d'Alexandre Ier." Kloocke 83–95.

Foyard, Jean. "Images de la femme chez Barrès." Guyaux 81–89.

Frigerio, Fabrizio. "L'Engagement politique de Denis de Rougemont." *Cadmos* 33 (Spring 1986): 115–124.

Fumaroli, Marc. *Quand l'Europe parlait français*. Paris: Fallois, 2001.

Gargett, Graham. *Voltaire and Protestantism*. SVEC 188. Oxford: Voltaire Foundation, 1980.

Gaudon, Sheila. "Anglophobie?" James 53–73.

Gay, Peter. *Voltaire's Politics*. New York: Vintage, 1965.

Geremek, Bronislaw. *The Common Roots of Europe*. Trans. Jan Aleksandrowicz. Cambridge: Polity, 1996.

Gide, André. "A propos des *Déracinés* de Maurice Barrès." *Essais critiques*. Paris: Gallimard, 1999. 4–8.

Girard, René. *La Violence et le sacré*. Paris: Grasset, 1972.

Girardet, Raoul, ed. "Le Programme révisionniste." *Le Nationalisme français (1871–1914)*. Paris: Armand Colin, 1966. 135–37.

Goodden, Angelica. *Madame de Staël: The Dangerous Exile*. Oxford: Oxford UP, 2008.

Granjon, Marie-Christine. "L'Allemagne de Raymond Aron et de Jean-Paul Sartre." Bock 2: 463–78.

Gsteiger, Manfred. "Réalité et utopie de l'Allemagne staëlienne." *Cahiers Staëliens* 37 (1985–86): 10–22.

Gunny, Ahmad. *Voltaire and English Literature*. SVEC 177. Oxford: Voltaire Foundation, 1979.

Gutwirth, Madelyn. *Madame de Staël, Novelist: The Emergence of the Artist as Woman*. Urbana: Illinois UP, 1978.

Guy, Basil. *The French Image of China before and after Voltaire*. SVEC 21. Genève: Institut Voltaire, 1963.

Guyaux, André, ed. *Barrès. Une Tradition dans la modernité*. Paris: Champion, 1991.

Gwynne, G. E. *Madame de Staël et la Révolution française*. Paris: Nizet, 1969.

Habermas, Jürgen. "La Paix perpétuelle: le bicentenaire d'une idée kantienne." *L'Intégration républicaine. Essais de théorie politique*. Trans. Rainer Rochlitz. Paris: Fayard, 1998. 161–204.

Habermas, Jürgen, and Jacques Derrida. "February 15, or, What Binds Europeans Together: Plea for a Common Foreign Policy, Beginning in Core Europe." *Old Europe, New Europe, Core Europe: Transatlantic Relations after the Iraq War*. Ed. Daniel Levy, Max Pensky, and John Torpey. London: Verso, 2005.
Hadidi, Djavâd. *Voltaire et l'islam*. Paris: Publications Orientalistes de France, 1974.
Halsall, Albert. *Victor Hugo and the Romantic Drama*. Toronto: Toronto UP, 1998.
Hartog, François. *Le XIXe Siècle et l'histoire. Le Cas Fustel de Coulanges*. Paris: PUF, 1988.
Hawley, Daniel. "L'Inde de Voltaire." *SVEC* 120. Oxford: Voltaire Foundation, 1974. 139–78.
Hay, Denys. *Europe: The Emergence of an Idea*. Edinburgh: Edinburgh UP, 1968.
Hayward, Susan. *French National Cinema*. London: Routledge, 1993.
Heater, Derek. *The Idea of European Unity*. London: Leicester UP, 1992.
Heine, Heinrich. *De l'Allemagne*. 2 vols. Paris: Renduel, 1835.
Hellman, John. *The Communitarian Third Way: Alexandre Marc's Ordre Nouveau, 1930–2000*. Montreal: McGill-Queen's UP, 2002.
———. *Emmanuel Mounier and the New Catholic Left, 1930–1950*. Toronto: Toronto UP, 1981.
Herder, Johann. *Against Pure Reason: Writings on Religion, Language, and History*. Trans. Marcia Bunge. Minneapolis: Fortress, 1993.
Hertzberg, Arthur. *The French Enlightenment and the Jews*. New York: Columbia UP, 1968.
Hofmann, Etienne and François Rosset. *Le Groupe de Coppet. Une Constellation d'intellectuels européens*. Lausanne: PU Romandes, 2005.
Hugo, Victor. *Œuvres complètes*. Ed. Jacques Seebacher and Guy Rosa. 15 vols. Paris: Laffont, 1985–90.
Hugo, Victor, and Victor Schœlcher. *Lettres*. Ed. Jean and Sheila Gaudon. Paris: Flohic, 1998.
Huré, Jacques. "Le Dernier des écrivains orientalistes." Guyaux 223–231.
Hutchison, Ross. *Locke in France 1688–1734*. *SVEC* 290. Oxford: Voltaire Foundation, 1991.
Ionesco, Eugène. "Préface pour *Rhinocéros*." *Théâtre complet*. Paris: Gallimard, 1991. 1405–06.
Irwin, Robert. *For Lust of Knowing: The Orientalists and Their Enemies*. London: Allen Lane, 2006.
Isbell, John. *The Birth of European Romanticism. Truth and Propaganda in Staël's* De l'Allemagne, *1810–1813*. Cambridge: Cambridge UP, 1994.
James, A.R.W., ed. *Victor Hugo et la Grande-Bretagne*. Liverpool: Francis Cairns, 1986.
Jaume, Lucien. *L'Individu effacé ou le paradoxe du libéralisme français*. Paris: Fayard, 1997.
Jáuregui, Pablo. "'Europeanism' versus 'Africanism': 'Europe' as a Symbol of Modernity and Democratic Renewal in Spain." *The Meaning of Europe*. Ed. Mikael af Malmborg and Bo Stråth. Oxford: Berg, 2002. 77–100.
Judt, Tony. *A Grand Illusion? An Essay on Europe*. New York: Hill and Wang, 1996.

———. *Past Imperfect: French Intellectuals, 1944–56*. Berkeley: California UP, 1992.
———. *Postwar: A History of Europe since 1945*. New York: Penguin, 2005.
Kant, Immanuel. *Toward Perpetual Peace, and Other Writings on Politics, Peace, and History*. Trans. David Colclasure. New Haven: Yale UP, 2006.
King, Norman. "Patrie et nation. Fictions Populistes dans le *Napoléon* d'Abel Gance et *La Marseillaise* de Jean Renoir." *Europe* 715/716 (Nov.–Dec. 1988): 68–75.
Kinsky, Ferdinand. "Où en est le fédéralisme de Denis de Rougemont?" *Cadmos* 33 (Spring 1986): 63–86.
Kirscher, Marie-Agnès. *Relire Barrès*. Lille: PU du Septentrion, 1998.
Kloocke, Kurt, and Simone Balayé, eds. *Le Groupe de Coppet et l'Europe. Annales Benjamin Constant* 15–16 (1994).
Kramer, Lloyd. *Lafayette in Two Worlds. Public Cultures and Personal Identities in an Age of Revolutions*. Chapel Hill: North Carolina UP, 1996.
Kundera, Milan. *L'Art du roman*. Paris: Gallimard, 1986.
Labroue, Henri. *Voltaire antijuif*. Paris: Documents Contemporains, 1942.
Lacouture, Jean. *Léon Blum*. Paris: Seuil, 1977.
Lacroix, Alain. *Constellation*. Meudon: Quidam, 2008.
Laforgue, Pierre. *Gavroche: études sur* Les Misérables. Paris: SEDES, 1994.
Lamartine, Alphonse de. *Œuvres poétiques*. Ed. Marius-François Guyard. Paris: Gallimard, 1963.
Lanson, Gustave. *Voltaire*. Paris: Hachette, 1946.
Las Cases, Emmanuel. *Le Mémorial de Sainte-Hélène*. 2 vols. Paris: Flammarion, 1951.
Laurent, Jacques. *Quand la France occupait l'Europe, 1792–1815*. Paris: Perrin, 1979.
Lavicka, Jan. "Voltaire et la Bohême." *SVEC* 219. Oxford: Voltaire Foundation, 1983. 105–15.
Leigh, John. *Voltaire: A Sense of History*. *SVEC* 2004: 05. Oxford: Voltaire Foundation, 2004.
Leriche, Françoise. "L'Obsession hugolienne de *la Recherche*." *Bulletin Marcel Proust* 40 (1990): 65–87.
Lestringant, Frank. *Le Cannibale. Grandeur et décadence*. Paris: Perrin, 1994.
Leuillot, Bernard. "L'Histoire réelle, telle qu'en Shakespeare." James 141–59.
Lévy, Bernard-Henri. *L'Idéologie française*. Paris: Grasset, 1981.
Lévy, David. *Voltaire et son exégèse du Pentateuque: critique et polémique*. *SVEC* 130. Oxford: Voltaire Foundation, 1975.
Lévy, Jacques. *Europe, une géographie*. Paris: Hachette, 1997.
Lotterie, Florence. *Progrès et perfectibilité: un dilemme des Lumières françaises (1755–1814)*. *SVEC* 2006: 04. Oxford: Voltaire Foundation, 2006.
Loubet del Bayle, Jean-Louis. *Les Non-Conformistes des années trente. Une Tentative de renouvellement de la pensée politique française*. Paris: Seuil, 1969.
Loyer, Emmanuelle. *Paris à New York. Intellectuels et artistes français en exil (1940–1947)*. Paris: Grasset, 2005.
Magnan, André. *Dossier Voltaire en Prusse (1750–1753)*. *SVEC* 244. Oxford: Voltaire Foundation, 1986.

Maillard, Pierre. *De Gaulle et l'Europe: entre la nation et Maastricht*. Paris: Taillandier, 1995.
Manent, Pierre. *Histoire intellectuelle du libéralisme*. Paris: Calmann-Lévy, 1987.
Marx, Karl. *The Eighteenth Brumaire of Louis Bonaparte*. Trans. Joseph Weydermeyer. New York: International, 1963.
Mason, Sheila. "Montesquieu's Vision of Europe." *SVEC* 341. Oxford: Voltaire Foundation, 1996. 61–87.
Masseau, Didier. *L'Invention de l'intellectuel dans l'Europe du XVIIIe siècle*. Paris: PUF, 1994.
Mauriac, François. *La Rencontre avec Barrès*. Paris: Table Ronde, 1945.
Mayeur, Jean-Marie. "Une Mémoire-Frontière: l'Alsace." Nora 3: 63–95.
Mehlman, Jeffrey. *Emigré New York: French Intellectuals in Wartime Manhattan, 1940–1944*. Baltimore: Johns Hopkins UP, 2000.
Mervaud, Christiane. "Des relations de voyage au mythe anglais des *Lettres philosophiques*." *SVEC* 296. Oxford: Voltaire Foundation, 1992. 1–15.
———. *Voltaire et Frédéric II*. *SVEC* 234. Oxford: Voltaire Foundation, 1985.
Metzidakis, Angelo. "Victor Hugo and the Idea of the United States of Europe." *Nineteenth-Century French Studies* 23.1–2 (Fall 1994–Winter 1995): 72–84.
Meyer, Henry. *Voltaire on War and Peace*. *SVEC* 144. Oxford: Voltaire Foundation, 1976.
Michel, Marc. "La Colonisation." Sirinelli 3: 125–63.
Miguet, Marie. "Proust et Barrès." Guyaux 287–306.
Miller, Christopher. *The French Atlantic Triangle: Literature and Culture of the Slave Trade*. Durham, NC: Duke UP, 2008.
Milza, Pierre. *Napoléon III*. Paris: Perrin, 2004.
———. *Voltaire*. Paris: Perrin, 2007.
Mommsen, Theodor. *The History of Rome*. Ed. Dero Saunders and John Collins. New York: Meridian, 1958.
Morin, Edgar. *Penser l'Europe*. Paris: Gallimard, 1990.
Morrissey, Robert. "Charlemagne." Nora 7: 630–73.
Mortier, Roland. *Clartés et ombres du siècle des Lumières*. Genève: Droz, 1969.
Mudimbe, V.Y. *The Idea of Africa*. Bloomington: Indiana UP, 1994.
Müller, Jan-Werner. *Constitutional Patriotism*. Princeton: Princeton UP, 2007.
Musset, Alfred de. *Œuvres complètes*. Ed. Philippe Van Tieghem. Paris: Seuil, 1963.
Nadeau, Maurice. *Histoire du Surréalisme* suivie de *Documents surréalistes*. Paris: Seuil, 1964.
Nash, Suzanne. Les Contemplations *of Victor Hugo: An Allegory of the Creative Process*. Princeton: Princeton UP, 1976.
Nietzsche, Friedrich. *Human, All Too Human*. Trans. Marion Faber and Stephen Lehmann. Lincoln: Nebraska UP, 1996.
Noiriel, Gérard. *Immigration, antisémitisme et racisme en France, XIXe-XXe siècle*. Paris: Fayard, 2007.
Nora, Pierre, ed. *Les Lieux de mémoire*. 7 vols. Paris: Gallimard, 1984–92.

Olivi, Bino, and Alessandro Giacone. *L'Europe difficile. Histoire politique de la construction européenne*. 3rd ed. Paris: Gallimard, 2007.

Ory, Pascal. *La Belle Illusion. Culture et politique sous le signe du Front populaire 1935–1938*. Paris: Plon, 1994.

Ory, Pascal, and Jean-François Sirinelli. *Les Intellectuels en France. De l'affaire Dreyfus à nos jours*. 2nd ed. Paris: Armand Colin, 1992.

Paxton, Robert. *French Peasant Fascism: Henri Dorgères's Greenshirts and the Crises of French Agriculture, 1929–1939*. Oxford: Oxford UP, 1997.

Pegg, Carl. *Evolution of the European Idea*. Chapel Hill: North Carolina UP, 1983.

Pellegrini, Carlo. "Stendhal contre Mme de Staël à propos de Napoléon." *Revue d'Histoire littéraire de la France* 66.1 (Jan.–Mar. 1966): 25–37.

Pellerin, Pascale. "Le *Voltaire antijuif* d'Henri Labroue: une escroquerie intellectuelle meurtrière." *SVEC* 2004: 07. Oxford: Voltaire Foundation, 2004. 173–85.

Pena-Ruiz, Henri, and Jean-Paul Scot. *Un Poète en politique. Les Combats de Victor Hugo*. Paris: Flammarion, 2002.

Perkins, Merle. "Voltaire and the Abbé de Saint-Pierre on World Peace." *SVEC* 18. Genève: Institut Voltaire, 1961. 9–34.

Petrovska, Marija. *Victor Hugo: l'écrivain engagé en Bohême*. Paris: Nizet, 1977.

Pithon, Rémy. "Cinéma français et cinéma allemand des années trente: de l'échange à l'exil." Bock 2: 587–99.

Poliakov, Léon. *Histoire de l'antisémitisme*. 4 vols. Paris: Calmann-Lévy, 1955–68.

Polowetzky, Michael. *A Bond Never Broken: The Relations between Napoleon and the Authors of France*. London: AUP, 1993.

Pomeau, René, ed. *Voltaire en son temps*. 5 vols. Oxford: Voltaire Foundation, 1988–94.

Portes, Jacques. "L'Epreuve de l'étranger." Sirinelli 3: 165–206.

Proust, Marcel. *Du côté de chez Swann*. 1913. *A la recherche du temps perdu*. Ed. Pierre Clarac and André Ferré. Vol. 1. Paris: Gallimard, 1954. 3–427.

Puymège, Gérard de, ed. *Du personnalisme au fédéralisme européen*. Genève: Centre Européen de la Culture, 1989.

Quinet, Edgar. *France et Allemagne*. Oxford: Clarendon, 1908.

Racine, Nicole. "La Revue *Europe* et l'Allemagne, 1929–1936." Bock 2: 631–58.

Ray, Satyajit. *Our Films, Their Films*. New York: Hyperion, 1994.

Rearick, Charles. *The French in Love and War: Popular Culture in the Era of the World Wars*. New Haven: Yale UP, 1997.

Réau, Elisabeth du. *L'Idée d'Europe au XXe siècle. Des mythes aux réalités*. Paris: Complexe, 1996.

Réau, Louis. *L'Europe française au siècle des Lumières*. Paris: Albin Michel, 1938.

Reid, T.R. *The United States of Europe: The New Superpower and the End of American Supremacy*. New York: Penguin, 2004.

Rémond, René. *Les Droites en France*. Paris: Aubier, 1982.

Renan, Ernest. *Qu'est-ce qu'une Nation? et autres écrits politiques*. Paris: Imprimerie nationale, 1996.

Renoir, Jean. *Ecrits 1926–1971*. Paris: Belfond, 1974.

———. *Ma Vie et mes films*. Paris: Flammarion, 1974.

Rivarol, Antoine de. *L'Universalité de la langue française*. Paris: Arléa, 1991.
Robb, Graham. *Victor Hugo*. New York: Norton, 1998.
Rolland, Romain. "Aux peuples assassinés." *Textes politiques, sociaux et philosophiques choisis*. Paris: Sociales, 1970. 151–59.
Romains, Jules. *Les Hommes de bonne volonté*. 27 vols. Paris: Flammarion, 1932–46.
Rosa, Guy. "Politique du désastre: Victor Hugo durant 'L'Année terrible.'" *Europe* 671 (Mar. 1985): 170–88.
Rosenblum, Joseph. *Practice to Deceive: The Amazing Stories of Literary Forgery's Most Notorious Practitioners*. New Castle, DE: Oak Knoll, 2000.
Rosset, François. *Ecrire à Coppet: nous, moi et le monde*. Genève: Slatkine, 2002.
Rougemont, Denis de. *L'Amour et l'Occident*. Paris: Plon, 1972.
———. *L'Aventure occidentale de l'homme*. Paris: Albin Michel, 1957.
———. *Le Cheminement des esprits*. Neuchâtel: Baconnière, 1970.
———. *Ecrits sur l'Europe*. Ed. Christophe Calame. 2 vols. Paris: Différence, 1994.
———. *Inédits*. Ed. Jean Mantzouranis and François Saint-Ouen. Neuchâtel: Baconnière, 1988.
———. *Journal d'Allemagne*. Paris: Gallimard, 1938.
———. *Les Mythes de l'amour*. Paris: Gallimard, 1961.
———. *La Part du Diable*. New York: Brentano's, 1944.
———. *Penser avec les mains*. Paris: Gallimard, 1972.
———. *Politique de la personne*. 2nd ed. Paris: "Je Sers," 1946.
———. *La Suisse, ou l'histoire d'un peuple heureux*. Lausanne: L'Age d'Homme, 1989.
Rousseau, André-Michel. *L'Angleterre et Voltaire (1718–1789)*. 3 vols. *SVEC* 145–47. Oxford: Voltaire Foundation, 1976.
Rousseau, Jean-Jacques. *Œuvres complètes*. Ed. Bernard Gagnebin and Marcel Raymond. 5 vols. Paris: Gallimard, 1959–95.
Roussel, Eric. *Jean Monnet*. Paris: Fayard, 1996.
Sabourin, Paul. *L'Etat-nation face aux Europes*. Paris: PUF, 1994.
Sadoul, Georges. *Le Cinéma français (1890–1962)*. Paris: Flammarion, 1962.
Said, Edward. *Orientalism*. 2nd ed. New York: Vintage, 1994.
Saint-Pierre, Charles de. *Projet pour rendre la paix perpétuelle en Europe*. Paris: Garnier, 1981.
Samuels, Maurice. "Renoir's *La Grande Illusion* and the 'Jewish Question.'" *Historical Reflections* 32.1 (Spring 2006): 165–92.
Schechter, Ronald. "Rationalizing the Enlightenment: Postmodernism and Theories of Anti-Semitism." *Postmodernism and the Enlightenment*. Ed. Daniel Gordon. London: Routledge, 2001. 93–116.
Schlegel, August-Wilhelm von. *A Course of Lectures on Dramatic Art and Literature*. Trans. John Black. London: Bohn, 1846.
Schlereth, Thomas. *The Cosmopolitan Ideal in Enlightenment Thought*. Notre Dame, IN: Notre Dame UP, 1977.
Schwarzbach, Bertram. "Voltaire et les Juifs: bilan et plaidoyer." *SVEC* 358. Oxford: Voltaire Foundation, 1997. 21–91.

Serman, William. "The Nationalists of Meurthe-et-Moselle, 1888–1912." *Nationhood and Nationalism in France*. Ed. Robert Tombs. London: HarperCollins, 1991. 121–35.
Sesonske, Alexander. *Jean Renoir: The French Films, 1924–1939*. Cambridge: Harvard UP, 1980.
Siclier, Jacques. "Le Cinéma." Sirinelli 2: 293–324.
Sidjanski, Dusan. "Penser avec les mains." *Cadmos* 33 (Spring 1986): 47–61.
Sirinelli, Jean-François, ed. *Histoire des droites en France*. 3 vols. Paris: Gallimard, 1992.
Sismondi, J. C. L. Simonde de. *De la littérature du Midi de l'Europe*. 2 vols. Bruxelles: Dumont, 1837.
Sokologorsky, Irène. "Victor Hugo et le XIXᵉ siècle russe." *Idéologies hugoliennes*. Ed. Anne-Marie Amiot. Nice: Serre, 1985. 191–98.
Solovieff, Georges. *L'Allemagne et Madame de Staël*. Paris: Klinsieck, 1990.
Song, Shun-Ching. *Voltaire et la Chine*. Aix-en-Provence: PU de Provence, 1989.
Sorlin, Pierre. *European Cinemas, European Societies 1939–1990*. London: Routledge, 1991.
Soucy, Robert. *Fascism in France: The Case of Maurice Barrès*. Berkeley: California UP, 1972.
———. *French Fascism: The First Wave, 1924–1933*. New Haven: Yale UP, 1986.
———. *French Fascism: The Second Wave, 1933–1939*. New Haven: Yale UP, 1995.
Sourian, Eve. *Madame de Staël et Henri Heine: les deux Allemagnes*. Paris: Didier, 1974.
Staël, Germaine de. *Considérations sur la Révolution française*. Ed. Jacques Godechot. Paris: Taillandier, 1983.
———. *Corinne ou l'Italie*. Ed. Simone Balayé. Paris: Gallimard, 1985.
———. *Correspondance générale*. Ed. Béatrice Jasinsky. 6 vols. Paris: Klincksieck, 1962–.
———. *De l'Allemagne*. Ed. Simone Balayé. 2 vols. Paris: Garnier-Flammarion, 1968.
———. *De la littérature considérée dans ses rapports avec les institutions sociales*. Ed. Paul Van Tieghem. 2 vols. Genève: Droz, 1959.
———. *Delphine*. Ed. Simone Balayé and Lucia Omacini. 2 vols. Genève: Droz, 1987.
———. *Dix Années d'exil*. Ed. Simone Balayé and Mariella Vianello Bonifacio. Paris: Fayard, 1996.
Starobinski, Jean. "Denis de Rougemont: 'Ecrire n'est pas un art d'agrément.'" *Table d'orientation. L'Auteur et son autorité*. Lausanne: L'Age d'homme, 1989. 159–80.
Stendhal. *Rome, Naples et Florence*. 1817. *Œuvres complètes*. Ed. Georges Eudes. Vol. 4. Paris: Larrive, 1951.
Sternhell, Zeev. *Les anti-Lumières, du XVIIIᵉ siècle à la guerre froide*. Paris: Fayard, 2006.
———. *La Droite révolutionnaire 1885–1914. Les Origines françaises du fascisme*. Paris: Seuil, 1978.
———. *Maurice Barrès et le nationalisme français*. Paris: Armand Colin, 1972.
———. *Ni droite ni gauche. L'Idéologie fasciste en France*. Paris: Seuil, 1983.
Storm, Eric. "The Rise of the Intellectual around 1900: Spain and France." *European History Quarterly* 32.2 (Apr. 2002): 139–60.
Sutcliffe, Adam. *Judaism and Enlightenment*. Cambridge: Cambridge UP, 2003.

Sutton, Michael. *France and the Construction of Europe, 1944-2007: The Geopolitical Imperative*. Oxford: Berghahn, 2007.
Szmurlo, Karyna. "Pour une poétique des langues nationales: Germaine de Staël." Kloocke 165–79.
Tagore, Rabindranath. *Nationalism*. London: Macmillan, 1917.
Taine, Hippolyte. *La Révolution*. Vol. 1. Paris: Hachette, 1882.
Tifft, Stephen. "*Drôle de guerre*: Renoir, Farce, and the Fall of France." *Representations* 38 (Spring 1992): 131–65.
Tilkin, Françoise. "L'Image des nations européennes dans les écrits personnels de Benjamin Constant." Kloocke 67–81.
Todorov, Tzvetan. *L'Esprit des Lumières*. Paris: Laffont, 2006.
———. *Nous et les autres. La Réflexion française sur la diversité humaine*. Paris: Seuil, 1989.
Traverso, Enzo. *À feu et à sang: de la guerre civile européenne 1914–1945*. Paris: Stock, 2007.
Triggs, Jeffery. "The Legacy of Babel: Language in Jean Renoir's *Grand Illusion*." *New Orleans Review* 15.2 (Summer 1988): 70–74.
Tronquart, Georges. *La Lorraine de Barrès. Mythe ou réalité?* Nancy: PU de Nancy-II, 1980.
Trousson, Raymond. *Le Tison et le flambeau. Victor Hugo devant Voltaire et Rousseau*. Bruxelles: PU de Bruxelles, 1985.
Truffaut, François. "Une Certaine Tendance du cinéma français." *Cahiers du cinéma* 31 (Jan. 1954): 15–29.
Valéry, Paul. "La Crise de l'esprit." 1919. *Œuvres*. Ed. Jean Hytier. Vol. 1. Paris: Gallimard, 1957. 988–1014.
Vallois, Marie-Claire. *Fictions féminines. Mme de Staël et les voix de la sibylle*. Saratoga, CA: Anma Libri, 1987.
Valois, Georges. *Le Fascisme*. Paris: Nouvelle Librairie Nationale, 1927.
Van Strien-Chardonneau, Madeleine. *Le Voyage de Hollande: récits de voyageurs français dans les Provinces-Unies, 1748–1795*. SVEC 318. Oxford: Voltaire Foundation, 1994.
Vercruysse, Jeroom. *Voltaire et la Hollande*. SVEC 46. Genève: Institut Voltaire, 1966.
Verdaguer, Pierre. "Denis de Rougemont et la nouvelle censure." *French Review* 59.2 (Dec. 1985): 258–66.
Villers, Charles de. *Philosophie de Kant*. Utrecht: Monde, 1830.
Viry-Babel, Roger. *Jean Renoir. Le Jeu et la règle*. Paris: Ramsay, 1994.
Voltaire. *Correspondence and Related Documents*. Ed. Theodore Besterman. *Complete Works*. Vols. 85–135. Oxford: Voltaire Foundation, 1968–.
———. *Œuvres complètes*. Ed. Louis Moland. 52 vols. Paris: Garnier, 1877–85.
Voyenne, Bernard. *Histoire de l'idée européenne*. Paris: Payot, 1964.
Ward, Patricia. *The Medievalism of Victor Hugo*. University Park: Pennsylvania UP, 1975.
Wasserstein, Bernard. *Barbarism and Civilization: A History of Europe in our Times*. Oxford: Oxford UP, 2007.

Wilberger, Carolyn. "Peter the Great: An Eighteenth-Century Hero of our Times?" *SVEC* 96. Oxford: Voltaire Foundation, 1972. 9–127.

———. *Voltaire's Russia: Window on the East*. *SVEC* 164. Oxford: Voltaire Foundation, 1976.

Williams, Alan. *Republic of Images*. Cambridge: Harvard UP, 1992.

Winock, Michel. *Histoire politique de la revue* Esprit, *1930–1950*. Paris: Seuil, 1975.

———. *Victor Hugo dans l'arène politique*. Paris: Bayard, 2005.

Wolton, Dominique. *La Dernière Utopie. Naissance de l'Europe démocratique*. Paris: Flammarion, 1993.

Zweig, Stefan. *The World of Yesterday*. Lincoln: Nebraska UP, 1964.

Index

Ackermann, Bruno, 138, 172n1, 173n5, 173n10–11, 174n24
Africans, 3, 13, 28–30, 42, 65, 66, 68, 70, 78, 79, 144, 165n11
Americans, 25, 40, 41, 58, 109, 110, 113, 114, 118, 123, 133, 138–40, 142, 143, 146, 148, 151, 155, 156, 170n7–8
Anderson, Benedict, 52, 148
Andrew, Dudley, 115, 124, 132
anticlericalism, 9, 27, 31, 34, 60, 161n35
anti-Semitism, 26–28, 84, 91–93, 126–27, 162n37, 169n23, 174n27
Arabs, 12–14, 116, 144, 147, 161n34

Balayé, Simone, 44, 162n1, 163n8, 163n17, 164n26, 164n29, 164n33
Bazin, André, 111, 170n10, 171n17
Benda, Julien, 138, 172n2
Besterman, Theodore, 7, 15, 20, 159n2, 160n3
Birnbaum, Pierre, 168n18, 169n25, 169n30
Bismarck, Otto von, 73, 100, 156
Blum, Léon, 81, 126–27, 133, 167n2
Bossuet, Jacques-Bénigne, 11–12, 28, 160n9
Buchsbaum, Jonathan, 118, 170n5, 171n14

capitalism, 20–21, 93, 119, 137, 143
Catherine the Great, 9, 14, 23–26, 28, 160n2
Céline, Louis-Ferdinand, 83, 127, 171n26

Chinese, 8, 12–15, 24, 27, 130, 160n9, 160n12, 160n14
Christians, 1, 9, 12–16, 20, 26–28, 31, 35, 42, 49, 58, 59, 68, 79, 138, 144, 147, 148, 161n34, 162n40, 167n8, 174n26
  Catholic, 16, 21, 27, 28, 31, 83, 87, 88, 101, 102, 138, 143, 145, 161n35
  Orthodox, 31
  Protestant, 11, 16, 17, 28, 31, 33, 35, 50, 84, 92, 93, 137, 138, 143, 145, 147, 173n18
Classicism, 21–22, 34, 68, 77, 164n37
colonialism, 5, 8, 15, 17, 20, 30, 39, 40, 58, 61, 64, 65, 68, 84, 105, 116, 118, 123, 133, 141, 148, 159n1, 170n38, 171n18
Commune, 57, 73, 78, 166n29, 169n27
communism, 24, 78, 82, 93, 111, 118, 138, 142, 145, 152, 154, 167n4
cosmopolitanism, 3–5, 8, 10, 13–15, 22, 31, 33–35, 53, 82, 84, 105, 141, 144, 156, 165n13

Dédéyan, Charles, 68, 161n24, 161n26, 165n10, 166n23, 166n25
Dreyfus Affair, 81, 84, 90, 91, 102, 103, 109, 167n2, 169n20–22
Drumont, Edouard, 91, 92, 106, 169n21
Dutch, 7, 8, 11, 17–18, 21, 23, 122, 147, 154, 159n2, 161n20, 166n27

English, 7, 8, 11, 13, 17–23, 34, 37, 39–41, 43–47, 49, 51, 66, 69–72, 75, 83, 84, 87, 96, 113, 123,

English (*continued*)
125–26, 128, 134, 140, 141, 159n2, 160n3, 166n20, 170n7, 171n18
anglomanie, 21–22
Enlightenment, 3–5, 7, 8, 24, 33, 35, 39, 49, 50, 86, 88, 90, 106, 159n5, 163n8
Eurocentrism, 5, 9, 12, 16, 31, 148

fascism, 82, 83, 86, 87, 89, 106, 112, 115, 119, 120, 131, 138–40, 142, 167n5, 168n13, 169n24, 170n39, 172n32
federalism, 58, 93, 123, 137–46, 148–50, 152, 155, 156, 166n17, 174n23–24
Fichte, Johann, 47, 51, 99, 164n35, 169n30–31
Franco-Prussian War, 5, 48, 51, 57, 65, 68–73, 79, 81, 84–86, 98, 99, 153, 166n29, 169n22, 169n27
Frederick the Great, 8, 9, 16, 22–26, 161n27

Gay, Peter, 9, 19, 161n21, 162n41
Gide, André, 81, 82, 167n4, 169n23
Goethe, Johann, 37, 49, 61, 96, 100, 164n28
Greeks, 13, 14, 25, 37, 49, 65, 86, 103–4, 106, 122, 144
Gutwirth, Madelyn, 45, 164n21, 164n23, 164n25
Gypsies, 3, 28

Habermas, Jürgen, 155–56, 160n15
Heine, Heinrich, 51, 53
Herder, Johann, 3–5, 97, 104, 157, 159n5, 169n30

Indians, 8, 12–14, 24, 27, 29, 40, 95, 106, 109, 113, 160n14, 170n7
Italians, 10, 33, 34, 36, 37, 40–46, 48–50, 52–54, 60, 66, 67, 72, 82, 83, 85–87, 94, 95, 101–3, 109, 113–16, 129, 131, 145, 159n2, 160n3, 164n25–26, 169n34, 170n10, 172n32

Jews, 3, 12, 14, 16, 20, 26–28, 41–42, 44, 67, 83, 89, 91–93, 99, 103, 126–27, 130, 134, 144, 160n9, 162n37–40, 169n23, 174n27
Judt, Tony, 140, 156, 173n13, 173n20, 174n2, 174n5

Kant, Immanuel, 3–5, 15, 47, 49, 50, 90, 96, 101, 103, 146, 157, 160n15, 168n15, 169n20

liberalism, 9, 20, 31, 34, 35, 37–39, 50, 53, 54, 57, 62, 65, 78, 79, 90, 143, 148, 163n15, 165n41, 165n13
Locke, John, 8, 19, 49–50, 161n25

Maurras, Charles, 83, 92, 106, 167n7
Mervaud, Christiane, 19, 161n27
Monnet, Jean, 87, 140, 153, 159n3
Montesquieu, 5, 17, 30, 36, 42, 87, 160n14
Moslems, 14, 25, 26, 28, 106

Napoleon I, 11, 31, 33, 34, 36–43, 45, 47–54, 57, 60–62, 64, 66, 68–71, 81, 86, 95, 99, 119, 160n8, 162n2, 163n11, 163n17, 164n29, 164n35–37, 165n12
Napoleon III, 57, 72–75, 153, 166n30–31
nationalism, 4, 33, 36, 39, 51–54, 59, 79, 82–89, 91–94, 96, 99, 106, 112, 113, 115, 118, 119, 121, 128, 134, 137, 142, 144, 145, 148, 155, 163n13, 168n13, 168n18, 169n30, 170n36, 170n39
Nazism, 5, 83, 112, 118, 121, 124, 125, 133, 134, 139, 142, 154, 167n5, 171n20
Newton, Isaac, 8, 18, 19
Nietzsche, Friedrich, 2, 5, 82, 103
Nord/Midi, 35–37, 42–45, 47, 49, 53, 60, 61, 68, 76, 78, 102

pacifism, 57–58, 85, 121
Poles, 26, 40, 41, 65, 66, 67, 72, 86, 127, 129, 161n33, 161n35, 166n17, 172n32
Pomeau, René, 19, 160n4–5, 161n23, 161n29, 161n31, 161n33, 162n41
Prussians, 5, 9, 22–24, 40, 48, 51, 57, 65, 68–73, 79, 81, 84–86, 96–100, 119, 124, 153, 160n2, 161n27–28, 166n17, 166n26, 166n29, 169n22, 169n27, 171n22

racism, 7, 29, 31, 42, 47, 89, 105, 106, 115, 116, 144
Renan, Ernest, 52, 89, 99, 154, 168n18
Rhine, 47, 55, 66–73, 76, 78, 84, 95–97, 99–101, 105, 166n23–24, 166n27
"Querelle du Rhin," 68–72, 100
Robb, Graham, 63, 73, 74, 165n5, 165n8
Rolland, Romain, 85, 123, 169n23
Romans, 10–13, 16, 24, 27–29, 39, 42, 43, 46, 49, 113, 144, 148
Romanticism, 4, 22, 31, 34–36, 42, 46, 49–51, 54, 55, 59, 61, 67, 68, 70, 74–77, 88–90, 95, 96, 101, 131, 132, 134, 163n8, 164n37
Rousseau, Jean-Jacques, 8, 15–17, 25, 36, 63, 90, 106, 160n14, 168n19
Russians, 7–9, 12–14, 17, 23, 24–26, 31, 34, 40, 41, 51, 66, 67, 70–72, 86, 105, 117, 120, 122, 123, 160n2, 161n32, 161n33, 166n17, 166n21, 170n36, 171n18

Sadoul, Georges, 118, 125
Said, Edward, 5, 105–6, 170n37
Saint-Pierre, Charles de, 15–17, 76, 160n16
Schlereth, Thomas, 8, 160n3, 160n7

Sesonske, Alexander, 111, 116, 118, 171n11, 171n17–18, 171n27–28, 172n35
Shakespeare, William, 7, 18, 22, 43, 53, 60, 62, 64, 66, 76, 77, 161n26, 166n20
slavery, 20, 30, 41, 42, 61, 68, 104, 162n43–44
Soucy, Robert, 82, 167n5, 168n13, 169n24
Soviets, 118, 119, 137, 142, 143, 146, 152, 154, 155, 167n4
Spaniards, 10, 30, 37, 60, 66, 70, 82, 85, 87, 94, 101–3, 105, 115, 116, 119, 120, 129, 131, 142, 159n2, 160n3, 166n19, 169n32
Sternhell, Zeev, 82, 84, 89, 139, 159n5, 167n5, 168n13, 169n24, 169n30

Taine, Hippolyte, 89, 168n19
Todorov, Tzvetan, 7, 168n18
Turks, 3, 13, 16, 25, 26, 28, 31, 66, 67, 70, 86, 105, 144, 159n1, 160n13, 161n33

Valéry, Paul, 1, 5, 85, 141, 144, 155, 159n6, 173n19

Wilberger, Carolyn, 24, 25, 161n32
Williams, Alan, 118, 171n24
Winock, Michel, 139, 165n2
World War I, 1, 65, 72, 81, 83, 84, 85, 92, 93, 96, 100, 102, 105, 106, 107, 109, 113, 116, 120–23, 125, 127, 132, 142, 153
World War II, 83, 87, 109, 112, 113, 116, 120, 134, 135, 139, 140, 141, 142, 152, 153, 154, 156, 174n23

Zola, Emile, 98, 102–3, 165n9, 169n20, 171n22